EUROPEAN NEONATAL RESEARCH

European Neonatal Research

Consent, ethics committees and law

Edited by

SU MASON
Head of Unit (Joint)
Northern and Yorkshire Clinical Trials and Research Unit
Academic Unit of Epidemiology and Health Services Research
University of Leeds, UK

CHRIS MEGONE
Senior Lecturer in Philosophy
School of Philosophy and Centre for Business and Professional Ethics
University of Leeds, UK

Ashgate

Aldershot • Burlington USA • Singapore • Sydney

Published by
Ashgate Publishing Limited
Gower House
Croft Road
Aldershot
Hants GU11 3HR
England

Ashgate Publishing Company
131 Main Street
Burlington, VT 05401-5600 USA

Ashgate website: http://www.ashgate.com

British Library Cataloguing in Publication Data
European Neonatal Research
   1.Neonatalology - Research - Europe - Moral and ethical
aspects 2.Informed consent (Medical law) - Europe
I.Mason, S. A. II.Megone, C.
174.2'8

Library of Congress Cataloging-in-Publication Data
European Neonatal Research / edited by S. A. Mason, C. Megone.
     p. cm.
   Includes bibliographical references.
   ISBN 0-7546-1301-1
    1.Neonatology--Research--Moral and ethical aspects--Europe. 2.
Infants--Research--Moral and ethical aspects--Europe. 3.Informed consent (Medical
law)--Europe. 4.Medical ethics--Europe. I.Mason, S. A. (Susan A.) II.Megone, C.
(Christopher)

RJ254 .I64 2001
618.92'01'07204--dc21
                                     00-054305

ISBN 0 7546 1301 1

Printed and bound in Great Britain by MPG Books Ltd, Bodmin, Cornwall

Contents

List of Contributors

Euricon Study Group

Management Team

Dr Susan A. Mason   Northern & Yorkshire Clinical Trials & Research Unit at the University of Leeds, UK

Dr Christopher Megone   Department of Philosophy, University of Leeds, UK

Mr Peter J. Allmark   Faculty of Medicine, University of Sheffield, UK

Professor Dag Bratlid   University Hospital, Trondheim, Norway

Professor Panagiota Dalla-Vorgia   University of Athens Medical School, Greece

Dr A. Bryan Gill   Leeds General Infirmary, UK

Mrs Patricia Morrogh   University College, Cork, Eire

Mrs Angela Phillips   Northern & Yorkshire Clinical Trials & Research Unit at the University of Leeds, UK

PD Dr Stella Reiter-Theil   Centre for Ethics & Law in Medicine, University of Freiburg, Germany

The late Craig Sykes   Northern & Yorkshire Clinical Trials & Research Unit at the University of Leeds, UK

Partnership

Dr Vineta Fellman   Hospital for Children and Adolescents, University of Helsinki, Finland

Dr Gorm Greisen   National University Hospital Copenhagen, Denmark

Dr Lena Hellstrom-Westas   University Hospital, Lund, Sweden

Dr Søren Holm	University of Copenhagen, Denmark, and University of Manchester, UK
Professor Anne Langlois	Department of Medical Ethics, Créteil, France
Dr Giuseppe Latini	The A. Di Summa Private Hospital, Brindisi, Italy
Dr Neena Modi	Hammersmith Hospital, London, UK
Professor Manuel Moya	University Hospital of San Juan, Spain
Dr Sophia Petmezaki	Mitera Hospital, Athens, Greece
Dr Aurora Plomer	Faculty of Law, University of Leeds, UK
Dr Glyn Russell	St Michael's Hospital, Bristol, UK
Dr C. Anthony Ryan	Cork Regional Hospital, Eire
Dr Elie Saliba	University Hospital, Tours, France
Professor Jan Helge Solbakk	National Committee for Medical Research Ethics, Oslo, Norway
Dr A. Michael Weindling	Liverpool Women's Hospital, Liverpool, UK
The late Professor Nils Svenningsen	University Hospital, Lund, Sweden

Partner Representatives

Mrs Nadège LeRoux	Research Centre for Medical Ethics and Public Health, Paris, France
Dr Nina Nelson	Department of Pediatrics, University Hospital, Linköping, Sweden

Legal Representatives

Judge Christian Byk	62 Bd de Port-Royal, Paris, France
Professor Carlos M. Romeo-Casabona	Chair of Human Rights and Genome Research, Bilbao, Spain
Dr Ciaran Craven	Law School, Trinity College, Dublin, Ireland
Professor Panagiota Dalla-Vorgia	University of Athens Medical School, Greece

Dr juris Marit Halvorsen *	Institute for Public Law, Oslo, Norway
Dr Hans-Georg Koch *	University of Freiburg, Germany
Ms Salla Lötjönen	University of Helsinki, Finland
Professor Linda Nielsen *	University of Copenhagen, Denmark
Dr Aurora Plomer	University of Leeds, UK
Associate Professor Elisabeth Rynning	Uppsala University, Sweden
Ms Elisabeth Gording Stang	Institute for Public Law, Oslo, Norway

* Provided legal information but not in attendance at Euricon legal colloquium.

Preface

The Euricon Project, *Is obtaining informed consent for neonatal research an 'elaborate ritual'? – A European Study*, was a three year European Union BioMed-funded study which commenced in 1996.

The conception of the study was at a meeting in Leeds, UK, of the European Neonatal Brain Club (an informal pan-European organisation) where, following a short presentation by Su Mason, a long plenary discussion was stimulated on the problems of obtaining informed consent for neonatal research. Here, it was agreed that this was a relevant question, which required study. At the same time Chris Megone was preparing a study of the work of European Research Ethics Committees (in some countries known as Institutional Review Boards or Scientific Ethics Committees), which are charged with the ethical review of medical research protocols such as randomised controlled trials on neonates. It was felt that this work dovetailed nicely with the examination of the issue of consent. Hence the Euricon project, with its twin strands of investigation, was born.

The project partnership (as stated in the list of contributors) comprised a multidisciplinary team of neonatologists, ethicists, lawyers and a sociologist specialising in European medical issues. Indeed, one of the features of this project has been the rich debate resulting from the bringing together of different disciplines, each with their own background and understanding of the issues surrounding informed consent for neonatal research.

This book brings together the various findings of the Euricon study. In section I, Allmark et al provide an introduction to the study and outline the ethical issues that impinge on the process of informed consent for neonatal research. The practical problems, encountered by both neonatologists and parents in a specific multicentre, neonatal trial, are outlined by Gill.

The second section of the book provides an analysis of European Research Ethics Committees, and their role in the ethical review of medical research protocols. It is based on data from the Euricon study. Megone et al discuss the structure, composition and operation of RECs throughout Europe and their position regarding informed consent in neonatal research.

xi

Holm and Solbakk provide their own individual critical ethical discussions on the participation of children in research studies and the resultant implication for RECs.

Section III provides a comparative analysis of the law governing informed consent in neonatal research within Europe. It starts with an overview of European legislation by Dalla-Vorgia et al. Subsequent chapters provide more detail on the law in specific European countries and analysis of some of the problems identified: Finland (Lötjönen), Greece (Dalla-Vorgia), Ireland (Craven), Norway (Halvorsen), Spain (Casabona), Sweden (Rynning), United Kingdom (Plomer). Finally in this section, Plomer provides a critical comparative analysis of two ethical frameworks: that of the USA Advisory Committee on Human Radiation Experiments of 1996, which claims to have identified fundamental, transcultural, transtemporal ethical principles and the 1997 Council of Europe's Convention on Human Rights and Biomedicine. Plomer describes how these frameworks underlie the regulation of research with children in Europe.

Section IV looks at the process of obtaining informed consent. Firstly, Mason et al describe the methods and results of the interviews performed with parents and clinicians as part of the Euricon project and discuss the implications of their findings.

The next two chapters are papers, representing personal viewpoints of the authors as opposed to findings of the study group as a whole. These were presented at the third Euricon colloquium and were designed to promote discussion. The first (Modi) takes the position that there are certain situations where a more flexible approach to informed consent might be better. Bratlid argues for improving the informed consent process by providing information to parents antenatally.

The final section of the book consists of the consensus statement on the conduct of the informed consent process of the Euricon research project. This statement is derived both from the empirical work and from reflection and discussion amongst the partnership at the three colloquia of the project. It addresses the issues of the requirement for informed consent, and the process of obtaining it, the structure of Research Ethics Committees and their role and practice. Finally, and importantly, issues which were widely discussed, but about which no consensus was reached, are outlined.

Su Mason PhD
Chris Megone DPhil

Acknowledgements

The editors gratefully acknowledge the contribution and partnership of the late Professor Nils Svenningsen, Lund, Sweden, to the interviews; of the late Mr Craig Sykes, NYCTRU, UK, to the study organisation; of Mr Dawood Dassu, NYCTRU, University of Leeds, UK, for the statistical analysis in Chapter 17; and of Mrs Alice Hamar for proof-reading original papers, and preparation of the text of this book for printing.

Funding

The editors gratefully acknowledge the grant from the European Union (Contract number BMH4 – CT95 – 0169 (DG 12-SSMA)), which supported the project, and the advice of Dr C Bardoux, Scientific Officer, European Commission.

PART I
BACKGROUND
INFORMATION ON
THE EURICON STUDY

1 Ethical Issues and Practical Problems in Obtaining Informed Consent for Neonatal Research

MR P.J. ALLMARK, DR S.A. MASON AND DR C. MEGONE

Method

The aims of the Euricon study were two-fold: to examine the validity of the obtaining of (parental, proxy) informed consent for neonatal research across Europe and to suggest practical improvements if necessary; and to examine the role of Research Ethics Committees (RECs), and their role in ethical review in Europe.

The study took a four-pronged approach to examining these issues:

1. Semi-structured interviews with 200 parents from nine European countries (Denmark, Finland, France, Germany, Greece, Italy, Spain, Sweden, UK) who had been asked for consent for their infant to take part in a research study, and with 107 clinicians who regularly asked for such consent.

2. Two separate postal questionnaires were sent to 44 RECs across 11 European countries (the above, and also Ireland and Norway) – the first examining their structure and their approach to the issues of neonatal consent and the second asking for a response to information sent to them on results from the above interviews.

3. Information on the law pertaining to this issue across Europe was supplied by legal representatives and explored at a colloquium.

4. Three colloquia were held. At these, the ethical, practical and legal issues concerning informed consent in neonatal research were examined in depth. The analysis of the responses from RECs, and the

structure of ethical review across Europe were also discussed. The colloquia were attended by the pan-European professionals (neonatologists, legal experts, ethicists and a sociologist) who made up the project partners – see the List of Contributors on page ix.

Medical Research and Randomised Clinical Trials

Progress in medicine is heavily dependent upon research. Research tests whether a treatment is effective, or whether one treatment is better than another, or whether patients do better with one operation or another, and so on. Such research is essential in developing better medical care, and in ridding ourselves of ineffective treatments. There are various stages in research on medical treatments. For example, one stage may often be the testing of a treatment on animals. But clearly at some point it is necessary to test treatments on humans. Thus in the case of illness in neonates, treatments need to be tested on neonates.

One particular method of research, which is thought by many to give the most reliable scientific evidence, is the randomised controlled trial (RCT). This involves testing treatments against each other and/or against a placebo. Patients are randomly allocated to treatment X or treatment Y and/or to receiving the placebo. Since bias should have been minimised due to the process of randomisation, when the researchers compare the outcomes for patients who got treatment X with those who had Y or only received a placebo, they are able to say which treatment, if any, is effective, and whether there were any unexpected side-effects.

Randomised Clinical Trials, Equipoise, and Random Allocation

Some may wonder how researchers can justify entering patients into such randomised controlled trials. One key condition that has been argued for is that those doctors undertaking the research must be in *equipoise* about the treatments that are being studied. This means that the doctors must:

1.   *Hope* (on the basis of support from prior evidence which is, however, insufficient for certainty) that the treatment being tested in the RCT is better than the best available treatment currently known (if they did not *hope* this, then they should not try out the new treatment at all); but also

2. *Accept that it is not yet known* whether this trial treatment is indeed better than the best currently available, since this trial treatment may turn out to have unexpected adverse side effects.

In some cases the best treatment currently available may only be best supportive care. If so the new trial treatment (plus best supportive care) may be tested against a placebo plus best supportive care. In either case, the point of the trial is to discover whether the new trial treatment is in fact better than the best currently available. The doctors must be in *equipoise* about the treatment, it is said, since if a clinician thought that one of the treatments being offered to his patient was probably better than the other, his duty to the patient would require him to offer only that treatment to the patient.

The randomising process of RCTs is scientifically beneficial in that it will reduce the chances of some hidden bias entering the study, and thus unduly influencing the results. The ethical justification for such a process can be connected to the fact that the researchers are in *equipoise* about the treatments. Their *equipoise* means that the doctors can defend the allocation of patients (who consent to take part in the trial) randomly between the treatments, since their present view is that they do not know which treatment will produce more benefit or least harm for the patient.

Consent to Research

Since the 1940s consent has been seen as central to any research on human beings, including medical research. In other words, research on human beings cannot, in general, take place unless the participants agree to that research. This requirement is reflected in European laws and in medical codes of ethics, such as the Declaration of Helsinki. Thus in the case of an RCT on human beings it has become an accepted requirement that patients entering the trial need to consent to undergo a research procedure of just that sort.

Consent and Neonatal Research

As explained above, Euricon has been looking in particular at parental consent to RCTs involving neonates. This case raises several difficulties. In the first place, what is involved here is sometimes termed 'proxy consent'. 'Proxy consent' occurs when a second party (in this case the parent or parents) agrees or refuses participation on behalf of the subject who may potentially enter the trial (in this case the neonate).

There is some question whether this procedure really counts as consent at all. For the neonate is not in fact giving its consent. Rather the parents are making a decision on behalf of their child (as to whether or not he should participate in the trial). If this is to be held as analogous to consent, the idea here must be that the parents are best placed to make a decision from the child's point of view, to decide as the child would decide. If this is what is going on, the procedure requires them to try to think what values the child would have, and how it would decide in the light of those values. However in the case of a neonate it is not plausible that the parents can be doing this. The neonate does not have any values yet, so the parents cannot be in a position to infer what they would be. The case differs from those of other non-competent patients such as coma victims, or patients suffering from senility, where it may be possible for relatives to judge what the patient would have wished, on the basis of their knowledge of the patient's values.

If so it may be better to see what the parents do here as a case of authorisation. The parents are acknowledged as the persons who have the authority to make the decision, on their child's behalf. This would be parallel to the way in which parents are agreed to have the authority to decide where their children are educated, for example, and other matters of their upbringing. For some philosophical purposes it is important to be clear on the nature of the parental role here. However in what follows we shall talk of the process as one of consent (though it is best understood as authorisation), to conform to usual practice. Consent is, in any case, a relevant concept in that what parents do is agree to, or refuse, their child's participation in the trial.

Euricon has been particularly concerned with a second (related) issue, namely whether any consent to, or authorisation of, neonatal research given by parents can count as informed consent (or informed authorisation).

The reason for this is that there is more to giving consent than someone simply saying 'go ahead'. Such an act of 'consent' would mean nothing if the person giving 'consent' had no real idea what the researcher was about to do; nor if the person consenting was frightened of the researcher; nor if the person consenting was unable to make proper decisions about himself (for example, because he or she was too young, or was mentally ill and in the neonatal case, for example, following a caesarean section a mother may still be under the effect of anaesthesia). Thus informed consent requires that: the consent be given voluntarily; the person giving consent has enough information to make an informed and reasoned choice; and the person giving consent be mentally competent to give that consent. In what follows these requirements have been specified in terms of the following criteria (Beauchamp and Childress, 1994; Neuberger, 1992):

1. Competence – the person giving consent must be mentally competent to do so;
2. Information – sufficient information must be received for the person to make an informed choice;
3. Understanding – the person's understanding must be sufficient for him to make a reasoned choice;
4. Voluntariness – the consent must be given voluntarily.

This is one account of the criteria that must be met if a person consenting is to count as having given informed consent. It should be noted that all these criteria specify a standard of perfection which is never completely met in practice. Furthermore, the extent to which the criteria *can* be met varies between trials. For example, in a randomised controlled trial that is both complex and in which parental consent must be gained very quickly, the amount of information about the trial that can be given to, and understood by, parents will be relatively less than in a less complex trial in which parents have plenty of time in which to consent.

Of course it is not only trials that differ from each other, so do parents. Parents vary in their intelligence, their ability to deal with stressful situations and so on. In the third colloquium we discussed whether it was acceptable for criteria to be met to a different extent in different cases *within* the same trial. The general feeling was that this was not acceptable. For example, the consent of a mother with a learning disability would be unacceptable if one could normally expect a higher level of competence from other appropriate mothers. If, on the other hand, all the suitable candidates for the trial were likely to have parents with a learning disability, then such a level of competence might be acceptable.

Difficulties for Consent in Neonatal Research

Given this account of the criteria for informed consent, it may be clearer why Euricon is concerned with the question of parental consent to neonatal research. For when parents give consent to such research it may be doubted whether any of the four criteria above are in fact met. (The practical problems in obtaining informed consent for a specific randomised controlled trial are discussed in Chapter 2.) Thus:

> The parents may be giving consent to researchers who are also responsible for the care of their baby. In such circumstances they may find it hard to refuse. So there may be some question as to whether the consent is voluntary (the fourth criterion).

> They may be asked to give consent within a fairly short time following the birth of their child (or following the discovery of illness in their child). But in order to be informed they need to receive full medical information about the research: the nature of RCTs in general, the nature of this trial, the risks and benefits involved, and so on. (Strictly, too, they need to try to think about the situation from the baby's point of view.) So there may be some question whether they have time to be properly informed (the second criterion) or fully understand what has been explained to them (the third criterion).

> Finally, the parents of sick neonates will obviously be in a difficult emotional situation. It may be difficult for them to take in information, or to reach balanced judgements. So the question arises as to whether they are mentally competent, in the circumstances, to give informed consent (the first criterion).

The Purpose of Consent in Neonatal Research

In neonatal research, consent can be seen as allowing the expression of the values of the person giving consent. In the light of what has been said about the concept of authorisation here, this can be taken as the parents expressing their values, playing their parental role in determining what happens to their child.   The value of seeking consent can be seen as (i) a matter of respecting the parental role (parental autonomy), (ii) a further protection of the child's interests in that parents can be expected to choose in what they perceive to be their child's interest.

The Aims and Works of RECs

Research Ethics Committees (RECs) have been set up in some form in many European countries during the last thirty years. Euricon has found that there is considerable variation in their geographical or institutional areas of responsibility, their structures and composition, their legal status and powers, and their funding, as well as in the decisions they reach. However they all have twin aims, namely to facilitate the carrying out of good quality medical research, but also to protect the (human) subjects of research. Often medical research requires them to find a balance between these two aims. Euricon has sought to cast some light on how committees are carrying out their tasks and to reflect on the structure of RECs, their role in the process of the ethical review of medical research, and how they carry out that role.

Objectives and Summary of Results of the Euricon Research Project

Against the background outlined above, the explicit aim of the Euricon project was to address the following connected questions arising in the European context (these are in bold type with the impact of the Euricon project summarised below each):

1. **Does the process of obtaining informed consent from parents on neonatal units lead to valid consent or is it merely an elaborate ritual? If so, what practical improvements can be suggested?**

Our research indicates that neither is valid informed consent always obtained on neonatal units, nor on the other hand is the process undertaken ever deemed a mere elaborate ritual. Parents are pretty much unanimous in valuing the involvement the process gives them, even in cases where they appear to have been very far from meeting the conditions necessary for their consent to be valid.

In fact only 29.5% of parents interviewed unequivocally gave a valid consent whilst over two-thirds had problems in one or more component areas. (The interview findings are described in detail in Chapter 17.) Practical improvements are outlined in the recommendations (Chapter 20).

2. **In the process of attempting to obtain consent what is/should be regarded as 'relevant and necessary information' to give to parents prior to the decision, and how is the digestion of that information assessed?**

The specific relevant and necessary information should include that recommended in the Declaration of Helsinki 1996. Euricon did not identify any further specific requirements. See Chapter 20 for a more extensive discussion on the method of obtaining informed consent.

There is no monitoring of the digestion of information. The process depends entirely on the ability of the person seeking consent to discern how much has been digested by the interviewee.

3.   How are health professionals trained in the process of obtaining informed consent?

There is no training of health professionals in the process of obtaining consent throughout the countries studied. The process might be improved by such training.

4.   What guidelines with regard to informed consent and neonatal research are laid down by Research Ethics Committees across Europe?

Findings are set out in Chapters 3 to 7.

5.   Does an examination of the application of research guidelines on neonatal units suggest that Research Ethics Committees are adequately in touch with clinical practice and the responses of parents? If not, what can be done to improve links?

The contrast between the information provided by the first questionnaire analysis and the information from interviews with clinicians and parents suggests that RECs may not be sufficiently in touch. Some suggestions are made to improve this.

6.   What are the legal requirements governing the criteria for informed consent in neonatal research across Europe?   What principles underlie those requirements?

These issues are set out in Chapters 8 to 16.

7.   Are there differing ethical and legal viewpoints between European countries on obtaining informed consent for research on neonatal units? What underlies any differences that do exist? Is greater consistency desirable? If so, how can it be obtained?

All the countries examined seemed to view the process as desirable; at least it was a requirement focused on by RECs in all those countries and it was also considered desirable by parents in all those countries. But there are considerable differences regarding the practice of obtaining consent from one country to another (see Chapter 4.)

In the chapters that follow we present the results of the project as they apply to our inquiry into the workings of RECs and our investigation of the problem of informed consent in neonatal research. In the last chapter of the book, in the consensus document, we provide a full account of how our results address the seven questions above.

References

Beauchamp T and Childress J. *Principles of Biomedical Ethics.* 4th edn. New York OUP 1994: 142-146.
Neuberger J. *Ethics and Health Care. The role of research ethics committees in the United Kingdom.* King's Fund Institute, London 1992.

2 The Practical Problems in Obtaining Informed Consent for a Neonatal Randomised Controlled Trial

DR A.B. GILL

The success of medicine, and in particular neonatal care, has arisen from the drive to provide care that is evidence-based. It is generally accepted that the most appropriate way to evaluate new treatments is in the form of a randomised trial. This could be either the evaluation of a new treatment versus conventional, or the comparison of two new treatments for a condition, or evaluation of a new treatment versus no treatment (placebo). There are many examples of neonatal randomised trials in the 1990s that have altered practice (Baumer, 2000; OSIRIS Collaborative Group, 1992; Ventriculomegaly Trial Group, 1994).

Fully valid consent from the parent(s) is deemed necessary in Europe (legally and ethically) for the majority of randomised trials in neonatal care (Kennedy and Grubb, 1994). The United Kingdom (UK) multicentre randomised controlled trial of a new modality of care for the newborn infant with severe respiratory failure is an example of a neonatal trial that presents many of the problems with obtaining fully valid consent (UK Collaborative trial of Extracorporeal Membrane Oxygenation (ECMO)) (Anonymous, 1996).

In keeping with the theme of the book, the aim of this chapter is to inform the reader of the structure and organisation of a specific neonatal trial that took place in the UK between 1992-1994 and to discuss the practical and ethical difficulties in obtaining consent for this trial.

What is ECMO?

Extra-corporeal Membrane Oxygenation (ECMO) is a form of lung-bypass. First developed in adult practice in the early 1980s it was introduced into neonatal practice in Europe in the late 1980s (Dworetz et al, 1989;

O'Rourke et al, 1989; Stolar et al, 1991). This technique oxygenates blood outside the body (and removes carbon dioxide) obviating the need for gas exchange in the lungs. Neonatal ECMO is most commonly used to support mature newborn infants. The principle is that a major vein and artery in the neck are cannulated. Blood is removed from the patient and passed over a special membrane surrounded by fluid through which oxygen is continually piped. The oxygen is exchanged with carbon dioxide by simple diffusion, thereby carrying out the normal function of the lungs.

Which Newborn Infants Require ECMO?

Prior to the UK collaborative ECMO trial, any fully mature (term) newborn infant with a specific lung condition in which gaseous exchange (normal lung function) was a problem despite full support via a ventilator could be considered for ECMO. In the UK this was only provided in one of three specialist centres. The types of clinical condition for which a baby would be considered for ECMO had a mortality approaching 50% with conventional management. Initial clinical observations and reports from around the world confirmed that many newborns appeared to benefit from this treatment although it was clearly recognised that death or side-effects did occur in a significant number. The major side-effect was the development of brain haemorrhage secondary to the requirement for the blood to be anticoagulated prior to it flowing through the ECMO circuit.

As a result clinicians within the UK responsible for the care of newborn infants needed to know whether ECMO was more advantageous (mortality and morbidity) than conventional ventilatory support for the mature newborn infant with respiratory failure of whatever cause. Doubts existed as to the value of this treatment for certain clinical conditions, for example, the infant with a diaphragmatic hernia. Concern over long-term disability, both neurological and respiratory, often resulted in infants not being referred for ECMO prior to the trial. In the climate of close financial control, concerns were expressed by the purchasers of health care as to the cost-benefit of this treatment. All these issues led to significant clinical equipoise for ECMO as a treatment modality for the sick newborn infant.

In 1992 the UK collaborative ECMO trial was set up to evaluate the clinical benefits of ECMO in the term newborn infant. The primary outcome measure of this study was death or disability at one year. Funding was obtained from the Medical Research Council, a government-funded agency for promoting research and development in Health Care in the UK.

Trial Design

Certain conditions existed for this trial:

- The newborn infant had to be more than 34 weeks gestation and have a birthweight of more than 2000 grams.
- The infant had to be suffering from severe respiratory failure.
- Those infants randomised to receive ECMO had to be transferred to one of five centres in the UK.
- Informed consent was required from the parents prior to entry.

Clinical Conditions

The clinical conditions were such that the majority of infants would have been expected to develop the condition leading to respiratory failure only in the first 24 hours after birth, i.e. they would not have been predicted prior to delivery. In addition many infants with these conditions were delivered following Caesarean section, often carried out as an emergency procedure under general anaesthetic.

The criteria for respiratory support were based on accepted clinical standards and infants were considered eligible for the trial if they met the above criteria.

Registration

When an infant was considered to have met the entry criteria for the trial, the attending clinician contacted the trial co-ordinating centre and identified the availability of an ECMO cot. Only if a cot was available were the parents then approached for consent.

Consent

Parents were approached for consent to the trial and given an information leaflet. Information on their baby's problem had normally been discussed prior to the reason for the trial being explained. Signed consent was obtained for entry into the trial prior to randomisation. Parents were informed that ECMO was not available outside the trial.

Randomisation

If parents agreed to entry into the trial, a second telephone call was made and randomisation was performed. Infants were assigned to either continuing the respiratory support in the referring centre or to transfer for ECMO to one of five centres in the UK. The receiving ECMO centre undertook transfer by road or air ambulance. Following randomisation parents were given an information booklet on the modality of care to which they had been randomised. If transfer occurred, the parents' travel and accommodation costs were met.

Outcome

In infants who died, consent was requested from the parents for autopsy. In the survivors, telephone contact was made with the parents after discharge home. After correspondence with the infant's General Practitioner and Health Visitor, further contact was made when the infant was aged four, eight and 11 months. The parents completed a postal questionnaire at about 11 months. At one year a full assessment of the infant's development was carried out by one of three specialist paediatricians. A study-specific garment was used in all the infants to hide the possible scars on the neck for those who had received ECMO.

Informed Consent Process

Parents were faced with their baby becoming very ill within the first 24 hours after birth. In the majority this was unexpected and the risk of their child dying was approximately 50%.

The clinicians responsible for their baby's care would have discussed the severity of their baby's problem prior to consideration for the trial. On being approached for consent it would have been necessary to explain the exact nature of ECMO therapy and the potential benefits and risks. Their baby's clinical state would be further explained, as would the reasons why entry into the trial was considered appropriate. Each parent was given an information leaflet explaining the trial.

Parental consent was requested for the entry of their baby into the randomisation process. It was explained that there would only be a 50% chance that their baby would be randomised to the ECMO treatment. Parents had to be informed that ECMO was not available outside the trial.

Following randomisation, parents were given a further information leaflet outlining the treatment arm to which their baby was randomised.

Results of the Trial

185 infants were enrolled into the trial, of whom 93 were allocated to ECMO and 92 to conventional treatment. Parents of 15 infants declined entry into the study. 70% of infants entered the study within 48 hours of birth, with 45% within the first 24 hours.

Of the 93 randomised to ECMO, 78 (84%) actually received the treatment. Of all the infants enrolled, 82 (44%) died. Overall 32% died in the ECMO group versus 59% in the conventional (control) group. $p=0.0005$. This suggests a highly significant benefit of ECMO in terms of mortality. This figure equates to one extra survivor for every three to four infants allocated to ECMO. Only one infant in each group suffered from severe disability at one year. In other words, the improved survival in the ECMO group was not at the expense of increased disability.

Discussion of the Problems with Obtaining Informed Consent

There are many potential problems with obtaining fully informed and valid consent in neonatal research, and these will be discussed in more detail elsewhere in the book.

The neonatal ECMO trial is a common example of neonatal randomised trials that exacerbate the difficulties of obtaining valid consent. Specifically, under the different criteria for valid consents (Beauchamp and Childress, 1994), namely competence, information, understanding and voluntariness, the following problems are apparent with this study:

1. *Competence* In virtue of the nature of the baby's condition the parents were approached within a short time after birth after discovering that their baby had developed a potentially fatal condition. In addition, on many occasions the mother would have had an emergency Caesarean section under general anaesthetic.

2. *Information and understanding* The parents had to receive a full explanation of this new treatment on top of an explanation about their baby's life-threatening condition. They would have been provided

with a number of different information sheets and the explanation of ECMO would have been necessarily complex. In addition they would have been informed that their child was not responding to conventional management, although 50% of infants would be randomised to continue with this form of treatment. They had to understand however that they were consenting to entry of their child into the randomisation process and that if their baby was allocated to conventional treatment there might have been little further treatment available. Snowdon et al (1997) have described elsewhere the limitations of understanding of the parents of babies in the ECMO trial. If allocated to ECMO, transfer to one of the five ECMO centres would have been required. This was potentially a risk to their baby as he/she was already critically ill. However in the trial no infant died during transfer to one of the ECMO centres.

3.   *Voluntariness* Parents were invariably faced with very little time in which to make their decision. Often this was less than two hours from being approached. Parents were informed that they could not have ECMO treatment outside the trial. By the nature of the trial it was not possible to withdraw from the actual treatment allocation since once ECMO had been started it would only be altered according to clinical response.

   The problems with this urgency and potential high-risk made the problems with obtaining consent difficult to overcome. It was clearly not possible to change the nature of the baby's condition thereby giving parents more time in which to decide. Most parents felt that they had little choice but to consent since ECMO was not available outside the trial. Having consented, once ECMO had been given it was not feasible to withdraw the child from this element of the study, although they could have declined to take part in the follow-up programme.

Multicentre trials carried out in neonatal care particularly in the acute situation will always have these problems with consent. If it is considered necessary to obtain full (legally) valid informed consent, then it will be necessary to identify solutions to these problems.

Conclusion

The UK ECMO trial was a well-conducted neonatal randomised trial that showed a significant benefit from the use of ECMO in term newborn infants. On the strength of this trial the majority of neonatal units in Europe now either provides or transfers newborn infants with respiratory failure for ECMO. Problems with consent are clearly seen with this type of urgent, high-risk trial. New ways of overcoming these problems need to be sought if fully informed consent is ever to be achieved. Such trials however are essential to evaluate best clinical practice.

References

Anonymous. UK collaborative randomised trial of neonatal extracorporeal membrane oxygenation. *Lancet* 1996; 348 (9020): 75-82.

Baumer JH. International randomised trial of patient triggered ventilation in neonatal respiratory distress syndrome. *Archives of Disease in Childhood, Fetal and Neonatal Edition* 2000; 82: F5-F10.

Beauchamp T, Childress J. *The principles of Biomedical Ethics.* 4th edn. New York. OUP 1994.

Dworetz AP, Moya FR, Sabo B et al: Survival of infants with persistent pulmonary hypertension without extracorporeal membrane oxygenation. *Paediatrics* 1989; 84: 1-6.

Kennedy I, Grubb A. *Medical law: text and materials.* 2nd edn. London. Butterworths 1994: 1052.

O'Rourke PP, Crone RK, Vacanti JP et al. Extracorporeal membrane oxygenation and conventional medical therapy in neonates with persistent pulmonary hypertension of the newborn: a prospective randomised study. *Paediatrics* 1989; 84: 957-63.

OSIRIS Collaborative group. Early versus delayed neonatal administration of a synthetic surfactant – the judgement of Osiris. *Lancet* ii 1992: 340:1363-1369.

Snowdon C, Garcia J, Elbourne D. Making sense of randomization; responses of parents of critically ill babies to random allocation of treatment in a clinical trial. *Social Science in Medicine* 1997; 45: 1337-1355.

Stolar CJ, Snedecor SM, Bartlett RH. Extracorporeal membrane oxygenation and neonatal respiratory failure: experience from the Extracorporeal Life Support Organisation. *Journal of Pediatric Surgery* 1991; 26: 563-71.

Ventriculomegaly Trial Group. Randomised trial of early tapping in neonatal post-haemorrhagic ventricular dilatation. Results at 30 months. *Archives of Disease in Childhood* 1994; 70: F129-F136.

PART II
RESEARCH ETHICS COMMITTEES IN EUROPE: THEIR ROLE IN ETHICAL REVIEW

3 The Structure, Composition, and Operation of European Research Ethics Committees

DR C. MEGONE, DR S.A. MASON, MR P.J. ALLMARK, PD DR S. REITER-THEIL, PROFESSOR D. BRATLID, PROFESSOR P. DALLA-VORGIA, MRS P. MORROGH, DR A.B. GILL, PROFESSOR A. LANGLOIS

Introduction

The protocols for all randomised controlled trials (RCTs) carried out in Europe must now, in practice, be submitted to appropriate local or regional research ethics committees (RECs) for ethical approval. The structure and role of RECs has developed in different ways in different European countries, but little is yet known about how these distinct systems work or their effectiveness as ethical regulators.

As has been indicated in Chapter 1, Euricon was a research project undertaken in eleven European countries, Denmark, Eire, Finland, France, Germany, Greece, Italy, Norway, Spain, Sweden, and the UK. One of its objectives was to analyse the nature of ethical and legal regulation of RCTs, as that regulation is currently constituted, across this broad range of European countries. Part of this work involved investigating the operation of RECs in these countries, examining their structures and their regulation of one important ethical issue, the obtaining of informed consent for neonatal RCTs. In particular, the aims here were fourfold: to examine the degree of uniformity of approach both within countries and across countries; to identify good practice; to consider to what extent RECs shared a common view of the purposes of ethical regulation; and to see to what extent they were equipped to carry out such purposes.[1]

The following three chapters all seek to contribute to the attainment of these aims. To our knowledge, the reports contained in these chapters constitute the first surveys providing any such comparison and analysis of procedures in RECs across European states.

The present paper is the first of two based primarily on responses to a single questionnaire, and analysing the work and effectiveness of RECs. It reports on the structure, composition, and operation of RECs in the eleven sample European countries. The information was provided by participant RECs themselves and by the ethical and legal expert partners in Euricon. As attention is now being given to the development of RECs both at European and national levels, the account presented and analysed here must be seen as a snapshot of a changing picture. It will be argued that, as things currently stand, the overall condition of RECs in Europe lacks uniformity. Nonetheless certain broad generalisations can be made concerning the legal status, area of responsibility, composition, appointment, funding, workload and training of committees. These might seem to be primarily practical issues but it will be suggested that, in order to deal with them coherently, theoretical questions as to the independence, expertise, authority, accountability, and democratic role of RECs must be addressed.

Method

Questionnaires were sent to RECs in each of the eleven countries represented in Euricon. The participating RECs were selected on the basis of their responsibility for the conduct of neonatal research in those hospitals from which we would draw clinicians and parents for subsequent interviews as to their attitude to informed consent. As will be seen, the structure of RECs across Europe entails that this method enabled an approach to be made to all, or nearly all the RECs in some countries, but only a proportion in others. Thus in Norway, Sweden, and Denmark, for example, there is a small number of regional committees (five, ten, and seven, respectively) reviewing all research in the country, whilst in countries such as France, Germany, Spain and the UK there are many more local or regional committees. The following table indicates the number of questionnaires distributed and returned (see Table 3.1).

Table 3.1 Questionnaires Sent and Returned

Country	Number Sent	Number Returned
Denmark	3	3
Finland	5	5
France	5	5 $(25)^2$
Germany	3	3
Greece	5	1^3
Ireland	5	4
Italy	4	4
Norway	5	4 $(+1)^4$
Spain	5	2^5
Sweden	4	2
United Kingdom	4	3
Total	48	36 (+1)

In total just over three quarters (77%) of the questionnaires sent out were returned, though one was answered in a letter. The questionnaires were sent out in 1996, and returns generally received by mid-1997 at the latest. (The results were only now publishable in order not to bias responses to a second questionnaire sent to RECs by Euricon.) The questions used in the questionnaire itself are included in Appendix I. The information from the questionnaires was supplemented by that from expert ethical and legal partners. The questions we asked those partners are also recorded in Appendix I.

Results and Discussion

This section has been divided thematically.

1. Legal Status

Background

The legal framework within which RECs operate has an obvious bearing on the degree of uniformity of operation. Euricon found that the greater the degree of uniformity in the constitution of RECs determined by law, the more uniform the responses on ethical questions from the RECs within that country. It is thus noteworthy that there is considerable variation between countries both as to the existence of a statutory requirement for RECs and in the scope of the law in determining the role of such committees.

Results

In six countries, Denmark, Eire, Finland, France, Germany and Spain, it appears that   RECs are required to exist by statute.[6] In the other five countries, Greece, Italy, Norway, Sweden, and the UK, there appears to be no such requirement, although in some of these the effect of a recent EU directive may have been to give them a *de facto* legal status.[7] In some countries, such as Denmark and France, the state has considerable powers as to their constitution, and proper functioning, whilst in the UK there are only guidelines on these matters from the Department of Health. Similarly there is no such prescription at all in those four other countries where RECs are not statutorily required to exist.

So far as the authority of the committees is concerned there is slightly less, though still notable variation. Where they are statutorily required (Denmark, Eire, Finland, France, Germany, Spain), legally stipulated forms of research must receive approval from them. In countries such as Norway, Sweden, and the UK, there is no legal requirement for researchers to obey RECs, but they gain some authority from other sources, First, journals require approval from committees before allowing publication of research work on humans. Second, in the UK, approval from RECs is required for any research that takes place on National Health Service premises.

Discussion

Should there be more uniformity in Europe on these points? At first sight greater uniformity as to the statutory existence of RECs might seem to make it less likely that there be parts of Europe in which unregulated trials could be carried out. However this issue is in fact entwined with the question as to what constitution and powers RECs should have (addressed in subsequent sections). Until or unless this latter question can be settled, a uniform legal requirement for their bare existence throughout Europe might only disguise a high degree of variation in practice.

2. Area of Responsibility

Results

Here too there is quite a degree of variation. RECs have either national, regional (for example, a major city or group of counties), or local responsibilities. Of those that are local there are two kinds, either those that oversee a local area (for example a 10-30 mile radius) or those that are institutionally based (for example, a hospital committee). The following table indicates the diversity of arrangements to be found.

Table 3.2   Areas of Responsibility for European RECs

Country	National	Regional	Local (area)	Local (institutional)
Denmark	Yes	Yes	No	No
Finland	No[8]	No	No	Yes
France	Yes	Yes	No	No
Germany[9]	Yes	Yes	Yes	Yes
Greece	No	No	Yes	Yes
Ireland	No	Yes	No	No
Italy	No	No	Yes	Yes
Norway	Yes	Yes	No	No
Spain	No	No	Yes	Yes
Sweden	Yes	Yes	No	No
United Kingdom[10]	No	Yes	Yes	Yes

At present only five countries have a national REC. Where such a committee does exist its role is not to review directly individual research protocols, but to provide co-ordinating and analytical support for regional or local committees. So far as the reviewing of protocols is concerned, countries are divided between those using regional committees and those using local (area or institutional) committees, though in Germany and the UK both regional and local kinds have a role. In the UK the regional committees (MRECs) have primary responsibility for multi-centre trials (trials taking place in five or more geographical areas), whilst in Germany there are local RECs attached to universities with research hospitals, RECs with regional responsibilities, and also federal RECs.

Related to this division between countries that rely on regional committees and those that rely on local committees, or a combination of the two, is a significant diversity in the number of RECs overseeing research. In those cases where committees are locally based, RECs are much more numerous, so there are probably still more than 200 RECs in the UK and they are very numerous in Germany and Spain. Even though France's committees are regional in the sense of having authority over more than a very local area, here too there are about 50 committees. These examples contrast sharply with the much lower numbers in Denmark, Sweden and Norway (see Method section).

Discussion

Given this diversity, which of these arrangements, if any, is most desirable? Should local or regional (or even national) committees be the preferred form of regulator, or should the regulation system find roles for more than one of these types?

This has been a point of considerable debate particularly from the perspective of researchers, some of whom have become hostile to regulation by local committees.[11] In the case of any research that must be carried out at multiple centres the existence of numerous local committees can greatly increase the workload on researchers who have to deal with them individually. The researchers' frustrations can only be increased if the committees' deliberations produce varied or even conflicting comments on the protocol. Regulation by regional committees might be thought to overcome these problems. Thus in Norway, for example, such multi-centre protocols are dealt with by just one regional committee which then has authority to act on behalf of all. The efficiency of this kind of process was one reason for the introduction of MRECs in the UK, which only had local committees prior to 1997.[12]

A second argument against local committees is that their members may be too close to those submitting research protocols to maintain proper independence. They may be unduly biased for or against researchers known to them. In response to this it can be argued that the local knowledge of such committees is one of their strengths. It can enable them to make informed judgements as to the reliability of researchers and as to whether the epidemiological characteristics of their area make it suitable for a particular research project. For the same reason they may also be more likely to know of other competing projects in the same field which would require the same patient population.

Nonetheless the first line of argument does have weight. If regional committees are a significantly more efficient mode of ethical regulation, that allows important research to proceed more speedily. However regional committees bring their own problems. If they are to be the sole reviewers of research protocols, their workload will become very large indeed. The Danish committees, for example, already have to look at approaching 1,000 protocols a year. It is hard to see how this amount of work can be carried out on an unpaid basis, in which case membership of the committee would have to be a professional task (or at least a form of employment). If this were the case the committees would have to be properly funded. Where should such funding come from? Furthermore if committee members are paid, that is likely to raise more sharply the question as to who should be on the committee (see '3. Composition', below).

This is one nest of issues raised by an argument in favour of using regional committees. Those who favour local committees might also argue that such committees can reflect the values of a local community. Regional committees, by contrast, might impose their different values on local areas. Underlying this line of argument may be a supposition from liberal political philosophy, namely that individuals, and communities, can adhere to a plurality of values. If on the other hand it is held that there is a set of shared values which binds together nation states, then there is less reason to worry about regional committees on this basis.[13]

The debate as to whether local or regional RECs are preferable ethical regulators is therefore quite complex. What then of national committees? If they were proposed as the forum for the direct review of research protocols, similar worries would apply to them as apply to regional committees. However they do not currently play such a role anywhere in the countries examined. Their role of co-ordinating and supporting the work of regional or local committees seems valuable. It can help these committees share ideas, and develop common approaches to ethical problems, thus improving the coherence and efficiency with which those committees conduct their work.

In sum, the debate as between local and regional committees raises issues which can be highlighted but not resolved here. However it would seem desirable to extend the use of national committees, working along the lines outlined here, beyond those countries currently employing them.

3. Composition

Results

The composition of committees varies considerably across Europe. In some cases, for example in Italy, Spain, and the UK, there is even variety between the committees within one country. Where the committees are legally regulated, as in France and Denmark for example, there is standardisation at least within the country. Table 3.3 below picks out some salient features of those RECs surveyed. Some further aspects of the variation are then noted.

Table 3.3   Membership of RECs

Country	Number of RECs surveyed	Number of committee members	Number of doctors as members (%)	Number of lay members
Denmark	3	7	42	4
Finland	5	7-13	>75	0-3
France	5 (25)	c.15	30-40	1-2
Germany	3	9-11	50	0
Greece	1	5	100	0
Ireland	4			
Italy	4	9-14	>40	0-2
Norway	5	6-7	33-50	2
Spain	2		>75	0-2
Sweden	2	7	>80	0-2
United Kingdom	3	10-16	>50	2-3

In our survey, committees varied quite significantly in size, containing between five and sixteen members. In some cases (in Greece, and in some of the Italian and Swedish committees, for example) the committee was made up entirely of hospital doctors.[14] Where there were members who were not hospital doctors, there was no uniformity in the criteria for their membership. In Denmark, for example, three in a regional committee were doctors, and the other four were appointed by the relevant regional council, without necessarily any particular specialist expertise. In other committees the membership was explicitly multi-disciplinary.

However whilst a commitment to multi-disciplinarity was quite common, there was considerable variation as to which disciplines should be represented on a REC. The French committees include quite a wide range of disciplines requiring there to be a general practitioner, a lawyer, an ethicist, a psychologist, a nurse, a pharmacist, and someone 'specialising in social affairs', as well as hospital doctors. Taking this range of disciplines as a starting point it was noteworthy that in general there were very few ethicists or lawyers to be found on the committees we surveyed. Likewise, psychologists and someone 'specialising in social affairs' were far from common. Both nurses and pharmacists or pharmacologists were more frequently to be found, but nonetheless a significant number of committees lacked them. Finally some committees also included two disciplines not required in France, namely statisticians and theologians.

The attitude to lay membership (where a lay person means simply someone who is not chosen for the sake of any special expertise he brings to the committee) was also variable. The case of Denmark has been mentioned. Here the committees were effectively composed only of doctors and lay members (though some lay members might happen to have had relevant expertise). In some other cases, by contrast, in committees in Finland, Germany, Greece, Italy, Spain and Sweden, there were no lay representatives at all. (However Finnish law now requires two lay members and Rynning reports Swedish committees as now including two to three lay members.)[15] In all other committees there was at least one lay member but, apart from the Danish and Norwegian committees, they were generally heavily outnumbered by members with medical expertise.

Very little attention seemed to be given to the question of whether there was a need for representation of ethnic or religious communities. In the UK this point is addressed in guidelines where it is explicitly suggested that members of committees should not see themselves as representatives but as wise independent judges.[16]

The one obviously uniform factor in our survey was the representation of hospital doctors in the membership of committees. Even where committees were not wholly made up of such doctors, very often they would constitute at least half of the membership.

Discussion

This degree of variety in composition suggests that there is rather limited agreement across Europe as to what expertise, if any, is required in order for these committees to be optimally effective. This may indicate some disagreement either as to the purpose of RECs, or as to what is required to achieve their purpose, or as to both.

The one area of clear agreement is that hospital doctors are required as members. This is reasonable given certain assumptions as to the tasks required of RECs. In most countries these committees assess the scientific validity and the value of proposed research. Considered from one perspective these are indeed ethical matters, since it would be wrong to ask subjects to enter research which is badly designed, or whose results are not of sufficient scientific importance. Putting the question of design more positively, the proper scientific construction of research is a significant protection for patients entering trials, and the committee should be equipped to judge this aspect of a protocol. Furthermore, even where results are important, properly informed medical judgements are needed in order to make a reasoned assessment of the risk/benefit ratio for the research. Clearly all these are matters on which medical experts, rather than laymen, are properly qualified to judge. Two points should be noted though. First, hospital doctors may only have specific medical expertise, for example oncology, so these rationales suggest committees might need to draw on medical expertise not necessarily found within the committee. Second, an argument of this sort would also seem to make a case for both statisticians and pharmacologists to be members of the committees. From this perspective it is already hard to see how committees comprised only of doctors are defensible.

Even if the above considerations make it essential to have hospital doctors on committees, it might be held that a preponderance of one discipline within the committees could make them give undue weight to perspectives shared by that discipline. For example, one might expect perhaps that medical researchers may give more weight than the public at large to the importance of progress in science.[17] Furthermore in many countries medical training involves little if any study of ethics, so that medically trained members of RECs may be less sensitive to the wider ethical aspects of the assessment of protocols.

Thus any plausible account of the purposes of an REC makes clear the necessity for hospital doctors as members, but suggests the need for other members too. The need for statisticians and pharmacologists has been addressed. Is the absence of ethicists and lawyers from so many committees defensible?

So far as ethicists are concerned, the importance of their presence in RECs presumably depends on whether they bring some relevant expertise to the committees. Some might hold that the necessary expertise is to be derived from experience of the problems researchers face in practice, and thus query whether the study of theoretical ethics is of much help for the sort of judgements that RECs make. But one might reply that study of medical ethics should help both with the identification of the types of consideration relevant to a REC's decisions, and with the kinds of reasoning that should be deployed by RECs. The obvious role for lawyers would be to determine whether proposed research was within the law. Whilst this is not sufficient to make research permissible it would appear to be a necessary condition for ethical acceptance. It was noteworthy that some committees appeared ignorant of aspects of the law governing some research in their countries.

If expertise is to be the rationale for having members of other disciplines on RECs, then one defence of the inclusion of a general practitioner, a psychologist, a nurse, someone 'specialising in social affairs', or a theologian, would presumably be that they could provide insights both as to the non-physiological effects of research on patients, and as to how to convey information about the research to the patients. (Representatives in some of these disciplines might also be thought necessary for the review of research in areas directly relevant to their expertise such as nursing or primary care studies.)

If committee membership is to be a matter of the expertise of members, then it might be suggested that lay members, specifically chosen without reference to expertise, do not have a role. It could be replied that the 'expertise' of lay members consists in assessing the effect of research on patients, and the provision of information to patients (the information sheet) from the average patient's point of view.

An alternative defence of lay membership might hold that their role was to make RECs more democratically representative, more representative of the community as a whole, or more accountable to the community as a whole. It might be doubted whether on either of these defences, in terms of expertise or democracy, lay representatives could really play the role required of them. Also, it might be pointed out that if membership of committees is to be thought of in terms of democratic representativeness or accountability, then the justification for having disciplinary experts on them would need to be reconsidered.

What this discussion brings out, however, is two possible ways of looking at the composition of RECs. In one view, RECs are repositories of expertise as to what research should and should not be allowed to proceed, from an ethical point of view. Their authority is based on this expertise. In another view, RECs represent the community from which they are chosen, and express that community's attitude to proposed research from an ethical point of view. Their authority then rests on their democratic representation, and they are accountable to that community. It might be said that there need not be a sharp distinction between these two ways of looking at things, but nonetheless this difference may both partially explain the differences in the composition of committees across Europe, and point to a deeper issue that needs to be resolved if preferable forms of composition are to be determined.

Furthermore the discussion here is not unconnected to that over the desirability of regional as opposed to local committees. The view of committees as repositories of expertise might be denied on the grounds that members will bring to their deliberations a plurality of potentially conflicting values. If so, it might be held that RECs should be accountable primarily to their communities and they can better achieve this if they are local. On the other hand if RECs are repositories of expertise then there is less reason to worry about their democratic accountability and more reason for them to operate on a regional basis.

4. The Appointment of Committees

Results

As might be expected, given the variation both in the area of authority and in the composition of RECs, there was some variety in the method of appointment of committee members. Table 3.4 below indicates the range of methods.

Table 3.4 Mode of Appointment to RECs of Committee Members

Country	Number surveyed	Mode of appointment
Denmark	3	Lay members by local council; medical members by the county on the advice of the Health Sciences Research Council
Finland	5	By chief hospital clinician, faculty board of the hospital, or the hospital authorities
France	5 (25)	By the state
Germany	3	By medical faculty and representative members of the university
Greece	1	By hospital
Ireland	4	By the Medical Research Board
Italy	4	By physician association; chairman of department with advice from current REC; hospital administration; hospital general manager
Norway	5	Ultimately by the Ministry of Education and Science
Spain	2	By the general manager of the local health service
Sweden	2	Doctors elected by medical faculty, lay members appointed by county council
United Kingdom	3	By health authorities, National Health Service trusts, medical boards, committees and schools
Total	37	

The varying methods of appointment broadly reflect the nature of the committee's composition. Where RECs are predominantly or wholly made up of doctors or those with medically related expertise, they are usually appointed by a medical body, or a representative of such a body; where there is a wider membership including lay members there is more likely to be some democratic or semi-democratic input with members being appointed by ministers, ministries, or regional councils.

Discussion

The appropriate mode of appointment for RECs depends on the approach to the previous questions about the role or purpose of the committees. If RECs are supposed to contain expertise, the method should be suited to identifying those with the relevant expertise. This may not necessarily be a matter of democratic election. If RECs are supposed to reflect the values of particular communities, or to be democratically accountable, then selection by direct popular elections, or by appointment by a democratically elected body, would seem more appropriate.

In either case, whether committees are viewed as bodies of experts, or as democratically representative, it will be important for their members to exercise independence. In the one case this would be a matter of exercising expertise properly, and in the other of properly representing the community, but both require independence. So a further constraint on the method of selection is that it should achieve the objective of appointing members who will exercise their judgement independently.

5. Funding

Results

In general, members of RECs in the countries Euricon examined are not paid. In some cases there is some reimbursement for the time spent on REC work, but in others there is none. For example, where hospital doctors are committee members the work is often seen as part of their job. In other cases, for example in the UK, membership is taken to reflect the goodwill of the voluntary contributor whether hospital professional or lay member. In all the countries surveyed there appears to be some administrative funding, but this is often minimal. The sources of such funding were the hospital or the state, or a charge on pharmaceutical companies (for their REC reviews), or a standard charge for any protocol reviewed.

Discussion

The degree of funding available is important since it affects how effective RECs can be. For example, even if committee members are not paid, funds might pay for secretarial support for a committee, removing such tasks from unpaid members, or possibly for bibliographic and expert support where members feel the need to call upon it.

If members were paid, this would significantly affect the time they could devote to the task. From the point of view of researchers this would have a bearing on the speed with which protocols are examined. It would also have a relevance to the time that committees could give to the review of each individual protocol, and thus to appropriate decision making. Both these points might in turn have a bearing on the status and authority of RECs, both amongst researchers and amongst the wider community.

However if funding is to be provided it is difficult to determine whence it should be sought. Both the option of charging pharmaceutical companies, and that of a standard charge for any protocol reviewed, raise the question of the protection of the independence of RECs. Committees might be tempted towards leniency to the principal sources of their funding. However if payment is to come from the state directly, or indirectly via hospitals, then RECs will have to compete for resources with all the other demands on the hospital or state purse and funding is likely to remain minimal.

6. Workload

Results

The information received from expert partners revealed that the workload of RECs is a significant problem in a number of countries. This was particularly noted by partners in Denmark, Sweden, and the UK. Clearly this matter is connected to the area of responsibility of committees, and to the question of payment for membership. The greater the breadth of area of responsibility, the more protocols a committee will have to review. Thus, as already noted, in Denmark individual regional committees are examining approaching 1,000 protocols a year. In the UK even some local RECs attached to university hospitals are reviewing more than 400 proposals per year.

Discussion

This raises the question whether it is feasible to have unpaid committees, and in particular unpaid regional committees of the sort found in Denmark. Even 400 protocols a year, let alone 1,000, is a huge burden of work for an unpaid committee to undertake.[18] This point is another that is relevant to the theoretical issue of the role RECs are supposed to play. If, for example, they are supposed to deliver independent, authoritative, expert judgement, do they have the time necessary to achieve that objective?

7. Training

Results

Although this is a matter beginning to receive attention, at the time of this survey our expert partners reported that in all participating countries the training available for members was either non-existent or very limited.

Discussion

The importance of this finding depends to some extent on what REC members are supposed to do. If there is no special expertise required, or none more than what they can be expected to bring to the task in virtue of their professional training, as for example in the case of a member who is a statistician, then it is not clear that there is much necessity for training. Similarly, it might be said, if members are simply supposed to be representatives of their communities, then there is no specific training that is needed for that role. In reply to this, though, it can be pointed out that there are certain crucial concepts which every committee member needs to grasp and reflect on, whatever their particularly expertise, and for the grasp of such concepts training may be of help. For example, members need to reflect on the nature of informed consent, the nature of a patient's best interests, the concept of the value of research, the difficulty of assessing risks and benefits, and so on. These important issues are not the sort that members can be expected immediately to grasp thoroughly, whatever their prior expertise, so training might focus on introducing committee members to these and other central themes in the ethics of research.

8. Concluding Discussion

This report has shown that in the eleven countries surveyed within Euricon there is significant divergence on three central issues relevant to the structure and operation of RECs, namely their area of responsibility, their composition and the method of selection of their members. In the discussion it has been suggested that these differences can be partially explained if they are thought of as, to some extent, reflecting two competing views of the nature and purposes of such committees. On the one hand there is the view of RECs as expert committees, delivering expert judgements, with members chosen for the expertise they bring to them, and thus in principle suitable for broad geographical areas of responsibility. On the other hand there is the view of them as democratically representative and democratically accountable committees whose role is to express the judgements of the relevant community on the ethical defensibility of the proposed research. On this view it might be held they should have narrower geographical areas of responsibility. It has been suggested that to resolve the issues raised by the different approaches currently found in the countries surveyed it will be helpful to explore further the differences between these conceptions.

These differences have repercussions for further issues such as to whom the committees are accountable and how, and what the source of the committees' authority is. On the expert model it seems that authority of committees rests in their expertise, and they need not be directly accountable to the community, whilst on the democratic model their authority would lie in the fact that they express the democratic will and their members would be directly accountable to the community. (Thus on the former model REC members would be more like judges, on the latter model more like local or regional councillors.) These lines of thought suggest at least, that on the expert model, the deliberations of RECs can be thought of as attempts to determine the correct or true answer, whilst the democratic model is compatible with REC judgements always being seen as merely consensus judgements, and thus just one amongst a plurality of possible consensuses.

These differences clearly have repercussions for what expertise, if any, there should be amongst the members of RECs. However it was argued that on either view of the purpose of RECs there were some good reasons for hospital doctors, statisticians, pharmacologists, lawyers and ethicists to be on the committees, and a rationale for members from other disciplines, such as nurses and General Practitioners, was also put forward. It was also noted that whichever conception of an REC was adopted, it would be necessary for members to exercise their roles independently, and thus selection procedures should respect that requirement.

On either model, it seems, connected difficulties regarding funding and workload, found throughout the eleven countries surveyed, need to be addressed if RECs are to work more effectively. Addressing these problems should allow committees to devote more time and thought to their decisions, and also enable protocols to be processed more quickly, to the benefit of researchers. It was also argued that on either model a case could be made out for the need for more training of committee members, though the distinct models would no doubt diverge somewhat in their understanding of the purposes of training.

A final suggestion regarding good practice applied to the institution of national RECs. It was suggested that these could be seen as playing a distinct role from regional or local RECs, and thus on either conception of these committees could be seen as a desirable institution, worth adopting in those countries currently lacking them.

In sum, in the light of divergent practices two possible views of the purposes of RECs have been outlined, with differing implications for the nature of desirable membership if those purposes are to be achieved, and for the method of selecting such members. Nonetheless the research has made it possible to identify a number of areas of good practice which could be more widely adopted by RECs.

Notes

1. Among other things, it will be helpful for researchers intending to undertake multi-centre research in different European countries, an increasingly frequent occurrence, to be aware of variations in the structure and outlook of RECs across Europe.
2. A French partner passed on copies of the questionnaire to other RECs.
3. We were only able to identify one operational REC in Greece prepared to reply to the questionnaire.
4. One Norwegian REC replied by letter rather than using the questionnaire.
5. We were informed by our Spanish partner that three other Spanish RECs had refused to pass the Euricon project (for reasons not forthcoming from the RECs) and thus refused to participate.
6. In Finland this has only become the case since the enactment of a new law in 1999 (see Chapter 9).
7. Within a personal communication from Clare Foster, Professor Ian Kennedy writes (of the UK case) that 'The Directive [91/507/EEC (Updated standards and protocols for the testing of medicines for human use) which came into force in 1993] and the regulation making it part of English law does not in itself address the legal status of ethics committees. It merely demands that they be used. By implication, of course, they must exist before they can be used. It does not follow, however, that the Dept. of Health (or the State) has an obligation to create them'.

8. In Finland there is a sub-committee on Medical Research Ethics of the National Advisory Board on Health Care Ethics which processes international multi-centre RCTs.
9. In addition, in Germany, there are private committees closely associated with research in the pharmaceutical industry.
10. At the time of our survey the regional committees in the UK (MRECs, which have responsibility for multi-centre trials) did not yet exist.
11. White, A. Ethics Committees: Impediments to research or guardians of ethical standards? *British Medical Journal* (1995), 311: p. 661; Ahmed, A., Nicholson, K. Delays and diversity in the practice of local research ethics committees. *The Journal of Medical Ethics* (1996), 22: 263-6.
12. But it is not clear that this has yet been fully effective in addressing researchers' worries. Joanna Tully, Nelly Ninis, Robert Booy, and Russell Viner. The new system of review by multicentre research ethics committees: prospective study. *British Medical Journal* (2000), 320: 1179-1182; Andrew L. Lux, Stuart W. Edwards, and John P. Osborne. Responses of local research ethics committees to a study with approval from a multicentre research ethics committee. *British Medical Journal* (2000), 320: 1182-1183
13. See further on this: C. Megone. Demokratie, Liberalismus, Kommunitarianismus: Bezuge zu lokalen forschugsethischen Komitees, in M. Kettner (ed.), *Angewandte Ethik als Politikum*, Suhrkamp Verlag, Frankfurt, 2000.
14. Though Swedish committees are now supposed to have 2-3 lay members, see Chapter 14.
15. See Chapters 9 and 14.
16. Department of Health, *Local Research Ethics Committees*, (1991, HMSO, London).
17. There is some evidence for this in our survey of the attitudes taken by committees to a sample RCT, which is reported in Chapter 4.
18. The introduction of MRECs (to review multi-centre trials) has not helped particularly with UK workload since these protocols are still reviewed by LRECs as well! For confirmation of this point, see Tully et al., *op cit* and Lux et al., *op. cit.*

Appendix I

The questionnaire on which these results are based contained four sections, one asking questions about the structure of the REC, two inquiring about the RECs attitude to informed consent in neonatal research, and a fourth asking about the RECs actual or hypothetical attitude to a case-study. Regarding the structure of RECs, it asked the following questions, covered in the paper: (this chapter?)

1. Is the responsibility of your REC local, national, institutional, or other (please specify)?

2. To indicate the structure of your committee please state its size and the expertise of each member (e.g. neonatologist, pharmacist, ethicist, layperson).
3. How is your REC funded?
4. Who appoints your REC?

In addition we asked our ethical, legal and neonatal expert partners for supplementary information on the following issues:

1. Is there a statutory (legal) requirement for RECs in your country? If so, what is it?
2. How are RECs funded in your country? Does the funding cover administrative costs only? Or does it cover the expenses of members? Or are the members paid?
3. How are members of RECs appointed? (It may be that there is wide variation, in which case the variety would be of interest.) Are RECs subject to much political influence in your country?
4. Do the RECs have responsibility for an institution (such as a hospital) only? Or are they responsible for a local area or region? Or are they national? Do members receive (any) training?
5. Are there any regulations concerning the make-up of RECs (such as that there must be a lay person, or a lawyer, or an ethicist as a member)? Do you know roughly what proportions of medical doctors and laity are to be found on committees in your country?
6. What is the power of RECs? Do their decisions have legal force?
7. How do RECs in your country take account of cultural diversity?
8. Are there any particularly noteworthy problems that RECs face in your country?
9. Are there any other features about RECs in your country which may be of interest to us?

We received answers to these questions from all countries except Greece.

4 The Attitudes of RECs in 11 European Countries to Informed Consent in Neonatal Research

DR C. MEGONE, DR S.A. MASON, MR P. J. ALLMARK, PD DR S. REITER-THEIL, PROFESSOR D. BRATLID, PROFESSOR P. DALLA-VORGIA, MRS P. MORROGH, DR A.B. GILL, DR S. HOLM, PROFESSOR A. LANGLOIS

Introduction

As was indicated in the introduction to Chapter 3, this chapter is one of three examining the workings of RECs in 11 European countries, and their effectiveness as ethical regulators.

The present paper is the second of two based on responses to a single Euricon questionnaire. It reports on the treatment by RECs, in the sample countries, of an important and difficult ethical issue, the obtaining of informed consent for neonatal RCTs. The information was provided primarily by participant RECs themselves, with minor additions from the ethical and legal expert partners in Euricon. As attention is now being given to the development of RECs both at European and national levels, the account presented and analysed here must be seen as a snapshot of a changing picture. It will be indicated that, with regard to the requirement for informed consent in neonatal research, attitudes vary a good deal both across Europe and within countries. However there are also some striking areas of uniformity. The results here provide a basis for comparison with those obtained from interviewing parents and clinicians about their experience of the process of giving, or seeking, consent.[1]

The following analysis identifies three main points about the situation revealed. First, on matters such as the defensibility of research on neonates without consent, or of research not aimed at the direct benefit of the neonate subject itself, disagreement between the committees is a matter of concern. Second, the responses serve to identify possible improvements in good practice with respect, for example, to the training of those obtaining consent, and to the monitoring of the implementation of REC regulations. Third, in the light of the response of the RECs to a particular RCT, one in which there were practical constraints on the informed consent process, RECs may need to attend more carefully to the practical requirements of implementing ethical regulations.

Method

Questionnaires were sent to RECs in each of the 11 countries represented in Euricon. The participating RECs were selected on the basis of their responsibility for the conduct of neonatal research in those hospitals from which we would draw clinicians and parents for subsequent interviews as to their attitude to informed consent. As will be seen, the structure of RECs across Europe entails that this method enabled an approach to be made to all, or nearly all, the RECs in some countries, but only a proportion in others. Thus in Norway, Sweden, and Denmark, for example, there is a small number of regional committees (five, ten and seven, respectively) reviewing all research in the country, whilst in countries such as France, Germany, Spain and the UK there are many more local or regional committees. The following table indicates the number of questionnaires sent out and returned.

Table 4.1 Questionnaires Sent and Received

Country	Number Sent	Number Received
Denmark	3	3
Finland	5	5
France	5	5 (25)[2]
Germany	3	3
Greece	5	1[3]
Ireland	5	4
Italy	4	4
Norway	5	4 (+1)[4]
Spain	5	2[5]
Sweden	4	2
United Kingdom	4	3
Total	48	36 (+1)

In total just over three-quarters (77%) of the questionnaires sent out were returned, though one was answered in a letter. The questionnaires were sent out in 1996, and returns generally received by mid-1997 at the latest. (The results were only now publishable in order not to bias responses to a second questionnaire sent to RECs by Euricon.) The questionnaire itself is included in Appendix I.

Results and Discussion

The section below has been divided thematically.

1. Method of Acquisition of Consent Permitted or Required by RECs

Results

The RECs were asked a number of questions about the procedures by which they require informed consent for randomised clinical trials on neonates to be obtained. Their answers are shown in two tables. The following table reveals whether committees required, or at least permitted, written consent; whether they required, or at least permitted, oral consent;

and whether they permitted one parent to express consent, or required it to be done by two.

Table 4.2   Informed Consent Requirments of RECs

Country (number of returns)	Written consent required or permitted	Oral consent required or permitted		Expression of consent by one parent permitted	Expression of consent by two parents required
Denmark (3)	Yes (all)		No (all)	Yes (all)	No (all)
Finland (5)	Yes (all)	Yes (3/5)	No (2/5)	Yes (2/5)	Yes (3/5)
France (5)	Yes (all)		No (all)	No (usually)	Yes (usually)
Germany (3)	Yes (all)	Yes (1/3)	No (2/3)	No (all)	Yes (all)
Greece (1)	Yes		No	No	Yes
Ireland (4)	Yes (3/4)	Yes (2/4)	No (2/4)	Yes (2/4)	Yes (1/4)
Italy (4)	Yes (all)	Yes (2/4)	No (2/4)	Yes (1/4)	Yes (3/4)
Norway (5)	Yes (all)	Yes (3/5)	No (2/5)	Yes (all)	No[6] (all)
Spain (2)	Yes (all)	Yes (all)		Yes (all)	No (all)
Sweden (2)	Yes (all)	Yes (all)		Yes (all)	No (all)
United Kingdom (3)	Yes (2/3)	Yes (2/3)	No (1/3)	Yes (all)	No (all)
Total	35/37	17/37	20/37	20/37	16/37

The next table shows whether committees required parents from whom consent was sought to be given an information sheet, and if so whether they required that parents read the sheet before deciding. It also shows whether the committees required parents to have time away from the requesting clinician in which to reflect.

Table 4.3 REC Requirements Prior to Parental Decision on Consent

Country (number of returns)	Must parents be given information sheet?	Must parents read information sheet?	Must parents be given time away before deciding?
Denmark (3)	Yes (all)	Yes (1/3)	Yes (2/3)
Finland (5)	Yes (all)	Yes (all)	Yes (3/5)[7]
France (5)	Yes (all)	Yes (all)	No (all)[8]
Germany (3)	Yes (all)	Yes (all)	Yes (2/3)
Greece (1)	Yes	No	Yes
Ireland (4)	Yes (3/4)	Yes (3/4)	Yes (3/4)[9]
Italy (4)	Yes (3/4)	Yes (2/3)	Yes (2/4)
Norway (5)	Yes (all)	Yes (4/5)	Yes (4/5)
Spain (2)	Yes (1/2)	Yes	Yes
Sweden (2)	Yes (all)	Yes (all)	Yes (all)
United Kingdom (3)	Yes (all)	Yes (all)	Yes (all)
Total	34/37	31/37	24/37

The following table shows that there was almost uniform agreement amongst RECs that consent should be sought from parents by the responsible researcher or the responsible clinician (which may often be the same person).

Table 4.4 Person Specified by RECs to Obtain Consent

Country (number of returns)	Do you specify who obtains consent?
Denmark (3)	Responsible clinician (1); No (2)
Finland (5)	Responsible clinician/investigator (all)
France (5)	The responsible investigator
Germany (3)	The responsible clinician (all)
Greece (1)	The responsible clinician
Ireland (4)	Clinician/investigator (all)
Italy (4)	The responsible researcher (3/4); No (1/4)
Norway (5)	The responsible investigator/clinician (4/5); No (1/4)
Spain (2)	The responsible clinician
Sweden (2)	The responsible clinician
United Kingdom (3)	The researcher or well-versed staff (1/3); No (2/3)

In addition we asked the committees whether there was any minimum information which they stipulated should be included in the information sheet. To this the variety of answers was great. Only in France, where the law stipulates the minimum information to be given, was there uniformity. The French law requires that every information sheet includes the research aim; that the trial involves randomisation; whether a placebo is being used; the expected benefits, and the foreseeable risks; any likely discomfort to the baby; any measures to reduce discomfort; the freedom to withdraw from the trial; the REC's opinion of the trial. In all the other countries there was diversity between the reporting RECs within the country as to what information was a minimum requirement. A small number of committees (for example, one in each of the UK, Germany, and Italy) made no stipulation at all.

Discussion

In all the countries examined, the requirement to obtain informed consent was viewed as extremely important by RECs. However these results indicate that the actual procedures by which consent is sought from parents are likely to vary quite a lot. How much does this variation matter?

Almost all committees permit written consent. Some require it, and do not permit oral consent. There are practical reasons for preferring written consent. The requirement for written authorisation emphasises the parent's responsibility for what is being permitted for the baby, and from the doctor's point of view it can serve as concrete evidence that consent has been sought. However there may be occasions when the timescale within which the research is to be undertaken is so short that only oral consent is possible, occasions where perhaps only the mother is available to give consent, and she is not in a position to write. Thus there may be grounds for allowing oral consent in certain circumstances.

Similar considerations apply to the division between the committees over whether one or two parents should give consent. Since many neonatal research proposals will be proposed in circumstances of some gravity, the decision as to whether to allow a child to participate or not will have a serious impact on the family. In such circumstances it is desirable for the whole family to be involved. On the other hand there may be good reason to allow one parent to consent where there are pressing reasons why both could not do so. This might be the case, for example, where only the father is available because the mother remains under the influence of a general anaesthetic following a caesarean delivery.

Almost all the RECs reporting required parents to receive an information sheet, and nearly as high a proportion stipulated that parents should read it. There is an obvious rationale for this in that the existence of such a sheet ensures a uniform core to the information any parent receives about the trial they are being asked to enter their child into. It also enables the committees to check both the content of that information and the way it is expressed.[10] There was a more significant division over the requirement that parents have time away from the researchers to consider this information. Only just under two-thirds of committees required this, and amongst those that did some did not specify any particular length of time, whilst in Ireland the law requires that parents be given six days to reflect (though it is possible for researchers to apply for this period to be reduced).

On the one hand there is good reason to allow people some such time away from the researchers. For most lay people the complexity of the information they are given about a trial will take time to digest, and time away from the researchers also allows them space to reach an independent decision. However, as has already been noted, in some neonatal trials the time available before the research must begin is very short. It may be for this reason that some of the RECs did not specify a length of time for reflection. If the first line of thought is correct though, that in turn raises the question of whether it is possible for parents to give valid consent when time is pressing, and there may not be time to grasp or reflect on the information given.[11]

The committees surveyed were pretty unanimous in expecting the responsible researcher or clinician to seek consent from parents. This might seem reasonable on two grounds. Clearly one might expect people in these positions to have a good understanding of the research to be conducted and thus to be in a good position to explain information to the parents. In addition the parents could be expected to trust the clinician in charge, and thus feel able to discuss the matter with him. On the other hand there might be some worry that parents could feel somewhat pressurised if their clinician was the person to obtain consent, either through feeling they should enter their child into the trial because they owed the clinician a debt of gratitude, or through believing that the care of their child might be adversely affected if they refused consent.[12]

On the face of it, it would be good practice if the RECs all shared a conception of the minimum information that should be given parents in an information sheet. Agreement on such a minimum information requirement in the patient information sheet would also help towards standardisation. Minimum standards for information are stated in codes governing research such as the Nuremberg Code, and the Helsinki Declaration. Given that these codes address the matter, it is somewhat surprising that there was not more uniformity amongst the RECs.

2.   The Training of Those Obtaining Consent

Results

Although the committees were largely uniform in stipulating who should seek consent from parents, none of the committees surveyed stipulated any training required for those carrying out the task. In Finland and Ireland some committees suggested that those seeking consent might have received relevant training in their medical education, but in general it was reported that there is no specific training for this work in any of the countries surveyed. Those asked to carry out the procedure are expected to learn 'on the job'.

Discussion

The argument in favour of training for this task is that explaining complex information to parents in difficult circumstances is demanding work, and involves communication skills, and that this is the sort of thing for which training is available. The RECs need not be concerned as to where such training is given - it is possible, for example, for such training to be included in general medical education - but it seems reasonable for RECs to consider whether the interviewer has the relevant skills.[13]

3.   The Monitoring by RECs of the Practical Implementation of the Constraints Laid Down

Results

Some committees in France, Greece, and Italy denied that the emotional condition of the parents was significant for their ability to give consent, but otherwise all agreed on the importance of parental understanding, voluntariness and emotional stability at the point of decision. However, of all the committees we surveyed, only one reported any monitoring of this. That committee was in the UK and mentioned an audit process.

Discussion

In the absence of an audit process it is obviously hard for RECs to determine to what extent it is possible for parents to gain adequate understanding to decide in an informed way whether or not to enter their child into a trial. Similarly it is difficult for committees to assess whether parents may sometimes suffer from problems of coercion, or whether their competence to decide is ever adversely affected by their emotional condition. The lack of monitoring thus means that committees may be out of touch with these aspects of practice, and so not in a good position to think through what is practically involved in meeting their stipulations.

At present it is difficult for committees to engage in such monitoring because of the problem of resources. They do not have the funding, or the time, to undertake this further task.[14] No doubt for this reason committees focus largely on the information sheet which they are in a position to check carefully. However the results of Euricon's interviews with parents and clinicians suggest that it can quite often be difficult to achieve in practice the standards for informed consent that RECs require. They also suggest that the information sheet plays a less significant role than might be expected.[15] It would therefore seem desirable for RECs to be in a position to monitor research that they approve. The results of such monitoring could inform the development and dissemination of guidelines on good practice for those seeking informed consent from parents. The monitoring could be achieved in various ways. (1) Questionnaires could be sent to parents by principal investigators on behalf of RECs, seeking information on their experience of giving consent. (2) At the end of trial recruitment, research groups could review their RCT from an ethical point of view and send a short report and recommendations to the appropriate RECs. (3) RECs could randomly monitor the practice of obtaining informed consent in RCTs directly (direct observation of practice).

4. The Views of RECs Regarding Research on Neonates Without Informed Consent Being Given

Results

The RECs were asked whether they would allow neonatal research to take place without informed consent and, if so, to what kind of research this would apply. Table 4.5 below presents the results.

Table 4.5 Neonatal Research Permitted without Informed Consent

Country (number of returns)	Would allow neonatal research without informed consent	Would not allow neonatal research without informed consent
Denmark (3)	(2/3) Only for epidemiological research or research using existing data	(1/3) Never
Finland (5)		(All) No
France (5)	(All) In emergency situations only.	
Germany (3)	(2/3) In emergency situations	(1/3) Never
Greece (1)		No
Ireland (4)	(1/4) Yes	(3/4) No
Italy (4)	(2/4) Yes: (1) extreme emergency (2) highly favourable cost/benefit analysis and impossible to tell parents	(2/4) No
Norway (5)	(1/5)	(4/5) No
Spain (2)	(1/2) In urgent situation	(1/2) No
Sweden (2)	(2/2) In very rare emergencies	
United Kingdom (3)	(1/3) Non-interventional studies	(2/3) No
Total (37)	17/37	20/37

Discussion

These results present a fairly sharp divide amongst the committees, with just over half never allowing neonatal research without consent, whilst just under half would permit it in restricted circumstances. This is an important matter and it is not clear that both approaches can be equally well justified.

The predominant circumstance in which such permission would be given was where the research could be defined as an urgent or emergency trial. These are two types of trial in which the time available to undertake the trial is limited, but the distinction between them is philosophically important. For the purposes of this study urgent trials are trials in which consent (if sought) would have to be obtained within a highly restricted timescale, for example, within 12 hours. For example, a trial where the treatment to be tested is only effective within a short timeframe following birth would be urgent. Emergency trials are those in which consent (if sought) would have to be obtained in such a timescale *and* the research concerns a treatment for a disorder that is life-threatening.

Given this distinction it is not plausible that a trial protocol's being *urgent* is sufficient reason to permit the research to be undertaken without consent. The mere fact that the research must be undertaken quickly does not justify proceeding without consulting the parents. However there is an argument in favour of permitting research without consent when the trial is an emergency trial. In an emergency it is accepted that standard treatment may be given to a patient without consent, so the researchers are justified in giving the standard treatment without consent. But in an RCT the researchers are unsure whether the standard or the novel treatment is better, so they are equally justified in giving the novel treatment without consent. If so, they are justified in entering the patient into a trial of these two treatments without consent (with the intention of giving treatment in the patient's best interests). This may be the line of reasoning which has prevailed in the discussion over the Council of Europe's recent Convention on Bioethics which would allow emergency trials on neonates without consent.[16]

If this line of reasoning is correct then any REC should be prepared to allow neonatal research without consent in the case of emergency trials. However it is not clear that the other kind of circumstance, cited by some committees, provides such a powerful reason. Some RECs would permit neonatal research without consent if the research were non-interventional, or epidemiological. But to this suggestion it might be replied that in these kinds of case the parental entitlement to keep their child's data private should not be overridden, so consent should still be sought.

5.   **The Views of RECs on Neonatal Research Which Does Not Involve Some Direct Benefit to the Subject of the Research**

Results

The committees were asked whether there were circumstances in which they would permit research on neonates which, whilst it would not benefit the neonate itself, was likely to make a contribution to the future treatment of others (sometimes termed 'non-therapeutic research'). Table 4.6 overleaf presents the results.

Table 4.6   Views of RECs on Permitting Research not of Direct Benefit to the Subject

Country (number of returns)	Would permit research not of direct benefit to the subject	Would not permit research not of direct benefit to the subject
Denmark (3)	(All) Yes: (1) if of benefit to other neonates; (2) if no harm or inconvenience to child	
Finland (5)	(All) Yes: (3) if no harm to child;	
France (5)	(All) Yes	
Germany (3)		(All) No
Greece (1)		No
Ireland (4)	(1/4) Yes	(3/4) No
Italy (4)	(3/4) Yes: (3) if no risk, no harm to child.	(1/4) An offence against law
Norway (5)	(All) Yes: (2) negligible harm/risk to subject; (2) considerable benefit; (2) consent of both parents.	
Spain (2)	(All) Yes (1) if harmless to subject; (1) subject to law.	
Sweden (2)	(All) Yes: if likely benefit outweighs risk.	
United Kingdom (3)	(All) Yes: (1) no risk; (1) scrutiny of risk; (1) no overt harm to subject	
Total	29/37	8/37

Discussion

Although this question did not directly concern the issue of informed consent, it investigated whether committees would permit consent to be sought for anything other than research which was of direct (probable) benefit to the subject.

The majority of committees surveyed would permit such research in certain circumstances. One line of reasoning draws attention to basic research, such as research on neonatal physiology or neurology. This research is designed to discover basic information, not to benefit the subject directly. However it is argued that such research is crucial to neonatology as a whole since this basic research must be undertaken if there are to be any advances in therapeutic research in neonatology.

The objection to this line of argument is that research which is not of direct benefit to the subject must therefore use the subject as a means to the achievement of some further end. The German committees, in particular, have been keen to draw a sharp line here with regard to non-competent subjects. This position can be buttressed by noting that there is a particular duty of care to non-competent subjects. In a similar way the recent European Convention on Bioethics has proposed allowing some basic research not of direct benefit to neonates, and the German contributors have again resisted this change. Once non-competent subjects are used as means at all, it may be held, it will be hard to prevent them being exploited more widely.

Many of the RECs which would allow such research tried to meet the above line of argument by specifying that any neonatal research not of direct benefit to the subject should bring no harm or risk to that subject. However it is not clear that such a demand is realistic, since any intervention (and indeed potentially even touching a neonate) will constitute some risk of harm to the subject. Thus if such research is to be permitted the stipulation would have to be that the risk be minimal, and outweighed by significant benefits to the wider community. If committees make that stipulation then they will have to develop some criteria for the assessment of minimal risk, and a basis for determining when the benefit to the relevant group is great enough to outweigh any such risk to the individual subject.

6. The RECs' Attitudes to a Specific Trial

Results

The REC was asked about its attitude to an actual neonatal trial that had in some cases already been submitted to the REC for approval. Where this had not occurred the REC was asked to answer as though approval for the trial was being sought. An outline of the trial was provided to all the RECs. The trial had a theoretical basis which would be relatively complex for a lay person to understand, and involved a single injection which had to be undertaken within four hours of birth, thus there was only that limited time for parents to decide whether to allow their child to participate or not. (It fell into the category of urgent research.) Table 4.7 below presents the results.

Table 4.7   RECs' Attitudes to a Specific Trial

Country (number of returns)	Would permit the research to be undertaken	Would not permit the research to be undertaken
Denmark (3)	(2/3) Unlikely but perhaps, would need more information. (1) Concerned about consent.	
Finland (5)	(4/5) Yes (1) consent no more important than usual.	
France (5)	N/R	
Germany (3)		(All) No: (1) Lack of adequate informed consent; (2) on scientific basis
Greece (1)	No decision. Informed consent not significant issue.	
Ireland (4)	(1/4) Yes	(3/4) No
Italy (4)	(1/4) Yes: consent no more significant than usual	(3/4) Would need more information
Norway (5)	(2/5) Yes: consent no more important than usual	(3/5) Would seek more information
Spain (2)		(1/2) More information required
Sweden (2)	(1/2) Yes: high scientific priority	
United Kingdom (3)	(2/3) Yes: (1) information sheet and need for rapid parental decision significant	(1/3) on scientific basis
Total	13/37	14/37

Discussion

Just over half the committees making their response known would not have permitted this trial. However only seven actually rejected it altogether, as the remaining seven wanted more information about aspects of the protocol. Of the seven who did reject it at this stage, three did so on the basis of the science in the RCT. Therefore only four specified any reason to do with the possibility of informed consent as a rationale for rejection. In the Irish case, as noted, the Clinical Trials Act requires those consenting to have six days to reflect, so that precluded these committees passing this protocol. (The one Irish REC that passed the protocol must have allowed a request for less time, as allowed by the act.) Thus just one committee rejected the protocol on the grounds of doubting the possibility of genuine informed consent in such a trial.

Of those committees that passed the protocol only two picked out the issue of consent as being a matter for concern, one of these specifying the time available for parental decision as an issue that was noted. This need not imply that other committees did not attend to this factor. A number said they would not give the matter of consent more importance than usual, but it may well be that for many of them this is always the most important issue.

The RECs were asked about this trial primarily in order to discover whether the limited amount of time available to parents to consent raised their (REC) concerns as to the possibility of informed consent in such circumstances. On the face of it four hours is rather a short time for parents, likely to be emotionally stressed, to digest complex information and reach a rational decision for their child. Interviews with parents and clinicians confirmed that urgent trials of this sort can make valid consent hard to obtain.[17] However only six committees in total specifically identified this problem and, of these, three did so because the law governing time available to those consenting is so stringent in their country.

RECs clearly consider the informed consent of parents is generally an important requirement if a trial procedure is to be ethically defensible. They give a good deal of time to scrutiny of the parent information sheet. However this last result may suggest that they are too impressed by the importance of the information sheet in achieving valid consent, and have not thought carefully enough about the way other factors may bear on the process of informed consent.

7.   Concluding Discussion

Multi-centre neonatal RCTs are regularly reviewed by RECs throughout Europe. This report has shown that there is some significant divergence in the attitude of these committees to the obtaining of informed consent for such trials. Thus researchers can expect somewhat different responses to their protocols. On some issues, such as whether research may be undertaken when it does not directly benefit the subject, or whether it may ever be undertaken without consent, these differences are important. The report has explored some of the arguments that might be put forward on either side, as a contribution towards deciding upon good practice in such matters. In other cases it may be less important to resolve the different approaches, or those approaches may need to be flexible according to circumstance, for example as to whether consent may be given by only one parent, as opposed to both.

On the other hand the report has revealed other areas where there is no divergence, but improvements in practice might be possible for all RECs. Thus it would be beneficial if RECs required that those seeking consent from parents had suitable training. It would also be beneficial if committees were given the powers and resources to monitor the implementation of their stipulations regarding consent. Committees generally note that valid consent requires (in addition to the provision of appropriate information) competence, understanding and lack of coercion, which may in turn require adequate time for reflection, and emotional equilibrium. However they are in no position to assess whether these latter criteria are met in practice. The unsurprising result may be that in reviewing consent they focus unduly on the aspect they can assess, namely the information sheet, and attend less closely to the other factors. Enabling them to undertake monitoring might alleviate this problem.

Notes

1. See Chapter 17.
2. French partner passed on copies of the questionnaire to other RECs.
3. We were only able to identify one operational REC in Greece prepared to reply to the questionnaire.
4. One Norwegian REC replied by letter rather than using the questionnaire.
5. We were informed by our Spanish partner that three other Spanish RECs had refused to pass the Euricon project, for reasons they did not pass on, and thus refused to participate.
6. For the Norwegian RECs, though, it is usually required
7. One specified at least 24 hours.
8. However the French Committees do require that parents be given time away to reflect if this is possible.
9. The Irish Clinical Trials and Drugs Act stipulates that patients/proxies must be given six days to decide, but researchers can apply to avoid this.
10. These results gather importance in the light of our findings from parents and clinicians as to what has been happening in practice. See Chapter 17.
11. This is a point where Euricon's research into the practical experience of parents and clinicians involved in giving and obtaining consent is highly relevant. See Chapter 17.
12. Once again this stipulation by RECs can be compared with the information revealed in the interviews with parents and clinicians in Chapter 17.
13. The recent *Report of a Review of the Research Framework in North Staffordshire Hospital NHS Trust* makes a similar recommendation at section 10.5.10 (NHS Executive West Midlands Regional Office, 2000).
14. See Chapter 3.

15. See Chapter 17.
16. Council of Europe. Convention for the Protection of Human Rights and Dignity of the Human Being with Regard to the Application of Biology and Medicine: Convention on Human Rights and Biomedicine.   European Treaty Series – No.164. Strasbourg: Council of Europe, 1997.
17. See Chapter 17.

Appendix 1

Regarding the attitudes of RECs to informed consent in neonatal research, our questionnaire asked the following questions:

Section A - Role of informed consent in research

1.   The following questions concern *the method* by which you require informed consent for randomised clinical trials on neonates to be obtained? *Do you specify*:
   a. that consent should be given in writing?
   b. that consent should be given by both parents or only one? If only one parent, do you specify the mother or father?
   c. that oral informed consent is sometimes acceptable? If so,
         i. in what circumstances would this be?
         ii. do you also require that such oral informed consent is documented?
   d. that parents receive an information sheet about the trial?
         i. If so, that the sheet is read by the consenting parents?
         ii. If not, does the REC have any other fixed procedure for the giving of information to parents?
   e. that parents are given a period of time away from the requesting clinician in which to decide whether or not to consent?
   f. who should obtain the consent?
   g. training for clinicians who obtain consent for research? If so, please describe.
   h. any 'minimum and relevant information' to be given to parents? If so, what is this?
   i. any other requirements?

2.   Does the REC have *written guidelines* concerning the obtaining of consent for research which they give to researchers? If so, please quote or attach a copy.

3. Once the research project has been approved by the REC do you do any *further checks or monitoring* of the consent process? If so, please describe.

4. Are there occasions where the REC would allow neonatal research to take place *without informed consent*? If so, to what kind of research would this apply? If not, why not?

Section B - Problems in obtaining informed consent

1. Do you have any procedures to ensure *that parents understand the information* given to them? If so, please specify what these are.

2. Does the REC monitor *whether consent is given freely* by parents? If so, how?

3. a. Does the REC consider *the emotional state of consenting parents* to be important when clinicians obtain informed consent?
   b. If yes, why?
   c. Do you have any procedures to monitor the emotional state of those giving consent?

4. If research was forbidden on the grounds that the parent's emotional state would render them unable to give informed consent, what would the REC envisage would be the *effect on neonatal research* in general?

5. Are there circumstances in which you would permit research on neonates which, whilst it *will not benefit the neonate* itself, is likely to make a contribution to the future treatment of others? If yes, are there any further conditions that you stipulate for such research?

Section C - A specific neonatal trial

The following questions referred to a specific neonatal trial that had in some cases already been submitted to the REC for approval. Where this had not occurred the REC was asked to answer as though approval for the trial was being sought. The trial concerned a procedure which would be relatively complex for a lay person to understand, and the procedure had to be undertaken within four hours of birth, thus there was only that time for parents to decide whether to allow their child to participate or not.

1. a. Has this trial been submitted to your REC for approval?
    b. If so, did your REC approve the trial?

2. What were (would be) the reasons for allowing/refusing this trial to proceed?

3. Was the issue of obtaining informed consent from the parents for this research a significant feature in the REC deliberations about this trial (or would it be)?

4. Were there directives laid down by the REC to govern the practice of clinicians in this trial regarding informed consent (or would there be)? If so, please specify.

5 The Views of RECs in Eight European Countries on the Process of Obtaining Informed Consent in Neonatal Research, and on the Structure and Organisation of RECs

DR C. MEGONE, DR S.A. MASON, MR P.J. ALLMARK, PD DR S. REITER-THEIL, PROFESSOR D. BRATLID, PROFESSOR P. DALLA-VORGIA, MRS P. MORROGH, DR A.B. GILL, DR S. HOLM, PROFESSOR A. LANGLOIS

Introduction

As indicated in the introduction to Chapter 3, this chapter is one of three examining the workings of RECs in 11 European countries, and their effectiveness as ethical regulators. As in the previous two chapters, the objective is to contribute to four aims which Euricon had: to examine the degree of uniformity of approach both within countries and across countries; to identify good practice; to consider to what extent RECs shared a common view of the purposes of ethical regulation; and to see to what extent they were equipped to carry out such purposes.

The present paper is based on information provided by participant RECs in eight European countries. The previous two chapters presented analyses of responses that RECs had already given to a first questionnaire. They were now sent a second questionnaire which sought their reflective views, in the light of further information from Euricon, on these matters of structure, composition and consent. Thus in response to the first questionnaire the RECs simply stated the facts about their current structure and composition. This second questionnaire sought their views as to the ideal structure and composition of an REC. In response to the first questionnaire they simply stated some of their current practices regarding informed consent. The second questionnaire sought their views as to how practice might be improved.

The primary objective of this second stage of research was to gain some insight into the reasoning processes of RECs. We wanted to discover the extent to which their answers revealed a consensus, and thus a likely common mode of reasoning, either on a substantive ethical problem or on their own mode of operation. A subordinate aim of the questionnaire was simply to reveal the committees' own perspectives on the way in which they could be improved and on the best way in which the process of obtaining consent to neonatal research could be approached.

The primary aims of RECs are two-fold, to protect the subjects of medical research, and to facilitate the furtherance of such research. Different committees, and committees in different countries, may have varied in the way they balanced these aims. Both the structure and composition of a committee, and the committee's mode of ethical reasoning, will affect how they pursue these aims. The main objective of our inquiry at this point then was to uncover something about how RECs themselves reflect on these matters. The analysis below highlights two main points. First, the committees responded in rather divergent ways to information about what seems to occur in practice when consent to RCTs is sought in the neonatal context. Second, there was considerable disagreement amongst the sample European committees both as to the ideal composition for an ethical review committee, and as to the way in which members should be selected.

What this may suggest is that there is not at present a common mode of reasoning amongst RECs either about ethical issues or about procedural issues, such as committee composition and structure. Of course this research is based only on responses from a small group of RECs, sampled by convenience. It cannot be claimed that this sample is typical of all European RECs, nor can we draw comparisons between RECs in distinct European states. However their participation in Euricon's work suggested these were likely to be thoughtful RECs that take seriously the issues raised. Thus we can note that even amongst such a thoughtful group, though small, there were quite significant differences of view on these matters, and that may be a cause for concern.

Method

A second questionnaire was sent to RECs in each of the eleven countries represented in Euricon. It was sent to the 37 RECs which had already responded to the first questionnaire sent by Euricon. Together with this second questionnaire they were sent a brief summary of some preliminary findings of the Euricon research project. These findings had two components. They included, first, a short précis of the analysis of the first REC questionnaire (see Chapters 3 and 4). The second component of the findings they received was based on the next stage of the project. In it we reported the preliminary analysis of a series of interviews with both parents who had been asked to give consent for their child to take part in neonatal research and clinicians who had experience of seeking such consent (see Chapter 17).

The participating RECs were selected on the basis of their responsibility for the conduct of neonatal research in those hospitals from which we had drawn the clinicians and parents who participated in the interviews just mentioned. As will be seen, the structure of RECs across Europe entails that this method enabled an approach to be made to all, or nearly all the RECs in some countries, but only a proportion in others. Thus in Norway, Sweden, and Denmark, for example, there is a small number of regional committees (five, ten, and seven, respectively) reviewing all research in the country, whilst in countries such as France, Germany, Spain and the UK there are many more local committees.

The questionnaire was sent out in English, following local advice that it would be understood, but was translated for Greece (see Table 5.1).

Table 5.1 Second Questionnaires Distributed and Returned

Country	Number sent	Number returned
Denmark	3	3
Finland	5	4
France	5	4[1]
Germany	3	3
Greece	1	0
Ireland	4	3
Italy	4	4
Norway	5	0
Spain	2	0
Sweden	2	1
United Kingdom	3	2 (+1)[2]
Total	37	24 (+1)

Thus the second questionnaire had a response rate of 64%.[3] The questionnaires were sent out in summer 1998, and returns generally received by the end of 1998.

Results with Associated Discussion

This section has been divided thematically, in accordance with issues raised in the questionnaire.

1. Competence

Results

The committees were given results from Euricon research which indicated that in the case of just over 70% of parents interviewed there was some doubt as to whether those parents had been competent to consent to their child's participation in research. This was usually either because of the short time the parents had had to reach a decision or because of the emotional condition they had been in at the time of deciding. The committees were then asked four questions in the light of this, and the following table summarises their responses.

Table 5.2[4] Summary of REC Responses Concerning Competence

1.	Sometimes parents are asked to give consent to neonatal research even though they are not really competent at the time they are asked to consent.	*Agree*	*17*
		Disagree	*4*
		Unsure	*2*
		Other	*0*
2.	It is reasonable for RECs to issue a statement on the information sheet which tells parents that the research has been considered and approved by a REC.	*Agree*	*16*
		Disagree	*4*
		Unsure	*1*
		Other	*1*
3.	All committees considering neonatal research should include a neonatologist.	*Agree*	*12*
		Disagree	*7*
		Unsure	*0*
		Other	*0*
4.	All committees considering neonatal research should include a 'family representative' to consider the research from the parents' point of view.	*Agree*	*8*
		Disagree	*13*
		Unsure	*0*
		Other	*0*

Discussion

The first question was one of several asked to find out the responsiveness of participating RECs to the information we had provided for them about the actual conduct of medical research. In the light of the information given to them, it is somewhat surprising that only three-quarters of the committees agreed that in neonatal research parents might *sometimes* not be fully competent to give consent. Since both the parental and clinician interviews for Euricon had shown that there are times when parents are not fully competent to consent (see Chapter 17), the remaining questions investigated the committees' response to suggestions that might address this problem. Thus one suggestion was that it would help parents trying to decide in difficult circumstances if they knew that the relevant research had been approved by an REC.[5] Although a majority favoured this suggestion, several noting that it would give parents more security in agreeing to participation, those that dissented raised two important points. First they queried whether such information might not coerce parents towards agreeing to their child's participation. Second, they pointed out that at present only a small proportion of parents profess to knowledge of RECs, so many would not be in a position to assess such information properly.

The latter two questions focused on ways in which the composition of RECs might be improved so that they would be better informed as to the circumstances in neonatal research where it would be difficult for parents to be fully competent to give their consent. Whilst a majority of committees favoured the inclusion of a neonatologist to assess relevant research, those that dissented suggested that it would be better for RECs to call on a neonatologist as an expert adviser where necessary. This approach might be thought more desirable if attention is also given to the optimum size for an REC if it is to carry out its function effectively. Representation of a range of medical specialities within the regular members might lead to unduly large committees (see below). On the other hand a possible disadvantage of expert advisers is that they may lack the range of experience regular committee members gain from reviewing a large number of protocols.

The majority of committees rejected the need for inclusion of a 'family representative' when neonatal research is being considered. Their grounds were that committees will invariably have other members with families, and that all members should see it as their role to protect research subjects, so there is no need for a special family perspective.

2. Information and Understanding

Results

The RECs were informed that whilst all participating committees required that parents be given information sheets about proposed research, the parents reported that in less than half of cases had they read the sheets prior to reaching their decision. They were also told that within the participating countries there was virtually no training for those who request consent from parents. The following table summarises their responses to questions that focused on these issues.

Table 5.3 REC Responses Concerning Information and Understanding

1.	Is it important that parents giving consent to neonatal research read the information sheet *before* giving consent?	*Yes 20* *No 1* *Unsure 1* *Other 0*
2.	Given that our evidence suggests that parents very often do not read information sheets before giving consent, what should be done to ensure that they do?	*See Discussion*
3.	Are there any other things that could improve parental information and understanding?	*Yes 14* *No 5* *Unsure 2* *Other 0*
4.	How do you believe researchers/clinicians learn to obtain informed consent?	*See Discussion*
5.	Should it be a REC requirement that those requesting consent from parents for neonatal research should have received training in doing this?	*Yes 7* *No 10* *Unsure 6* *Other 0*
6.	If your answer to 5. was *No, Unsure, Other*, do you believe the current system is satisfactory?	*Yes 7* *No 5* *Unsure 4* *Other 0*

Discussion

Committees were in fact unanimous in their view of the importance of information sheets. The two that dissented to the first question only thought the sheets insufficient, but agreed they were necessary. In the face of the fact that they appear widely unused at the relevant time, the committees made several suggestions, including the following: that the research should be explained orally first, and then the parents be given the information sheet; that the person seeking consent should discuss the contents of the sheet with the parents prior to their reaching a decision; and that the parents should sign to say that they had read the sheet. The advantage of an information sheet is that it provides a uniform amount of information to all parents, and that information can be checked by RECs. The suggestions made by the committees are all sensible, but once this information is explained, or supplemented, orally by the clinician, as they suggest, the uniformity of the printed sheet is to some extent lost, and it is more difficult for RECs to monitor what parents are being told. So there is not an easy solution to the problem of ensuring that all parents are adequately informed.

Given this, it was perhaps disappointing that a third of committees responding could not suggest any other way to improve parental understanding. Of those that had further ideas, several suggested that there should be an independent person available, someone not involved in the research, with whom parents could discuss the practical aspects of research participation.

Almost all acknowledged that there is virtually no training available for those who have the task of seeking informed consent from parents. The consensus was that those obtaining consent generally learn by experience at present. Clearly such a method has pitfalls, especially if the experience is not well guided. However there was significant division as to whether RECs should in future require that those seeking consent have appropriate training. Committees who favoured a training requirement suggested it should focus on communication skills, but might also cover the ethical and legal principles governing the consent process. A further suggestion was for specific training in dealing with sensitive matters. If such training were available, then checking that interviewers had undergone it would be an additional burden for RECs. However if these skills are indeed desirable, and can be acquired through training, it would be a relatively simple matter for RECs to monitor.

The variety of responses to these questions suggested there was no general consensus amongst the committees surveyed as to how to convey information to parents optimally.

3. The Voluntary Aspect of Consent, and the Monitoring of the Consent Process

Results

Another important requirement of genuine informed consent is that the consent be given freely. The committees were informed that Euricon had found that parents sometimes reported feeling coerced, and also that RECs surveyed had been almost unanimous in reporting that they did not monitor what actually happened on the ground when research teams engaged in the process of seeking consent. The table below reports their responses to questions asked in the light of these points.

**Table 5.4   Summary of REC Responses Concerning Voluntariness
and Monitoring of the Consent Process**

1.	Do you believe that parents sometimes give a consent to neonatal research which is not completely voluntary (e.g. because they believe that the care of their child will be adversely affected if they refuse)?	*Yes 12* *No 7* *Unsure 3* *Other 0*
2.	It is clear that RECs require that the consent which researchers obtain from parents is a voluntary consent. However, do you think it is part of the REC's role to *ensure* that parental consent is given voluntarily?	*Yes 11* *No 12* *Unsure 0* *Other 0*
3.	Should there be some monitoring of the oral interaction which occurs between the parents and the clinician/researcher during the consent process?	*Yes 6* *No 13* *Unsure 4* *Other 0*
4.	If your answer to 3. is *No, Unsure, Other*, do you believe the current situation is satisfactory?	*Yes 10* *No 5* *Unsure 1* *Other 1*
5.	If you believe the current situation is not satisfactory, what else should be done to ensure that an informed consent to neonatal research projects is given by parents?	*See Discussion*

Discussion

Given the information produced in the Euricon parental interviews, it is striking that nearly half the committees did not concede that parents might sometimes be under some coercion in giving their consent. It is also striking that the committees are so divided on this point, with the remaining half of the committees supposing it to be fairly clear that coercion does sometimes occur. These RECs suggested that coercion might occur because the parents feared that a refusal on their part might compromise their baby's care, or because they might feel they owed the clinician gratitude.

There was also notable division on the question of monitoring the voluntary aspect of consent. Those committees who felt this was not the REC's role suggested either that such a procedure would be unenforceable, or that the responsibility for ensuring voluntary consent should lie with the senior researcher. Those committees who saw RECs as having a monitoring role in ensuring that consent was voluntary, suggested that committees might check this via a post-project questionnaire to parents.

The question of monitoring was pursued further in questions 3 and 4 in Table 5.4. Once again, despite the fact that Euricon's evidence suggests that there was some doubt as to whether 70% of the parents interviewed had in practice given genuine informed consent, the committees were divided as to whether RECs should monitor to what extent their stipulations are adhered to. In fact a similar number rejected the need for monitoring of the oral interaction, but fewer were definitely in favour of such monitoring.

Many of those who rejected REC monitoring felt it to be impractical. There might be two reasons for this. One is simply the matter of resources. At present RECs, which are generally composed of persons acting in an unpaid capacity, do not have the wherewithal to carry out such monitoring. However some committees also noted specifically the difficulty of observing such a sensitive interaction as that involved in obtaining consent, without interfering in it.

Those who felt monitoring should be undertaken, but not by RECs, suggested it should fall to senior doctors, nurses, or relatives to do this. But it is not clear that the first two are sufficiently independent of the research team to carry out this role, nor that relatives would have the expertise to do it, or the independence from the family. It is also very unlikely that doctors or nurses would have the necessary time.

The responses to these questions may reflect the practical difficulties involved in RECs undertaking the monitoring of what in fact happens when consent is sought from parents. However in the absence of such monitoring it is hard to see how RECs can be aware of the practicality of the constraints they lay down on researchers who seek consent from parents. It is certainly surprising that a high number of those committees that denied the need for RECs to carry out monitoring appear to have done so because they took the current situation to be satisfactory (see response to question 4 in Table 5.4). For reasons indicated above, the Euricon research had made clear that there were a number of difficulties in the parental consent process, enough to make it implausible that the current situation is acceptable. On the other hand those committees that rejected monitoring but felt the present situation to be unsatisfactory had only limited ideas as to how to improve it. One suggested the need for more information in the media about the conduct of RCTs, but it is not clear that this would address the specific difficulties parents face in deliberating about neonatal research.

4. Particular Problems in Obtaining Consent to Neonatal Projects

Results

The Euricon research had suggested that the validity of parental consent appeared especially questionable in research where time was short and their child was seriously ill. In light of this the committees were asked about their views on such research.

Table 5.5   Summary of REC Responses Concerning Problems Associated with the Consent Process in Neonatal Research

1. Is it unrealistic to expect informed consent to neonatal research in emergencies or where the time available for gaining consent is very limited?	*Yes 11* *No 12* *Other 0*
If your answer to 1. is *Yes* then: 2. Should the research go ahead without parental consent?[6]	*Yes 5* *No 9* *Other 0*
3. If you believe the research should go ahead without parental consent, what extra safeguards, if any, should be put in place?	*See Discussion*

Discussion

The division amongst the committees on the first question raises two worries. First there is the mere fact of their wide divergence on an important matter relevant to the ethical conduct of research. Second there is the fact that twelve committees appear simply to have ignored data derived from interviews with two hundred parents. Nor does this data fly in the face of common sense. One might expect time constraints, and the serious state of the neonate, to have an adverse effect on a parent's ability to process information rationally.

In response to the second question, nearly half those committees who had expressed doubts about the possibility of genuine consent in these circumstances were inclined to allow the research nonetheless. Several suggestions were made as to how to alleviate the absence of consent: that the REC should be more stringent in assessing whether such research could go ahead; or that parents should be advised ante-natally of the possibility of such research. Whether or not these suggestions seem acceptable, perhaps the most important point to note here is that the Euricon parental interviews found that more than 95% of parents wished to be asked for consent to their child's participation in research. At present, therefore, it seems unlikely that allowing research to proceed without consent would withstand public scrutiny.

The responses of the RECs to these questions, and those responses discussed in the previous section, raise a number of issues. First, if RECs are not able to monitor what happens in practice when consent is sought, are they well equipped to carry out one of their main objectives, that of protecting subjects, and is this incapacity a clear hindrance to their work? Second, if the committees surveyed are so divided on the questions of whether genuine consent to neonatal RCTs is always possible, and whether the process of seeking such consent needs monitoring, is it plausible that the REC system in Europe as a whole is currently well equipped to achieve its main goals (at least with respect to neonatal research)?

5. The Role and Structure of RECs

Results

The first REC questionnaire, and expert partners within Euricon, had provided information as to the size, composition, and method of selection of RECs, and concerning important aspects of their working practices (see Chapter 3). This information was reported to the RECs. The second questionnaire aimed to elicit their views on the diversity of structures currently to be found and on good practice in their functioning. Their views on the size, composition, and mode of selection of committees, and on good practice, are outlined below in Tables 5.6 and 5.7.

Table 5.6[7]   Summary of REC Responses Concerning Structure and Method of Appointment

REC Size

1.   What is the most desirable total number of members on an REC? $7 - 15^8$

2.   How many of these should be lay members? $0 - 3^9$

REC Composition

3.   Who should be represented on a REC (please tick appropriate box)?

	Essential	Desirable	Not needed
Medical doctor (hospital based)	23	0	0
General practitioner	9	7	7
Nurse	14	4	4
Pharmacologist	15	6	2
Statistician/ research methodologist	8	7	5
Psychologist	6	7	9
Ethicist	12	4	5
Clergy	3	9	9
Lawyer	12	3	6
Lay person	17	3	3

On method of appointment to RECs:

4.   Should there be uniformity in the method of appointment to RECs?   *Yes 11*
No   6
Other 2

5.   What is the most desirable method of appointment of *professional* members to RECs?

(The numbers under *Yes* reflect those RECs who chose a method as one of their three most favoured methods. The numbers under *No* reflect those who had considered that method completely unacceptable.)

	Yes	No
Appointment by chairperson of the REC	7	5
Election by all members of the REC	10	5
Recommendations by government health department	9	3
Appointment by professional organisations	10	-
Advertise for, then interview, applicants	4	4

Table 5.6 continued

6.   What is the most desirable method of appointment of *lay* members to RECs?

(The numbers under *Yes* reflect those RECs who chose a method as one of their three most favoured methods. The numbers under *No* reflect those who had considered that method completely unacceptable.)

	Yes	No
Appointment by chairperson of the REC		
Election by all members of the REC	3	5
Appointment by political bodies (such as local political parties)	4	4
	3	7
Advertise for lay people in local press and interview them	4	5
Recommendations by government health department	5	5
Appointment by patients' organisations	8	2

Table 5.7   Summary of REC Responses Concerning Problems Associated with the Consent Process in Neonatal Research

1.   The time your REC is able to give to the assessment of each protocol is adequate to achieve satisfactory ethical review of the protocol.

Yes 18
No 2
Other 1

2a.   Is there any merit in the idea of European harmonisation in the composition of RECs?

Yes 12
No 6
Other 5

2b.   Is there any merit in the idea of European harmonisation in the method of appointment of members to RECs?

Yes 7
No 8
Other 5

3.   Should REC members be paid?

Yes 7
No 13
Other 0

4.   Should members of RECs be unpaid but receive compensation for time spent on REC work?

Yes 15
No 5
Other 2

5.   If RECs are to be funded, where should the funds come from?

See Discussion

6.   What form of administrative support would most improve the working of RECs in your country?

See Discussion

Table 5.7 continued

7. Is it desirable to have uniformity in the decisions made by different RECs within a country?	*Yes 16* *No 4* *Unsure 2* *Other 0*
8. Should there be a National Research Ethics Committee to ensure more uniformity in decision making?	*Yes 15* *No 6* *Unsure 0* *Other 0*
9. If your answer to 8 is yes, how should the National Committee achieve this objective?	*See Discussion*

Discussion

Once again the most important point here, which holds even though the numbers are small, is the degree of disagreement amongst committees that are likely to have given thought to their responses. In this case the differences may well reflect principled differences in reasoning as to the authority, accountability and democratic role of RECs.

Table 5.6 shows that whilst there was broad agreement on a desirable size for RECs, there was less agreement as to what categories of profession should be represented on it, and less still as to how the members should be selected.

The consensus favoured a size of seven to fifteen members, with almost all agreeing that there should be lay members and that these should be two or three in number. Unsurprisingly, since our earlier research had found significantly more than 50% of current members to be hospital doctors, there was unanimity that hospital doctors are essential members of the committees. This is perfectly reasonable since RECs must clearly have the expertise to assess the medical value of projects, and their design, and hospital doctors can contribute significantly in these areas.

However, there was otherwise widespread disagreement. It is hard to explain some oversights. Given the need to assess the design of a project, its risks and benefits, and its value, it is surprising that a number of committees did not consider a pharmacologist or a research statistician essential members.

Conversely, the degree of disagreement on other aspects of both composition and mode of appointment may more clearly suggest that the committees do not share a common view as to what is required of committee members, where the authority of committees lies, and to whom they are accountable.[10]

For example, the split as to whether committees should or should not contain lawyers and ethicists may reflect a disagreement as to whether committees should be viewed simply as groups of wise men, or perhaps representatives of interest groups, or whether they should be seen as a set of experts. This division on principle may also underlie the differences of view as to how both professionals and lay members should be appointed. The view that RECs should be groups of experts might lead one to suggest the appointment of professionals by professional organisations. For it could be argued that such organisations are best placed to select experts. The fact that this was the one method of appointment no REC rejected completely, suggests that some at least may have had this line of reasoning in mind. On the other hand none of the other methods of selecting professionals as committee members would necessarily be effective methods for selecting an expert. Yet each of the other methods was favoured by some committees. So those committees may simply have viewed their professional members as randomly selected members of their groups, or just independent wise men (not necessarily medical ethics experts) from within that profession.

A different principle to adopt in selecting committee members sees those members as representing interest groups. This principle might be the one held by committees who favoured the appointment of lay people by patients' organisations. For such lay members could be seen as representing patient's interests. Yet another principle of selection would hold that REC members are democratically accountable to the community. This principle might be cited in defence of the appointment of members by political bodies or by the government health department, methods also favoured by some RECs.

In other words there might be three or four principles used to defend different compositions for committees, and different ways of selecting committee members. The diversity in the responses given may well reflect different views amongst the RECs as to which of these principles, and associated positions about the authority and accountability and democratic role of committees, is most defensible.

Such differences may not in themselves be a bad thing, but the issues may need more explicit and more public debate. For example, although question 2a in Table 5.7 reveals that a majority favoured more European harmonisation in the composition of RECs, it is not clear it is desirable to attain this without there first being greater clarity as to whether committees are to be viewed as groups of experts or not, and where their authority and accountability lie.

A second point,[7] was that committees very often favoured the size, structure and mode of appointment that was exhibited in their own committee. Despite the fact that they were made aware of the diversity to be found around Europe, few seem to have given much reflection as to whether their own present structure was in fact optimal for the function they understood a REC to be serving. This need not be a bad thing. One explanation for the phenomenon would be that all the committees were absolutely clear as to the principles underlying their own composition and method of selection, and convinced of the correctness of these principles. However another less satisfactory possibility is that the committees were satisfied with the practical effectiveness of their own operation, and for that reason simply did not attend to the principles which might defend their structure.

The analysis thus far has suggested two main points in this area about the thought processes of participant RECs. First there is the possibility of a conscious or unconscious adherence to a variety of principles regarding their composition and selection; and second the possibility of some complacency with regard to the potential uncovering of better principles and better structures. Three further aspects of the results tabulated in Table 5.7 might supplement this analysis.

First, it was somewhat surprising that almost all committees felt themselves to have adequate time to consider all protocols at present. Previous findings (see Chapter 3) had been that most committees were significantly overworked, often because members were performing the work voluntarily. Thus one would have expected committees to have reported such overwork. This response might be seen as further evidence of an unwillingness to reflect on possible improvements in committee structures.

The RECs' answers to questions 6 to 9 in Table 5.7 can also be considered in connection with the question of the principles that might underlie the composition and method of selection of committees. Administrative support was seen as desirable for help with training, with the development of common guidelines on practice, and with the facilitation of joint meetings with other committees. National Committees were favoured for similar purposes (there was no call for National Committees to replace regional or local committees and thus become the sole national reviewer of protocols), and there was a significant majority in favour of greater uniformity in decision-making.

Such support for greater uniformity in decision-making under the direction of guidelines from National Committees might seem most congenial to a view of RECs as groups of experts selected for their expertise, so as to come up with the correct ethical review of protocols. But as has been seen, the views of committees regarding structure and selection did not all cohere with this understanding of a REC. This raises the question whether all the RECs were, consciously or unconsciously, adhering to a consistent set of principles on these matters.

Third and finally, the answers given to question 5 in Table 5.7 also have some bearing on the reasoning exhibited by the committees. The general idea of funding committees is consistent with the idea of paying members for their expertise, but also with other understandings of RECs . For example, it might be argued that democratically accountable representatives should be paid for that role, as councillors are now, or that citizens simply undertaking the role of exercising judgement in these matters should be compensated for that. However the committees were divided in their opinion as to the most suitable source for funding. Some suggested fees from applicants for protocol review could be used, while others favoured calling upon the resources of the state. The latter group felt this source would be a better guardian of the independence of the committees, and this suggests a further principle relevant to the selection of committee members. REC members, whether experts or democratic representatives, should be independent judges. Thus the division over answers to this question may indicate that some committees were giving more weight than others to this principle.

In sum then, the responses discussed in this section suggest a range of possible principles that may be informing the reasoning of RECs as to their own role and structure. They may also indicate that in some areas that reasoning may on occasion be somewhat inconsistent or somewhat complacent.

6. Conclusion

The sample size here is small and the numbers do not permit generalisation. Nonetheless the degree of diversity of opinion found among such a small and thoughtful group is worthy of attention. The responses analysed permit the identification of possible differences in reasoning both on a substantive ethical issue, parental informed consent to neonatal research, and on the meta-issue of the role and structure of RECs. Furthermore the responses suggested some insensitivity, even amongst a group likely to be conscientious, with regard to observational information concerning the informed consent process.

To what extent are these matters for concern? One might consider this with regard to the question of how well committees, which reason in such ways, can collectively achieve the two main aims of RECs, namely protecting the subjects of medical research, and facilitating the conduct of such research. If the differences do reflect differences in principle, but some of the RECs are unconscious of the principles that govern their reasoning, this is a cause for some concern. For committees that cannot make explicit their reasoning will find it hard to react to new information, whether about the structure of other committees or about the practice of informed consent. This in turn will make it hard for them to reason about how to carry out their two main aims. Even if the committees are conscious of the differing principles that govern their approaches to these matters, that may still be a cause for some concern. Such differences require a wider public airing both from the point of view of researchers, who have an interest in understanding how their protocols are approached, and from the point of view of the general population, who constitute potential subjects of research and have an interest in understanding how the committees approach the matter of protecting subjects.

Thus the possible deficiencies in RECs' modes of reasoning even in such a small group may be indicative of areas where there is room for improvement in pursuit of their main aims. It might also suggest caution as to whether RECs are presently equipped to take on further roles, for example as the body to which it would be reasonable to delegate the task of consenting to research participation on behalf of incompetent subjects.

Notes

1. During the course of the Euricon inquiry the French RECs, Comités Consultatifs de Protection de Personnes se prêtant à la Recherche Biomédicale (CCPPRB), received a letter advising them not to comment on their own practices, and thereafter we received no further questionnaires.
2. The third UK REC did reply, but declined to complete the second questionnaire. No reply was received from other committees that failed to fill in this second questionnaire.
3. In the case of the first questionnaire, we had sent out questionnaires to 48 committees in the participating countries, but only 37 of these replied, so the second response rate involved a reply from just over half of the committees who had been sent the first questionnaire.

4. In this and subsequent tables the answers sometimes number less than 24 as some RECs did not respond to all the questions asked.
5. In France this is already required by law.
6. Three committees answered this question despite answering *No* to the previous question.
7. It was striking that in their responses committees very often favoured the size, structure and mode of appointment that was exhibited in their own committee.
8. There was quite wide agreement (16 committees) on a size of eight to fifteen, but in two countries a smaller number, seven at most, was felt appropriate (five committees in all expressed this latter view).
9. There was widespread agreement (16 committees) that between one and three lay members was appropriate, though three committees felt that lay members were not required at all, and three committees felt they should constitute half the committee.
10. One small point of interest was that whilst 11 committees favoured greater uniformity in the method of appointment of RECs (and six did not) only seven favoured more European harmonisation on this matter (and nine did not). It is not clear what explains this apparent discrepancy.

6 The Role of RECs in Europe in the Ethical Review of Paediatric Research: a Critical Discussion

PROFESSOR J.H. SOLBAKK

Introduction

According to the Declaration of Helsinki medical research involving human beings should comply with four morally relevant principles and/or distinctions: first, the principle of free and informed consent; second, the distinction between therapeutic research and non-therapeutic research; third, the assessment of potential risks versus presupposed benefits; and last, but not the least, the principle that concern for the interests of the research subject should always prevail over the interests of science and society.

Bearing this normative framework of the Declaration in mind, three claims will be made about medical research involving children. On the basis of these claims, five implications for the future role of RECs in ethical review of paediatric research will be discussed.

The first claim is that a common interpretation of the Declaration of Helsinki is that children should not be involved in *non-therapeutic* research. Such an interpretation, however, is not only incompatible with the moral intentions embedded in the Declaration of Helsinki; it may also systematically undermine the scientific foundations of paediatric medicine. Consequently, 'protecting' children from being involved in non-therapeutic research may be said to represent an *unethical defence*. A different way of framing this argument would be to say that although there may be morally relevant differences between children and adults, as subjects of medical research they should be treated as *methodological equals*. That is, gaining knowledge about children's diseases requires the same methodological procedures as those required in medical research aimed at understanding adults' diseases.

My second claim is that the concept of 'minimal risk' that is applied in therapeutic research involving children is too *narrow*. Consequently, children suffering from serious diseases for which there are no existing cures, are systematically denied the right to 'take therapeutic risks'. According to the Declaration of Helsinki medical research involving human subjects cannot legitimately be carried out unless the importance of the objective is in *proportion* to the inherent risk of the subject. I can see no reason why one should abstain from the proportional kind of risk-assessment when it comes to therapeutic research involving children. In other words, the concept of minimal risk should remain within the context of non-therapeutic research, where it rightly belongs.

The third and most controversial claim is that the protection of children's rights to participate in medical research may not be the only need today; it is also due time to raise the question whether children have a certain degree of *social obligation* to participate in medical research, not for their own benefit, but for the possible benefit of other children.

First Implication

The first implication relates to my claim about children's social *obligation* to participate in medical research. A common interpretation of the *role* of Ethical Review Committees is that it consists in safe-guarding the physical, psychological, and social *welfare* of research participants, in terms of ensuring 'that the potential risks, discomforts, and inconveniences can be justified by the anticipated benefits that are likely to result from the research', and in protecting participants' *rights* to be 'fully informed' and 'to withdraw from the study at any time' as well as their right to 'privacy and confidentiality'.[1]

The rights and welfare argument in relation to paediatric research should, however, not be restricted to those children who act as research participants. Ethical Review Committees should also take on the responsibility of securing that children - as well as other vulnerable groups - are not, in the name of safety, *arbitrarily denied* access to investigational procedures that may benefit such groups. Otherwise phrased, Ethical Review Committees should not only consider their role in emphasizing the *value* of research on children, but also their role in propagating individual participation in research as a *social obligation*, not for the common good of society, but for the possible benefit of future patients.

Second Implication

A second implication related to the social obligation argument as well as to my first two claims, is that 'Ethical Review Committees should not only consider it an "advantage"',[2] but an *ethical obligation* to include - as consultants (or full members) - patients (or patient-representatives) of vulnerable groups.

Third Implication

The third implication I want to draw attention to, relates to my claim about considering children as *methodological equals* to adults, in the sense that children should not be systematically 'protected' from participating in non-therapeutic research that involves a risk level *greater than minimal risk*. By this I do not intend to violate the widely accepted principle that children should not be involved in research that might equally well be carried out with adults.[3]

What I aim at are non-therapeutic research situations where this option is not available, and where the level of risk goes beyond that of 'minimal risk'. Such situations are described in The United States Health and Human Services Regulations, which are more permissive than, for example, the guidelines from British paediatricians or the Council of Europe's Convention on Human Rights and Biomedicine. According to the US guidelines:[4]

> Greater than minimal risk and no prospect of direct benefit to the subjects but likely to yield generalizable knowledge - research is permitted as long as the risk is only a minor increase over minimal risk, the information is of vital importance to understanding or ameliorating the subject's condition, the intervention presents experiences that are reasonably commensurate with the subject's actual situation, and adequate provisions are made for consent from (usually) both parents and for paediatric assent.

The CIOMS guidelines from 1993 also favour such an approach, arguing that 'when an ethical review committee is persuaded that the object of the research is sufficiently important, slight increases above minimal risk may be permitted'.[5]

According to Baruch A. Brody, the author of the most recent book on *The Ethics of Biomedical Research,*[6] and my own guide into the jungle of national and international guidelines involving paediatric research, there is a *double* problem involved in those regulations that do not accept a level of risk beyond minimal risk in non-therapeutic research. They underestimate both the necessity of more thorough research on children and that of differentiating between groups of children:[7]

> The first [point] is that most (with the exception of the HHS regulations and the International Harmonization Guidelines) do not do justice to the *needs* for research on children, although they talk about its importance. They are just too restrictive on non-therapeutic research, especially on older children. This leads to the second point. All of these policies treat *all minors alike*. This seems wrong. As minors get older, their assent should become of greater significance and this should allow them, with parental consent, to assent to participate in nontherapeutic research whose risks are more than minimal, with the risk level approaching that for which adults can volunteer as the minors get closer to full maturity[emphasis mine].

I agree with Brody that such an approach should be implemented, but only under the auspices and competent guidance of independent review committees.[8]

On a more general level I agree with the proposed § 6.3 in the draft guidelines from CIOMS/WHO, where the responsibility of ethical review committees in *consideration of justice* is underlined:[9]

> Ethical review committees should in general strive to ensure that no one group or class is under-represented or over-represented in research carried out in the country, locality, or institution in which the committee is situated.

> Justice requires that the benefits and burdens of research be distributed fairly among all groups and classes in society, including age, sex, economic status, and ethnic or racial identification.

Fourth Implication

The fourth implication relates to my claim about the unacceptability of operating with the notion of 'minimal risk' as standard within the context of *therapeutic* research on children, as this will systematically deny children the right to a *proportional* kind of risk assessment as well as the right to *take therapeutic risks*. I am therefore pleased with the CIOMS guidelines from 1993, where risks in relation to paediatric research are justified in a *proportionate* way,[10] as is the situation with adult research participants: 'Risks are to be justified in relation to anticipated benefits to the child'.

As observed by Michael A. Grodin and Leonard H. Glantz,[11] dying children as subjects of research represent a particular ethical challenge for three reasons:

> First, they suffer from conditions that researchers feel a profound imperative to cure or ameliorate. Second, parents may be less capable of making protective decisions because they will often embrace any option that presents even the remote possibility of preserving or prolonging their child's life. Finally, dying children are subject to significant physical invasion and psychological stress as a result of their conditions. Additional invasions for research purposes constitute added burdens to an already burdened child. As a result of these factors, researchers and reviewers must be scrupulous in assuring that neither parents nor children are exploited.

Although I am sympathetic to the precautions advocated by Grodin and Glantz, I think they should have underlined the special responsibility of *independent* ethical review committees in handling such cases. There may not only be a need to protect a child against unnecessary burdens, or to safeguard the right of parents to make protective decisions; it may also be necessary to defend the *freedom* of physicians, 'to use a new diagnostic and therapeutic measure, if in his or her judgement it offers hope of saving life, re-establishing health or alleviating suffering', as stated in the Declaration of Helsinki.[12] Only in this way, I believe, may a child's right to take therapeutic risks become a viable and desirable right.

Fifth Implication

The fifth and last implication relates to an *unintended side-effect* of the practice of selecting adults as research participants when research might equally well be carried out with children. According to Brody this has led to the paradoxical situation that children are often exposed to 'unnecessary risks' in the name of safety, because clinical decisions are made 'without appropriate guidance from research'.[13] 'Children', he says, 'are in this way therapeutic orphans'.[14] According to Brody, two strategies have been tried out to cope with this problem. The first is the *extrapolation* strategy, while the second is the *starting-with-children* strategy.[15]

The problem with the strategy of extrapolating from studies performed in adults, according to Brody,[16] is that it implies exposing children to 'greater risks to get quicker benefits'. The case of using chloramphenicol for neonatal sepsis at a dosage extrapolated from older children and adults is mentioned as a typical example of such a strategy resulting in life-threatening side effects for the neonates due to their immature system of detoxification.[17]

I agree with Brody that the starting-with-children-strategy seems to be more justifiable than the classical 'protectionist view', as this alternative approach signals that it is due time that children are treated as methodological equals.[18] As observed by Brody, both in the 1993 CIOMS guidelines as well as in the 1997 proposed Canadian Code there is evidence of such a shift taking place:

> The participation of children is indispensable for research into diseases of childhood and conditions to which children are particularly susceptible.[19]

> Children should not be excluded from participating in research that is potentially directly beneficial to them as individual participants and, with appropriate safeguards, indirectly beneficial to them as a group.[20]

Personally, I am also sympathetic to Brody's argument that an even stronger stance in favour of the starting-with-children strategy would be appropriate; especially when it comes to diseases affecting a substantial number of children, they should be involved as research participants on equal terms with adults.[21] This would certainly imply a shift in policy about risk-safety-standards; 'refusing to accept a lesser degree of evidence of an appropriate risk-benefit ratio in paediatric use' and insisting on an 'appropriate involvement of children in the crucial clinical trials'.[22]

If this argument about the higher justifiability of the starting-with-children approach is valid, then ethical review committees should also feel obliged to protect children from becoming 'therapeutic orphans', by insisting on the inclusion of children as research participants in initial trials designed to obtain approval. In this way ethical review committees would also comply well with the observations made in the draft guidelines of CIOMS and WHO, that scientific and ethical review cannot - and in fact *should not* - be clearly separated.[23]

Notes

1. CIOMS/WHO, *Guidelines for Ethical Review Committees* (Draft), 24 March 1998, § 5.
2. As expressed in the CIOMS/WHO draft guidelines, § 4.1 (b).
3. See for instance, *CIOMS' International Ethical Guidelines for Biomedical Research Involving Human Subjects*, Geneva 1993, guideline 5.
4. *United States HHS Regulations*, Appendix 3.1, § 46.406.
5. CIOMS 1993, guideline 5, p. 21.
6. Oxford University Press, New York, Oxford, 1998, pp. 127-128.
7. Ibid.
8. Brody 1998, p. 128.
9. CIOMS/WHO 1998, § 6.3, p. 6.
10. CIOMS 1993, guideline 5, p. 21.
11. *Children as Research Subjects. Science, Ethics, and Law*, Oxford University Press, 1994, p. 217.
12. World Medical Association, *Declaration of Helsinki* (1964, 1975, 1983, 1989, 1996), II. 1.
13. Brody 1998, p. 177.
14. Ibid., p. 177.
15. Ibid.
16. Brody 1998, pp. 178-179.
17. Ibid.
18. Ibid.
19. Commentary to Guideline 5.
20. *CANADA*, 1997, Article 6.6.
21. Brody, 1998, p. 179.
22. Ibid.
23. Draft guidelines CIOMS/WHO, §4.1 (a).

7 The Role of Research Ethics Committees and of the Law in the Ethical Review of Medical Research: a Critical Discussion

DR S. HOLM

The Present and Future Role of RECs

The Research Ethics Committee (REC)[1] is a key component of all modern regulations and declarations concerning the ethical conduct of biomedical research.[2] The constitution of RECs, their composition, and their methods of work vary quite widely between the different European countries, as has been documented in the EURICON project.

In most countries the main role of RECs is to approve or reject biomedical research projects based on an ethical analysis of the research protocol. This analysis will usually look at:

- The importance of the research question
- The scientific quality of the protocol
- The inconveniences and risks involved for research subjects
- The information given to research subjects
- The procedure for obtaining consent after information is given.

A project may be rejected on the basis of problems in any of these areas.

In some countries approval is legally required before a project may be initiated, whereas in other jurisdictions the approval is given in the form of guidance to the researcher, but even where only guidance is given it often has the same effect as approval/disapproval, since most research institutions do not allow their researchers to perform projects against the guidance of the RECs. Over the years the quality of this approval process seems to have increased, and many RECs have developed detailed guidelines for the ethical conduct of research which ensure that the protocols are already of a good standard when they are first submitted. In most countries within the European Union it is thus today impossible to get approval for research which is ethically sub-standard, or to perform research without approval.

The future European Union Good Clinical Practice (GCP) directive will probably ensure more similarity in the constitution and operation of RECs and, it is hoped, should thus further promote the quality of the approval procedure. The legal and ethical justification for the approval procedure is that it can protect the research participants from taking part in projects that are ethically or scientifically problematic. There are, however, three possible functions for RECs that have not received as thorough a consideration in the literature as their role in approving research and making sure that informed consent is obtained and documented. These three roles are:

- Democratic legitimation of research
- Approval of research projects in cases where consent cannot be obtained
- Monitoring of the compliance with approved protocols.

This chapter will look more closely at the possible justification for extending the roles of RECs to these three areas, and at how this could be done.

RECs as Democratic Institutions

Biomedical research involving human subjects is a social practice that relies on social acceptance for its continuation and flourishing. This social acceptance has to encompass both the goals of the activity and the way the activity is conducted. In a very early paper on medical research ethics Hans Jonas pointed out that research and development is always an optional goal.[3] It is not incoherent or irrational to think that no more medical research should be performed, as long as one is willing to accept also that no more medical progress will be made. But then it is not irrational not to wish for progress! The RECs probably have only a minor role to play in explaining the general goals of biomedical research to the public, but they do have potentially very important roles to play with regard to the social acceptance of the goals of specific projects and the conduct of research. We know that recruitment rates to biomedical research have been falling steadily over the last 10-20 years and, unless this trend is reversed, it will lead to serious problems concerning both the pace of biomedical progress and the generalisability of those results that are generated.[4-16]

Although the approval procedure could be analysed purely in terms of protection from problematic research, the presence of lay members on most RECs points to another possible function. What are the lay members there for? The most minimal interpretation of their role is that they are there simply to ensure that the information given to prospective research participants is understandable by 'ordinary people' and not too filled with medical jargon. On this minimal interpretation the role of the lay person would be purely as a 'linguistic sounding board'. However, some countries have a majority of lay members on their RECs, and in most countries lay members are not chosen on the basis of their ear for language, so it is not unreasonable to suggest that they also perform other roles. But what roles?

If we re-conceptualise RECs not only as formal approval bodies, but as institutions within a democratic framework which at the same time regulates and legitimises biomedical research, we may become clearer about the role of both the RECs themselves and their lay members. When a REC approves a project it is not a neutral administrative act, it is also an implicit endorsement of the project and its qualities, or that is at least the way it will seem to the outside observer. RECs carry the honorific 'ethics' in their name, and something that is approved by an ethics committee must *ipso facto* be ethical! RECs may not want their approval to have this implication of endorsement, but it is difficult to avoid, and it is worth considering whether it cannot be used constructively. Can we imagine a situation where REC approval actually functions as a partial legitimisation of the specific research project?

The most common public worries about biomedical research are that research is only carried out to promote the career of the researchers or to promote the interests of the pharmaceutical industry. According to these worries, the researchers are not really interested in helping patients, or solving those health problems that are seen as important from the point of view of society. Many research projects are therefore performed that are really unimportant, and where the participation of research subjects is therefore wasted.[17-20,21] How would a REC have to appear, and what would it have to do, in order to be able to allay these public worries?

First, it would probably have to be (and be seen to be!) totally independent of research interests. This indicates that the members of RECs should not be appointed by the research institutions themselves, but through some independent mechanism. It further points towards a very substantial representation of non-researchers on the RECs. It is 'common knowledge' that doctors (and other researchers) are as thick as thieves, and this common knowledge will affect the perception of RECs, whether or not it is actually true! In this context it is not enough to argue that researchers are honourable persons, who would never let their own interests or the interests of their colleagues influence their decisions on RECs, if the public is not fully convinced by the argument.

Second, the non-researchers would have to be elected to the REC by a mechanism that is transparent and accepted in the society where the REC is operating. The non-researchers will have to be independent, to be beyond reproach and to be people who are seen as truly representing the public interest. Different methods may suit different societies but just co-opting the 'great and the good', or the local vicar does not add much democratic legitimisation.

Third, RECs would have to be very open about their methods of working and the reasons for specific decisions. Only by aiming at complete transparency can the necessary confidence be developed in the public.

Fourth, many RECs would have to become tougher in their rejection of research protocols that are deemed either to be methodologically poor, or to give only very limited benefit to society. People who are willing to become research subjects are a scarce resource and, just like other scarce resources, it should be protected and used wisely and not squandered on projects without clear benefit. A potential research subject should not have to worry about whether or not the project in which he or she is being asked to participate is of good scientific quality and likely to produce beneficial scientific results. The fact that it has been approved by a REC should be conclusive evidence of scientific quality and expected benefit.

Fifth, RECs would have to engage in public discussion and consultation concerning contentious research projects, and contentious justifications for research projects. Whether a research project is socially acceptable in a certain society, and whether it will add or detract from the general acceptance of biomedical research, is not always a question which can be answered by pure conceptual analysis or by applying a set of rules and guidelines. Some societies may accept certain kinds of research which would be deemed unacceptable in other societies, and certain justifications for research may be acceptable in some societies but not in others (e.g. research with the primary aim of benefiting the national pharmaceutical industry). As democratic institutions RECs would have to consult those people on whose behalf the decisions are made, in order to be able successfully to claim that they represent these people.

These five requirements that RECs would have to fulfil before they could gain a stronger role in the democratic legitimisation of research would in many instances necessitate radical changes in the structure and function of existing RECs, and it is therefore doubtful whether RECs will take on this role in the future.

Research without Consent, and the Role of RECs

As the empirical parts of the EURICON project have amply demonstrated, there are areas of important biomedical research where it is impossible to get a valid informed consent from the research subjects (or, as in the case of neo-natal research, their proxies). This problem will occur in situations where the information and decision-making process is impaired by severe time constraints, or by the physical or mental state of the potential research subject or their proxy. A classic example outside the field of neonatology is research into acute treatments of myocardial infarction, where the patient is in pain, has problems with breathing, is afraid of dying, and has to make a decision about participation in a quite complicated research project within a very short time. In such a situation it is rather obvious that although it may be possible to get the patient to say either 'yes' or 'no' to participation in the research, a given consent will not really be fully informed and fully reflective.

But we need to perform research into conditions of this type if we are ever to be able to offer better treatments to the patients. If we insist on informed consent in these situations we will create a situation where no research can be carried out on the groups or conditions in question, and where no new well-tested treatments will be introduced. Those who cannot give consent will be protected, but the protection will harm them, or their group, in the long run (the 'golden ghetto' problem). It could be argued that it will always be possible to do the appropriate research in similar groups with consent, or do it by different methods, but such an argument is hard to sustain. Research on treatments of severe stroke can, for instance, be tried out in animal experiments, or in human trials in people with mild stroke, but the final test of efficacy will have to be done in the relevant patient group. Some jurisdictions simply do not allow research without full informed consent, and they will in the end have to introduce treatments that are not properly validated, unless they can 'borrow' research results from more permissive jurisdictions.

We therefore need to look critically at when it should be permissible to perform research without full informed consent. In the following sections this question will be discussed with special emphasis on situations where full informed consent is not available, but where the prospective research participants are nevertheless not fully incompetent. In these situations the research arguably should require something other than informed consent from the potential research subjects themselves.[22] A number of options seem to be open here:

- Proxy consent
- Retrospective consent
- Assent with later ratification
- Research without consent.

In order to choose between these options, we need to know what the requirement for informed consent is supposed to achieve in the normal case. This is a topic on which there is not total agreement in the literature, partly because informed consent has both a legal and an ethical function and a very long history.

The concept of informed consent to research has gradually been developed since it was first clearly enunciated in the 1947 Nuremberg declaration after the trial of the Nazi doctors who had performed experiments in the concentration camps. Informed consent does, however, have ancient roots in the prohibition found in most legal systems against touching another person without permission. Since 1947 informed consent has been incorporated as a basic principle in the Helsinki I & II declarations of the World Medical Association and in many national and international regulations of biomedical research including the recent European convention on bioethics.[2,23-25]

The concept of 'informed consent' has now almost reached the status of an infallible dogma in biomedical research ethics. It is seen as a necessary and perhaps even sufficient condition for the ethical acceptability of the enrolment of a person as a research subject. This is not the case in many other areas of research involving humans (e.g. in the social sciences).[26]

Philosophically, informed consent can be given both deontological and consequentialist justifications. It can be seen as a basic requirement of the respect we owe other persons, or it can be seen as a way for an agent to further his or her life projects. On both justifications, however, it is the case that a key function of informed consent is to allow persons to make sure that important decisions about them and their lives are taken on the basis of their own values and preferences, and not based on other peoples' values and preferences. Through the consent process the individual prospective research subjects are able to apply their own values in the assessment of the benefits and burdens of the research. This is important because the idea that there is an 'objective' assessment of benefits and burdens applicable to all persons is problematic. Legitimately, there can be quite different ideas about whether the benefits outweigh the burdens, when this is seen both from a personal point of view, and from an impersonal point of view. This can be shown formally within the framework of rational choice theory, but can also be brought out by two banal examples: to a member of Jehovah's Witnesses the fact that a project will improve blood transfusion techniques is not a positive benefit, and to a person with severe needle phobia (or a very low pain treshold) the fact that a project involves 'only' two extra blood samplings may be a major burden. A somewhat less banal example is that some persons simply may not value medical progress very highly; they may be content with the present state of medical knowledge, and for them the balancing of benefits and burdens will again differ from that of medical researchers who usually value progress highly.

In situations where consent cannot be gained it would thus seem that proxy consent, where the proxy has knowledge of the values and preferences of the patient, is the best option. By using a proxy we can get closest to the decision the patient would have made had he or she been competent.[27] However, this kind of proxy consent, usually labelled 'substituted judgement' in the literature is probably not easy to gain in the kind of research situation we are discussing here. There may be no suitable proxy available in an acute situation and, even if a person is available he or she may well be so concerned about the state of the patient that the quality of information processing and consent again becomes problematic. It is, furthermore, not very likely that the average person has ever discussed his or her views about medical research with even close relatives. Relying on proxy consent in the acute situation will thus either again be reliance on a fiction, or it will be an option available only in a very few circumstances.

This necessitates a move to one of the other three options. Research without any form of consent or assent is clearly problematic, especially in situations where the patient is fully conscious and can express views and preferences. This seems to leave either retrospective consent or assent with later ratification as options.

The main problem with retrospective consent is that it is not really consent. If I 'act now and ask later', the person I act upon may later accept my actions, or even say that he or she was glad that I acted, but that is not the same as the person having given consent. This is clearly seen if we note that the opposite situation may also occur. The person may not accept my actions, and may be angry because I acted. Retrospective consent can therefore not function as a prospective justification of an act, but only as a retrospective justification (or perhaps more accurately redemption of, or excuse for) the act.

The second remaining option is assent with later ratification. This would involve a two-step process. At the time of entry into the study the prospective research participants are informed that one of the 'treatment' options involves participation in an experiment, and are given very basic information about the major risks and inconveniences in the project. They are then asked to assent to or decline participation in the experiment. If a patient assents he or she is enrolled in the study. At a later time when the patients who assented are in a condition such that real informed consent is possible, they are given full information about the study and are asked to ratify or reject their previous assent. If the assent is rejected all data about the patient are removed from the trial files. This two-step process has one major advantage over retrospective consent in that it allows patients who for various reasons do not want to participate in research to have this preference respected. No one ends up participating in research directly against their will, and by requiring later ratification of the assent it is also ensured that those who, on reflection, do not want to be associated with a specific research project can have that preference respected. No one will therefore be in a situation where they can truthfully say 'They made me participate in research, and I knew nothing about it. They simply used me as a human guinea pig!' This model is therefore the one which best fulfils both the deontological and consequentialist justifications of the requirement for consent.

In many jurisdictions in Europe there is at present no possibility of implementing assent with later ratification because the law explicitly requires full, informed consent. This leads to a situation where some research projects are carried out built on a fiction of consent or where important research is not carried out because of consent problems. What safeguards would have to be put in place before assent with later ratification could be a reasonable option to implement in law?

First there would have to be close scrutiny of those projects where assent would be sought instead of consent, to assure that the departure from consent was really warranted. This would have to involve three separate questions: 1) Is it true that consent cannot be obtained? 2) Is the project sufficiently important to allow the departure from full informed consent? and 3) Are there specific elements in the project which makes relying on assent problematic? Making sure that these three questions were answered convincingly would be a natural role for a REC.

We need to be certain that the 'easy' option of assent with later ratification is only used in those circumstances where it is truly impossible to obtain consent from the prospective research participants. The researchers themselves are not the right people to judge when this is the case, because of their clear interest in making the project run as easily and smoothly as possible. There will probably be cases where it is difficult practically to get consent, but where it can be done if enough effort is made, and the REC should make sure that such cases are distinguished from those where consent is genuinely impossible.

The REC should also make sure that permission to use assent with later ratification is only given in cases where projects have a realistic chance of solving an important research question. Just as research involving children is only (or should only be) allowed if it can solve an important research question with relevance for children, research without full informed consent should only be allowed in other groups under similar conditions. This also entails that the projects have to be well designed and of a size that allows unequivocal conclusions to be drawn.

Projects may also contain specific elements that make them unsuited for any departure from full informed consent. Assent with later ratification is most suitable for simple and not very controversial projects. If the risks of a project are high and at the same time of a very technical nature the project may be unsuitable for assent. The same could be true of projects that include very intimate physical examinations, or have very controversial goals.

The use of assent instead of consent also highlights the question of who should give the information, and who should gain and document the assent. With regard to standard consent there are already discussions as to whether it is preferable that the information is given by someone who has no personal interests in the success of the project (an 'independent person'), and not by the researcher as is usually the case now. For instance, it has been suggested that the information should be given by the patient's general practitioner, or by specially trained nurses. This question of independent information becomes even more important in situations where it is *a priori* accepted that communication is difficult, and where something less than full informed consent is therefore allowed. It is, however, at the same time important to note that many of the relevant projects concern situations and conditions that occur suddenly, unexpectedly and at very inconvenient times; it may therefore be very difficult to find a suitable, and sufficiently knowledgeable independent person. If assent with later ratification was made a legal option RECs should, however, be given the power to put down stringent requirements for the information process both with regard to who should give the information, and with regard to what information should be given and how.

We have discussed above a number of conditions that have to be fulfilled for research without consent to be ethically acceptable. But unfortunately these conditions alone are not sufficient for research without consent to be acceptable. There is one further condition which has to be fulfilled, and this is unfortunately a counterfactual condition. We have to take into account that the public perception of individual research projects may affect the public perception of medical research as such, and that such long-range negative effects can entail that even if an individual research project is ethically acceptable seen in isolation, it may nevertheless be problematic seen in a larger perspective. Before we allow a medical research project without full informed consent to go ahead, we therefore have to answer the following question: 'What will happen when the design and conduct of this study becomes public knowledge? Will subjects feel that they have been deceived or used as human guinea pigs?'

The need to answer this question indicates that any body making such decisions will have to consult with persons in the prospective group of research participants in order to get a legitimate basis for a decision. Current RECs may therefore not be suitably constituted.

Monitoring the Conduct of Research

In many countries RECs have a right and an obligation to monitor how the approved research projects are actually conducted, but this monitoring role is in many cases much less developed. If monitoring is performed it is often based only on annual or final reports from the researchers themselves. In most countries we are thus in a situation where it is ensured that the research protocols are ethically acceptable, but where there is no direct control to ensure that the research is conducted according to the protocols and that there are no ethically problematic breaches of the protocols. This can in certain respects be compared to a situation where sensible speed limits are set and the quality of cars inspected, but the speed of motorists is never measured and speeding tickets are only issued in cases where an accident has occurred.

Other agencies than RECs may in some cases perform monitoring of biomedical research. This is the case for instance with all GCP compliant research, where the sponsor (often the pharmaceutical industry) is required to ensure both adequate monitoring and auditing of the research. The aims of this monitoring are, however, not primarily to ensure ethically acceptable conduct of the research, but to ensure the scientific validity. There are also many biomedical research projects that are not subject to the GCP rules, since their purpose is unrelated to the development and registration of new pharmaceuticals.

How can the monitoring role of RECs be developed in the future? There seem to be two possible ways to go. The first of these possible developments involves more and more detailed regulation of specific aspects of the research design, patient information etc. When research 'scandals' are unveiled a standard response from politicians is 'We must have stricter regulation', but it is doubtful whether this is actually a correct and useful response. Many of the 'scandals' concern research projects that have either never been approved by a REC or are conducted in breach of the approved protocol. It is, to put it mildly, unclear why and how stricter regulation can help in such cases. The more reasonable response seems to be to punish the transgressors (partly for reasons of future deterrence), and to ensure better control in the future, so that no unapproved research can be conducted, and breaches of the approved protocols can be detected and rectified. Stricter regulation without increased control may even in some circumstances be counterproductive because it can increase the incentive to try to circumvent the REC system, either by re-describing research as 'quality control' or 'routine data collection for statistical purposes', or by cutting corners in the actual conduct of research.

What would be involved if RECs took the second route and began to monitor research projects?   Many models can be envisaged, but a comprehensive monitoring of research projects must involve at least three components:

- The researchers' self-assessment of compliance with the protocol
- Site visits to control documentation and data-protection issues
- Surveys of patients.

The first of these components would be the easiest to implement, but would give the least reliable data. Researchers could simply be sent a standardised questionnaire at the end of their project, asking simple questions about consent and information procedures, etcetera. Although such a process will not generate absolutely reliable data because of problems of self-incrimination, it is not worthless. It becomes important because if researchers are asked about their consent procedures, their recruitment problems, their data protection measures, and so on, they are given a chance to reflect upon their own practice and the practice of their co-workers; this can, at least in some instances, lead to beneficial changes in practice. In the long run, the mere fact that researchers know that they will be asked such questions may also lead them to ensure proactively that they comply better with the regulations than in a situation where they know that there is no control.

The second and third components are more difficult to implement, and require a much greater investment of resources, but they are important nevertheless because they give a more accurate picture of the ethical conduct of research. By implementing direct control of a proportion of all research projects, the REC will be able to detect if there are clear breaches of the rules and regulations governing research. Furthermore, the REC will be able to get a better feel for how the research is conducted within the different research institutions active in a given area, and this information may be valuable in the assessment of future research protocols.

It could be argued that the monitoring function should be separate from the RECs, and that it is a natural function of, for instance, the bodies that authorise health care professionals. The conduct of unethical or unapproved research is a breach of professional duty, and should be controlled and sanctioned as any other kind of professional misconduct or malpractice (for example, by official censure or removal of authorisation). This argument is not unreasonable but, if a separation between the approval and monitoring functions was implemented in this way, it would probably lead to an under-utilisation of the information produced by the monitoring exercise. The authorising bodies are usually only interested in clear cases of professional misconduct, since it is only such cases that can form the basis for action against individual health care professionals. The RECs are (or should be) interested in a much broader range of information including the clear cases of misconduct, but also cases of exemplary or innovative research practice, and cases where the rules are not clearly broken but just bent in problematic ways. It is this broad range of information which will allow a REC to identify areas of research practice where intervention or guidance is necessary.

In order for RECs to fulfil such a monitoring role, and to utilise the information gained constructively, they must be given certain powers. The legislation or regulations governing RECs must clearly state that 1) RECs have a duty to monitor approved projects, 2) RECs have a right to access and collect the information that is necessary to fulfil the duty, including a right to perform the necessary inspections at premises where research is taking place, and 3) RECs are given authority to apply a range of sanctions to researchers who perform research that contravenes the regulations or the approval that has been given. RECs would also need more staff and more money, since good monitoring of research performance is very labour intensive.

Notes

1. In some countries the committees are known as Institutional Review Boards, and in others as Scientific Ethical Committees.
2. Faden RR, Beauchamp TL. *A history and theory of informed consent*. New York: Oxford University Press, 1986.
3. Jonas H. Philosophical Reflections on Experimenting with Human Subjects. In: Freund PA (ed.). *Experimentation with human subjects*. London: George Allen and Unwin, 1972. (p. 1-31).
4. Blichert-Toft M, Mouridsen H, West Andersen K, From the Danish Breast Cancer Cooperative Group (DBCG). Clinical trials. *Seminars in Surgical Oncology* 1996; 12: 32-8.
5. Hunter C, Frelick R, Feldman A, Bavier A, Dunlap W, Ford L et al. Selection factors in clinical trials: results from the Community Clinical Oncology Program Physicians Patient Log. *Cancer Treatment Reports* 1987; 71: 559-65.
6. Jack W, Chetty U, Rodger A. Recruitment to a prospective breast conservation trial: why are so few patients randomized? *British Medical Journal* 1990; 301: 83-5.
7. DeVita V. Breast cancer therapy: exercising all our options. *New England Journal of Medicine* 1989; 320: 527-9.
8. Zelen M. Strategy and alternate randomized designs in cancer clinical trials. *Cancer Treatment Reports* 1982; 66: 1095-100.
9. Anonymous. DBCG (Danish Breast Cancer Cooperative Group) *1977 - 1997 Jubilee publication*. Copenhagen 1998: 19-20, 48-9.
10. Fisher B. On clinical trial participation (editorial). *Journal of Clinical Oncology* 1991; 9: 1927-30.
11. Antman K, Amato D, Wood W, Corson J, Suit H, Proppe K et al. Selection bias in clinical trials. *Journal of Clinical Oncology* 1985; 3: 1142-7.
12. Benson III A, Pregler J, Bean J, Rademaker A, Eshler B, Anderson K. Oncologists' reluctance to accrue patients onto clinical trials: an Illinois cancer center study. *Journal of Clinical Oncology* 1991; 9: 2067-75.
13. Taylor K, Kelner M. Informed consent: the physician's perspective. *Social Science and Medicine* 1987; 24: 135-43.
14. Edwards S, Lilford R, Hewison J. The ethics of randomised controlled trials from the perspectives of patients, the public, and healthcare professionals. *British Medical Journal* 1998; 317: 1209-12.

15. Ganz P. Clinical trials: concerns of the patient and the public. *Cancer* 1990; 65: 2394-9.
16. Verheggen F, Nieman F, Jonkers R. Determinants of patient participation in clinical studies requiring informed consent: why patients enter a clinical trial. *Patient Education & Counselling* 1998; 35: 111-25.
17. Madsen S, Holm S, Riis P. Ethical aspects of clinical trials: the attitudes of the public and out-patients. *Journal of Internal Medicine* 1999; 245: 571-9.
18. Cassileth B, Lusk E, Miller D, Hurwitz S. Attitudes toward clinical trials among patients and the public. *JAMA* 1982; 248: 968-70.
19. Bevan E, Chee L, McGhee S, McInnes G. Patients' attitudes to participation in clinical trials. *British Journal of Clinical Pharmacology* 1993; 35: 204-7.
20. Rossel P, Holm S. How does the public perceive the motives of medical researchers for doing research? *Bulletin of Medical Ethics* 1999; 146 (March): 16-7.
21. This is a simplified and thereby slightly caricatured version of the public's worries. It furthermore only mentions the negative side, and it is clear that the public also has positive perceptions of biomedical research.
22. We could maintain the fiction that we are obtaining informed consent when patients say 'Yes' in such situations, but it seems less than desirable.
23. Evans D, Evans M. *A Decent Proposal – Ethical Review of Clinical Research.* Chichester: John Wiley & Sons, 1996.
24. Council of Europe. Convention for the Protection of Human Rights and Dignity of the Human Being with regard to the Application of Biology and Medicine: Convention on Human Rights and Biomedicine. *European Treaty Series - No. 164.* Strasbourg: Council of Europe, 1997.
25. Council of Europe, Directorate of Legal Affairs. *Explanatory Report to the Convention for the Protection of Human Rights and Dignity of the Human Being with regard to the Application of Biology and Medicine: Convention on Human Rights and Biomedicine.* DIR/JUR (97) 5. Strasbourg: Council of Europe, 1997.
26. Kimmel AJ. *Ethics and values in applied social research.* Newbury Park, CA: Sage Publications, 1988.
27. Buchanan AE, Brock DW. *Deciding for Others – The Ethics of Surrogate Decision Making.* Cambridge: Cambridge University Press, 1989.

PART III
COMPARATIVE ANALYSIS OF THE LAW ON INFORMED CONSENT IN NEONATAL RESEARCH WITHIN EUROPE

8 Overview of European Legislation on Informed Consent in Neonatal Research[1]

PROFESSOR P. DALLA-VORGIA, DR S.A. MASON, DR C.
MEGONE, MR P.J. ALLMARK, PROFESSOR D. BRATLID, DR A.B.
GILL, MRS P. MORROGH, DR A. PLOMER, PD DR S. REITER-
THEIL, ON BEHALF OF THE EURICON STUDY GROUP

Introduction

As part of the Euricon project, legal representatives from eleven European countries (see List of Contributors, p. viii) were invited to a colloquium to report, discuss and analyse European legal frameworks governing informed consent for neonatal research. The first author (PDV) presented a general overview of European law, which is the basis for this report. Furthermore, specific supplementary information from different countries was given by legal representatives from these countries, and is summarised in the table.

Legally and ethically, informed consent of the subject is a requirement for biomedical research. However there are differing interpretations in European Law of this requirement for neonatal research. Increasingly, to answer many neonatal research questions, there is a need for multinational recruitment to randomised controlled trials and studies, and thus a need for investigators to be aware of the differing, relevant, national legislation.

The aim of this paper is to discuss areas of consistency and inconsistency in the law or practice governing informed consent for neonatal research in ten European countries (Denmark, Finland, France, Germany, Greece, Ireland, Norway, Spain, Sweden, and the United Kingdom). In particular, the following areas are examined: whether there is specific law governing informed consent for research and, if so, what it is; the ethical review system, whether there are specific requirements for consent, whether benefit for the individual child is a specific requirement, and whether research of no direct benefit (so called non-therapeutic research) is legally permitted in minors – for example the taking of extra blood samples purely for research purposes.

The Law Governing Neonatal Research Across Europe

A variety of laws and a plethora of ethical and professional guidelines govern the conduct of research within individual countries and across Europe.

The Declaration of Helsinki, first adopted by the World Medical Assembly in 1964 and last amended in 1996, acts as a universal, ethical guide. Throughout Europe, Research Ethics Committees (RECs) require that research trials and studies comply with this Declaration. Further guidance is proffered in the 1989 United Nations Convention on the Rights of the Child.

The principles of the Declaration of Helsinki have been incorporated into the International Conference on Harmonization *Guidelines for Good Clinical Practice* (ICH GCP). American and Japanese, as well as the European regulatory authorities, have adopted the latter to which all regulatory trials must comply in order to be granted authorisation to market a medicinal product.

A further measure to introduce harmonization across Europe for the conduct of research is the Council of Europe's 1997 *Convention for the Protection of Human Rights and Dignity of the Human Being with Regard to the Application of Biology and Medicine*.

Article 16 of the Convention sets out general conditions to research on human beings:

i.   there is no alternative of comparable effectiveness to research on humans,

ii.   the risks are not disproportionate to the potential benefits of the research,

iii. the research project has been approved by the competent body after independent examination of its scientific merit, including assessment of the importance of the aim of the research, and multidisciplinary review of its ethical acceptability,

iv.   the persons undergoing research have been informed of their rights and the safeguards prescribed by law for their protection,

v.   the necessary consent has been given expressly, specifically and is documented. Such consent may be freely withdrawn at any time.

The Convention further sets out restrictions for research on persons not able to consent, such as neonates. This research may only be undertaken when:

i.   the above mentioned general conditions on research are fulfilled,
ii. the results of the research have the potential to produce real and direct benefit to their health,
iii. research of comparable effectiveness cannot be carried out on individuals capable of giving consent,
iv. the necessary authorisation has been given specifically and in writing.

Exceptionally, research which does not have the potential to produce results of direct benefit to the health of the child is authorised in Article 17 of the Convention if additional conditions are satisfied:

i.   the research has the aim of contributing, through significant improvement in the scientific understanding of the individual's condition, disease or disorder, to the ultimate attainment of results capable of conferring benefit to the person concerned or to other persons in the same age, category or afflicted with the same disease or disorder or having the same condition,
ii. the research entails only minimal risk and minimal burden for the individual concerned.

A new European Union Directive is being amended currently which includes both the ICH GCP guidelines and the above Convention. It is designed to regulate clinical trials further, but probably will be limited to those used to develop medicinal products within the pharmaceutical industry and thus will harmonize regulation of this type of trial across Europe.

Non-pharmaceutical research is subject to less standardisation. For this, investigators should comply with the Declaration of Helsinki if not also the above Convention for the Protection of Human Rights. However, different cultural and religious contexts, professional practices and historical antecedents have resulted in variations in practice and law throughout Europe. Differences and similarities in five areas governing informed consent for neonatal research across ten European countries are summarised in the table. A wider discussion of the differing legislation and its implications for neonatal research is presented in Chapters 9 to 16.

Legislation on Research

Six of the ten countries examined (Germany, Greece, Ireland, Norway, Spain, and Sweden) have specific legislation governing pharmaceutical trials. The laws of Denmark, Finland and France cover other types of research as well, and the United Kingdom has no legislation specific to research but relies on general principles of law, for example, governing protection against bodily harm.

Ethical Review System

Research involving humans is reviewed independently by multidisciplinary Research Ethics Committees in all countries except Greece where this is carried out more usually by Scientific Committees (which are not multidisciplinary). Here, as in Norway and the UK, review is not a statutory requirement, as it is for all research in Denmark, Finland and France. In Germany, Ireland, Spain, Sweden and Greece, Research Ethics Committee review is a legal requirement for clinical trials involving medicinal products; for the last country, control is by the National Drugs Organisation.

Consent

Proxy consent by legal guardians is the norm for neonatal research. Five countries accept this from one adult, but in Denmark, if parents share custody, consent from both adults is necessary, otherwise the research cannot be conducted. In Finland and Germany, only in exceptional circumstances when emergency treatment is required, can consent from one parent be accepted. In France and Sweden consent from both parents is the norm.

Most countries permit enrolment into research without consent where this is not feasible, as part of emergency care. This is not allowed in Denmark nor Ireland where legislation concerning consent for research is stringent.

In Ireland, a further legal stipulation requires that following informed consent to a clinical trial, a six-day period should elapse before the trial can be commenced. This provision can be amended, if dictated by the trial protocol, by application to and with the approval of the Irish Medicines Board.

Requirement for Benefit of the Child

All ten countries require a potential of direct benefit for a child to be entered into a trial or research study, either through general or specific research legislation.   Thus proxy consent is not without some legal limitation.

Clinical trials specifically provide legal uncertainty since, due to their necessary condition of therapeutic equipoise, it follows that at the time of recruitment it is unknown whether a treatment arm will confer benefit, no benefit, or perhaps even harm to the patient.

Research of No Direct Benefit Permitted

Linked to the requirement for direct benefit to the child is the issue of whether a country's law will permit   research of no direct benefit to children (so called non-therapeutic research).

Most of the ten countries will permit research of no direct benefit in minors with the stipulation that it must involve no more than minimal risk (an uncertain and subjective criterion).

Finland, France, Greece, Norway and Spain follow the *Convention for the Protection of Human Rights* and permit a wider community and scientific viewpoint, allowing research of no direct benefit if the child's inclusion might result in increased knowledge about the illness to the benefit of other children (but again provided that no more than minimal risk is involved).

Research of no direct benefit in children is not permitted in Germany and Ireland.

Discussion

Increasingly, European countries collaborate in research projects. This is due to scientific ties and co-operation between various European research centres and also to the need for multinational research which is increasingly required in order to recruit sufficient patients to attain results with statistical significance.

Although European countries share a common cultural heritage and many similarities in their legal regulations of various subjects, they also have many differences in their legal systems, their laws, their codes of practice and even practice itself. In research this is reflected in the Declaration of Helsinki which is generally accepted in Europe, while specific types of research, like research concerning minors or emergency research are not regulated in the same way in different countries. Even in countries where regulation seems similar, there might be differences in the interpretation, based in some cases on court decisions or official guidance, and in other cases on the cultural background of those involved in research. Physicians who conduct research are not always aware of the legal framework and it is the Research Ethics Committees that have to examine the legality along with the ethical acceptability of the research project, and their practice differs in turn.

The European Union and the Council of Europe are working in the direction of harmonization of the existing legislation and professional rules on research in humans. *The 1997 Convention for the Protection of Human Rights and Dignity of the Human Being with Regard to the Application of Biology and Medicine* has already been signed by twenty-eight countries and ratified by six, proceeding to become their internal law and it is expected that more countries will do so in the near future. Also the protocol on research which will be an adjunct to the Convention is almost ready and this will give guidance to researchers all over Europe.

However, even if harmonization is achieved, differences that are based on fundamental and often deep beliefs of the people will not easily be changed. Even the issue of informed consent which is a legal requirement in most countries might be considered less important by some doctors who believe in the significance of research and consider that it would be extremely difficult for them to obtain consent in certain situations.

Harmonization of legislation concerning research in humans is a desirable aim and we should work in this direction. However, while we must be realistic in accepting the differences between people and countries, we should uphold the application of important general principles, such as those contained in the Declaration of Helsinki and the Convention on Human Rights, which will best protect human beings.

Conclusion

The vulnerable population of neonates and their parents must be given adequate legal and ethical protection in the matter of research. However, investigators must be allowed to answer important research questions without the limitation of excessive legislative restriction, since failure to research issues specific to the neonate will not be in the best interests of that group.

In order to recruit sufficient patients to attain statistical power to answer relevant research questions within a meaningful time frame, multinational research is increasingly required. The legislative application of ethical principles varies across Europe. This environment of legal variety in the matter of proxy consent for neonatal research results in differing practical implications for the conduct of pan-European research.

Summary of Legal Requirements in Europe for Research in Neonates

Country	Legislation on research	Ethical review system	Consent	Benefit of the child requirement	Research of no direct benefit in minors permitted
Denmark	Yes (Act No.503 of 24 June 1992 as amended by Act No.499 of 12 June 1996)	Regional Research Ethics committees review all bio-medical research projects on live-born human subjects	With proxy consent risk evaluation is stringent. (Report No. 1335 of April 1997 by commission of Minister of Research and Minister of Health). Consent from both parents required where custody is shared. If one parent withholds consent, research cannot proceed	Yes	Yes, when only minimal risk involved
Finland	Finnish Medical Research Act 1999	Medical Research Act regulates RECs. Each of the 20 hospital districts to have at least one REC. Duties and composition regulated	Written proxy consent by guardian or legal representative following information (Medical Research Act 8(3) and 6(2). Both parents to consent unless health care procedure is 'routine' or welfare of child demands immediate decision. (Child Custody and Right of Access Act 1983.) Research Act permits research without consent in situations of 'urgency; and expectation of 'immediate benefit to the patient's health'	Research should directly benefit child's health or be of special benefit to other children or those with the same state of health and not possible to use other research subjects	Yes, provided only minimal risk of harm or distress, benefit to similar groups, and if unable to use other research subjects

Country	Legislation on research	Ethical review system	Consent	Benefit of the child requirement	Research of no direct benefit in minors permitted
France	1988 specific legislation on research	Regional Committees	Written proxy consent by those legally responsible (usually both parents). Research can be commenced without consent in cases of emergency; then consent from 'members of the family' should be sought	Research must aim to provide a direct benefit to the health of the minor. However placebo-controlled trials permitted (guidebook of Department of Health)	Yes, provided there is only minimal risk expected and research will benefit other children with the same disease, handicap and age or there is no alternative solution
Germany	Law governing clinical trials of drugs and medicinal products provides rules for involvement of minors	Submission of research protocols to RECs required by law for clinical trials of drugs and medicinal products. Declaration of Helsinki and professional rules for physicians require submission to RECs for other research projects	Proxy consent for minors from both parents (if share custody). Presumed consent permitted in cases of clinical emergency	Yes. Child must be expected to derive therapeutic, diagnostic or prophylactic advantage. There is some question of whether placebo-controlled clinical trials are legal for neonates	No
Greece	Specific legislation on clinical drug trials	Scientific Committees instead of RECs. Research Ethics Committees only function in a few hospitals. In clinical drug trials control by the National Drugs Organisation	Proxy consent required (by legal representative)	Not specifically mentioned for research but stated in general legislation	Yes, for diagnosis or prevention of diseases applicable to the child

Country	Legislation on research	Ethical review system	Consent	Benefit of the child requirement	Research of no direct benefit in minors permitted
Ireland	All pharmacological research controlled by the control of Clinical Trials and Drugs Acts 1987-1990, as amended by the Irish Medicines Board Act 1995. Non-pharmacological research regulated by common law principles, the constitution and professional canons	Yes – RECs review medical research. Competence of RECs for clinical trials must be approved by the Irish Medicines Board. Clinical trials need permission (including approval of investigators' indemnity arrangements) from the Irish Medicines Board (prior to REC approval). The statutory requirements only relate to clinical trials involving pharmacologically active preparations. Medical Practitioners bound by 'A Guide to Ethical Conduct and Behaviour and to Fitness to Practise of the Medical Council'	Proxy consent by person independent of investigator. A six-day period must elapse after patient or patient's legal representative has been given information about a trial prior to commencement of the trial. This provision can be amended with the permission of the Irish Medicines Board. 'Therapeutic privilege' has no role in obtaining consent to participation in research. Consent to participation in research is required even in a clinical emergency	Yes	Not clear. Lawyers have divided views. It may be permitted if interventions are minor with negligible risk and if increase in scientific knowledge gained which may benefit other children
Norway	Specific legislation on clinical drug trials (Dec 4th 1992 No.132) Legal obligations governed by general principles of law, specifically individual autonomy. Penal Code offers protection against bodily harm and mental coercion. Courts apply provisions of the Declaration of Helsinki	Five regional RECs cover the country. No statutory status but their mandate imposes review by one of these committees on all research involving humans. No local hospital or other committee acknowledged in the system. Small country and research community said to be surveyable	Proxy consent for minors (aged less than 18 years)	Yes, in Act on Children and Parents and Act on Legal Guardianship	Not clear. Lawyers have divided views. It may be permitted if interventions are minor with negligible risk and if increase in scientific knowledge gained which may benefit other children

Country	Legislation on research	Ethical review system	Consent	Benefit of the child requirement	Research of no direct benefit in minors permitted
Spain	Specific laws of 1990 and 1993 regulate clinical trials on drugs and these stipulate requirements for minors	Ethics Committees for Clinical Research in all hospitals where research is carried out	Proxy consent by legal representatives (Royal Decree, art.12.1 stipulates requirements of proxy informed consent). Before research starts, the proxy consent by the legal representative is communicated to the Public Attorney (Royal Decree, art.12.5). Consent may be dispensed with in an emergency when research concerns the specific interest of the health of the child and if there is Research Ethics Committee approval. Retrospective consent of the legal representative is then requested as soon as possible (Royal Decree, art.12.6)	Yes, within general legislation	Yes, provided there is adoption of measures to guarantee that risk will be minimal and relevant knowledge about the illness will be obtained

Country	Legislation on research	Ethical review system	Consent	Benefit of the child requirement	Research of no direct benefit in minors permitted
Sweden	No specific legislation. Patients right to self-determination governed by Act on Professional Activities in Health and Medical Services (1998:531) and Health and Medical Services Act (1982:763). Medical Products Act (1992:859) regulates pharmaceutical clinical trials	No statutory regulation for RECs however, ten regional RECs connected to six faculties of medicine covers biomedical research on humans. However, there is no explicit legal demand for REC approval for non-pharmaceutical regulatory research. REC status is only advisory. Co-ordination of the independent RECs is provided by the Medical Research Council's National Board for Research Ethics. No appeal can be made to the latter for an individual case. For clinical trials on drugs, the permission of the Medical Products Agency is required by law	Oral consent is allowed Parents and Children Code regulates rights and duties of custodians of minors. Both custody holders to consent unless health care procedure is minor or best interest of the child demands immediate decision. Sometimes unclear whether or not consent of one parent sufficient. In extraordinary situations, patients unable to give consent may be included if trial is linked to treatment of patient's illness, has REC approval and might benefit the patient	Yes, following Sweden's ratification of the UN Convention on the Rights of the Child (1989) – Article 3.1 states that the best interest of the child must be a primary consideration in all decisions concerning children	Yes, provided no more than minimal risk involved
United Kingdom	No specific legislation and no specific case law. Legal rights and duties based on common law principles governing medical treatment and general principles in the Children Act 1989	No statutory basis for ethical review but approval of (LRECs and MRECs) required for research which is publicly funded or conducted on NHS premises	Consent of person legally responsible for the child required. Consent in writing not legally required	Yes. Welfare and best interests of child must be protected	Probably not permitted.

Notes

1. Chapter 8 has been reproduced in similar form in *Archives of Disease in Childhood*, 2001; 84: F70-73.

References

Bonati M, Choonara I, Hoppu K, Pons G, Seybert H, Closing the gap in drug therapy. *Lancet* 1999; 353: 1625.

Council of Europe. Convention for the Protection of Human Rights and Dignity of the Human Being with Regard to the Application of Biology and Medicine: Convention on Human Rights and Biomedicine. European Treaty Series – No.164. Oviedo, Spain. 4 April 1997.

International Conference on Harmonization *Guidelines for Good Clinical Practice* (ICH GCP). The Association of the British Pharmaceutical Industry, London, 1997.

Mason SA. Obtaining informed consent for neonatal randomised controlled trials - an 'elaborate ritual'? *Archives of Disease in Childhood* 1997; 76: F143-F145.

McHaffie HE et al. Withholding/withdrawing treatment from neonates: legislation and official guidelines across Europe. *Journal of Medical Ethics* 1999; 25: 440-446.

Royal College of Paediatrics and Child Health. *Safeguarding informed parental involvement in clinical research involving newborn babies and infants. A position statement*. Royal College of Paediatrics and Child Health, London. December 1999.

World Medical Assembly. *The Declarations of Helsinki*. Ferney-Voltaire, France: The Association, 1964; amended in 1975, 1983, 1989 and 1996.

9 The Regulation of Neonatal Research in Finland

MS S. LÖTJÖNEN

Medical Treatment versus Medical Research

When treating neonates in ordinary medical practice, Finnish law authorises the custodians of the neonate to act as his or her proxies without strict guidelines to follow. Section 7(2) of the Act on the Status and Rights of the Patients (the Patient Act)[1] states:

> if a minor patient cannot decide on the treatment given to him or her, he or she shall be treated in mutual understanding with his or her custodian or legal representative.

The term 'mutual understanding' has been interpreted to require either specific nor written consent.[2]

If the child takes part in medical research, different provisions of law are applied. The most important piece of national legislation in this regard is the Finnish Medical Research Act (the Research Act) that entered into force on 1 November 1999.[3] The Act includes provisions on research ethics committees, informed consent and proxy decision-making for both minors and adult incompetents. As in medical treatment, the custodian or the legal representative of the child has the power to decide on the child's participation in the trial; however, in research, stricter limits have been set than in medical treatment.

According to the Research Act, minors may be research subjects only where it is not possible to obtain the same scientific results using other research subjects and where the risk of harming or distressing the research subject is minimal. Additionally, the research should be likely to be either (1) of direct benefit to the research subject's health, or (2) of special benefit to the health of people in the same age group or with the same state of health. The latter provision explicitly allows non-therapeutic trials on minors to be conducted in Finland.

121

In the following, I will view some of the basic elements of medical research on minors in Finland, emphasising the aspects that touch on research on neonates specifically. Generally, the same legal rules apply to neonates as to other minors. Some differences can still be seen, for example, with regard to the scope of persons eligible to make decisions on the child's behalf. On the other hand, the question of self-determination of the subject can be left aside in the case of a neonate. Authority to consent on behalf of the child, the formal and material requirements as well as limits of proxy consent will be examined, together with the relevance of consent in situations of urgency. A brief overview on control mechanisms other than decision-making by a proxy will also be provided.

Who Can Act as a Proxy for a Neonate?

According to section 8 of the Medical Research Act,

> [Where the minor does not have the capacity to make an independent decision on his or her participation]..minors may be research subjects only where written consent for this has been given by their custodian or legal representative after being provided with the information referred to in section 6 (2).[4]

While there is no question of the incapacity of a neonate to give his or her consent independently, the question of who is eligible to act as the child's custodian still remains. The central legal source is then the Child Custody and Right of Access Act.[5] According to the Act, the custodians of the child are his or her parents or other persons to whom the custody of the child has been granted by the court.[6] Where the parents are not married to each other at the time of the child's birth, custody shall be vested in the mother. If the parents are married to each other at the time, custody shall be vested in both parents.[7] With respect to neonates of up to 30 days of age, the procedures that enable unmarried fathers to act as their legal custodians have rarely been enforced. Therefore, where the parents of the neonate are not married, there is a strong presumption of the mother being sole custodian; thus she has the authority to make decisions on the child independently.

If both of the parents act as custodians, they can only make decisions concerning the child together.[8] There are two kinds of exceptions to this rule. Firstly, there are the general provisions of authorisation. A custodian may by his or her status represent the child independently in health care if the procedure is of such a routine nature that the other custodian may be assumed to consent. Routine procedures include such measures as an ordinary health check or a minor intervention. Authorisation may also occur when one custodian constantly allows the other to take care of the decision-making concerning the child's health. In the above-mentioned situations, barring anything contrary coming to the fore, health care personnel can accept one custodian consenting alone.[9]

The second exception to the rule is statutory. The Child Custody and Right of Access Act, section 5(2) states:

> if one of the custodians is unable to take part in the making of a decision owing to absence, illness or some other reason and if a delay in deciding the matter would be detrimental, his consent on the matter shall not be necessary. A matter of great importance for the future of the child, however, may only be decided jointly by the custodians unless it is manifest that the best interests of this child require otherwise.[10]

Again, it has been considered that routine procedures which bear no risk to the child can be safely conducted on him or her, if the other custodian cannot be contacted.[11]

The above-mentioned authorisation of one custodian to act as sole proxy for the child has been written with standard medical care in mind, and no legal evaluation has been made thus far regarding its applicability to medical research. The central questions seem to be whether medical research by its (experimental) *nature* can be considered to be 'a routine procedure' and whether the other custodian can be assumed to consent. A further question is that if participation in research includes only *measures* similar to routine procedures, such as taking blood samples, would it render the same rules applicable to research as in ordinary care? It is likely that the more pragmatic view which puts an emphasis on the invasiveness of the procedure will be adopted. The practical consequences of requiring two signatures for even the most minor procedure would be disproportionate to the interest that the rule was made to protect. Therefore, I would argue that what has been said on medical treatment should apply to medical research as well in terms of authorising one custodian to act alone. This is also how the situation is viewed in practice.

Nevertheless, the research team can only rely on these exceptions to the extent that they assume the consent of both custodians. The other custodian should be made aware of the child participating in research as soon as possible and, if either of the custodians should withdraw his or her consent at any stage prior to the completion of the research, the child may not be subjected to any further procedures other than those related to the care of his or her health.[12]

An interesting question is whether the proxy could authorise a person other than a custodian to act on behalf of the child, for example in a situation where the father is not known (or not married to the mother) and the mother is suffering from post-operational fatigue which deteriorates her capacity to give a fully informed consent to enrol her child in research, but, at the same time, she is deemed competent enough to authorise a third person to do it on her behalf. This situation has not been addressed properly in academic literature, although in daily life authorisations of child care happen all the time: in day-care nursery, on children's visits to relatives, etc. No exact rules on whether such an authorisation could take place in medical research can be given here. One issue is clear, however: authorisation must not be given to a person with a conflicting interest, such as somebody from the research team. Even the treating physician as a possible substitute for a custodian would be questionable. If authorisation is necessary, the authorised person should be one close to the patient, such as the child's biological father (if not a custodian already by marriage) or some other relative or a close friend that the mother has named.

Requirements for Consent

The formal requirements for valid informed consent in neonatal research fundamentally follow the same criteria as consent by an adult subject, except that consent is given by a proxy. Medical research on human beings may not be conducted without a *written* informed consent by the research subject or by her proxy.[13]

The basic requirement of *voluntariness* to medical procedures is already secured as a right to physical integrity at the constitutional level, although the Constitutional provisions do not specifically address medical research.[14] Nor does the wording of the Research Act directly state this requirement. However, the Research Act does emphasise the subject's right to withdraw from research at any point prior to the completion of the research which, if interpreted in the light of the international and national regulations, is regarded as encompassing the idea of voluntariness.[15] Furthermore, according to the Decree[16] given to substantiate some of the provisions of the Research Act, the issue must be specifically addressed in the consent form. The relevant provisions are applied with regard to consent of both a subject and a proxy.

It may be viewed as peculiar that voluntariness is not addressed as such in the wording of the Act unlike in some of the most central international conventions and guidelines on the subject.[17] However, there is no question about the importance of the requirement both in academic writings and in practice. Voluntariness is additionally safeguarded by prohibiting any payments to research subjects other than in compensation for expenses, loss of earnings or other inconvenience suffered as a result of the research.[18]

The issue of *competence* does not normally arise in connection with adult proxies consenting on behalf of their child, but in some circumstances it may come up, for example when the parents are so upset about the health of their child that their judgement may be impaired or when the mother is still in the process of recovering from anaesthesia. In the Research Act, the question of competence of the *research subject* him or herself is addressed in sections that handle adult incompetents and minors. Section 7 concerning adult incompetents does not give any content as to the evaluation of competence. However, the matter is to some degree illuminated in section 8, which deals with minors. One should note here, however, that since adults enjoy a presumption of competence, the standard of competence may be biased in favour of the adult when minors and adults are compared.

In both medical treatment and medical research, the test for competence is *understanding*. With reference to the Research Act, the extent to which a minor is able to use her right to self-determination depends on her age, maturity and capacity to understand the meaning of the research procedure.[19] In the evaluation, the nature of her illness and the research are determinative. For example, if the research is likely to benefit her health, a 15-year-old may in most cases give her consent to research independently, although her custodian will be informed of the procedure. If this criteria is applied to evaluating the competence of *a proxy* (for example, a mother suffering from a post-operative fatigue and the shock of having heard upsetting news on her child's possible brain damage), one should disregard the age and maturity factors (assuming the mother is of legal age), and focus on her capacity to understand instead, emphasising both the condition of mother and child and the nature of research. This would result in a lower standard of capacity required from the proxy when research is likely to benefit the neonate.[20]

The capacity to understand is naturally related to the nature of *information* given to the proxy and to the way the information is delivered. According to section 6 of the Research Act, subjects

> shall have their rights, the purpose and nature of the research and the procedures it involves properly explained to them. The potential risks and harm shall also be properly explained. This information shall be given in a way that research subjects are in a position to give their informed consent as regards issues connected with the research that have a bearing on their decision-making.

By section 8(3), the same standard of information is applied to information provided to proxies as to subjects themselves. It seems, therefore, that the extent of information delivered follows what is called the 'subjective standard', i.e. the standard of information is evaluated by the needs of the research subject rather than by using a physician-based evaluation.[21]

What would then be the minimum standard of information that the proxy must be able to understand in order to give a valid consent under Finnish law? One could interpret the Act strictly and say that the proxy should understand all the information given to her if it has a bearing on decision-making, but in urgent situations this might be very hard to achieve. At the time of deciding whether to enrol the subject in research or not, the nature and purpose of research as well as the potential risks and harms of the procedure could be suggested as forming the essence of the information given. The person making a decision should also always be made aware of her right to withdraw her consent. Even though the wording of the Medical Research Decree includes some further requirements on the information provided, such as information on data protection, these could be said to have only an indirect effect on the validity of consent. If the situation is such that time does not allow ensuring that the proxy has completely understood these details, one could exceptionally allow these facts to be explained (again) at a later stage. In no case should any of the above-mentioned information be withheld altogether from either the subject or the proxy. [22]

The Governmental Bill for the Research Act[23] seeks to explain what has been meant by 'information shall be given in a way that research subjects are in a position to give their informed consent'. The information should, according to the Bill, be given both orally and in writing so that the person consenting would have a chance to absorb the information properly.

The more demanding the participation in research is considered to be both physically and mentally, the more important it is to let the person making the decision thoroughly weigh her options.[24]

Emergency

Sometimes the legal proxy either may not be present or is clearly deemed incompetent to understand even the essence of the research suggested by the research team within the given time. The general consent provisions in the Research Act (section 6) bear an exception to the rule of informed consent:

> Exceptions to this [research subject's informed consent in writing] may be made where consent cannot be obtained owing to the urgency of the situation and the patient's state of health, and the measure is expected to be of immediate benefit to the patient's health.[25]

The question arises, however, of what is meant by the notions of 'urgency' and 'immediate benefit to the patient's health'. As informed consent is the cornerstone of the rights of the research subject in medical research, any exceptions should be given a very narrow interpretation. When seeking guidance from the Governmental Bill for the Act, a reference is made therein to victims of an accident and conducting research in emergency situations.[26] Therefore, the notion of 'urgency' is not intended to be seen from the researcher's point of view or to be used solely because the legal proxies are not available at the time, rather the exception is limited to those situations where the health of the neonate urgently requires action to be taken.

What then does the notion of 'immediate benefit' stand for? Although in itself the ethics of using placebo controls can be questioned in some cases, in research conducted under the rule of urgency, placebo controls should under no circumstances be used where an accepted treatment already exists. If, however, no accepted treatment exists, the situation is evaluated differently. Guidance will again be sought from the Governmental Bill which states that the exception of urgency applies only to those situations where it is presumed that the result of treatment would be the same or better compared with treatment given without the subject taking part in research.[27] Therefore, in the case of placebo-controlled trials, there seems to be no (legal) hindrance for trials under the rule of urgency where no accepted treatment exists and the measure is expected to be of immediate benefit to the patient's health.

Applying this rule in practice, in cases other than placebo controls, is not necessarily as simple as it may initially appear. The risk-benefit calculation very often blurs the comparison of the results of the two alternative treatment procedures. Although new treatments would not be sought unless their results were presumed to be better, they often involve risks and side-effects which either are unknown or may be more harmful than the side-effects of the traditional treatment. How can the results of the two then be compared? No definite answers can be given here, but it is precisely this sort of risk-benefit calculation that lies within the realm of decision-making of the custodian of the child and, unless the new procedure is the child's only choice to survive or escape a serious danger to her health, new treatments with more significant risks should not be conducted without proxy consent, even in emergency situations.

Limits of Proxy Decision-making

The general provisions on the duties of the custodians in child law state that the custodians shall safeguard the child's development and well-being while having the best interests of the child as the first and paramount consideration.[28] However, the provisions of the Research Act make an exception to the strict interpretation of the best interests principle by allowing medical research on minors not only for personal health benefit but also for people in the same age group or with the same state of health. The relevant subsection reads:

> ... the research should be likely to be of direct benefit to the research subject's health or the research should be likely to be of special benefit to the health of people in the same age group or with the same state of health.[29]

A question arises on the interpretation of the scope of people belonging to the 'same age group or with the same state of health'. The Governmental Bill for the Act states that, with regard to studies in genetically inherited diseases, the members of a family that may carry the carrier-gene could form a group with the same state of health.[30] The Parliamentary Committee on Social Affairs and Health in its report emphasises that 'the same age group' should not be interpreted to mean specifically the group that took part in the research but more generally children of the same age as those who took part in the research when it was initiated.[31] However, what was meant by the kind of 'special benefit' related to the health of people in the same age group or with same state of health is not explained either in the Bill or in the Committee Report.

Two additional criteria are viewed with regard to the limits of conducting research on a minor:

> Minors may be research subjects only where it is not possible to obtain the same scientific results using other research subjects and where the risk of harming or distressing the subject is very low.[32]

The criterion under which minors may be subjects only where it is not possible to obtain the same scientific results using other research subjects, I shall call the criterion of 'societal necessity'. It can be understood on two levels. Firstly, it encompasses the idea of using human beings, in general, as the last option for achieving the desired results. If the same results can be yielded using laboratory experiments or animal testing, the research should not be conducted on any human being, much less on a minor. Secondly, if the same results can be achieved using adults as research subjects, minors should not be taken as research subjects. An exception to this rule may be if the research is conducted on a very rare illness and there are not enough adult patients to satisfy the statistical requirements for an accurate result.[33] Even under this exception, the requirement of 'societal necessity' is fulfilled, although it is now interpreted more broadly.[34]

The other precondition for medical research on minors is that the research may only entail a minimal risk of harm or distress to the child. In the Research Act there are no additional criteria as to what constitutes or qualifies as a minimal risk, but as the Act was prepared with regard to the future implementation of the Council of Europe Convention on Biomedicine and Human Rights, one may look to the Biomedicine Convention for more guidance.[35] The Explanatory Report to the Convention narrates the precondition for minimal risk (Art 17, para 2) to include a single blood sample from a child, and gives a few other examples which also meet the criteria.[36] As the Finnish Medical Research Act has only entered into force in November 1999, it is difficult to evaluate how the minimal risk criteria is going to be interpreted in practice in Finland.

Other Control Mechanisms on Medical Research on Neonates

The Medical Research Act also regulates ethics committees.[37] Each hospital district (total 20 in the country) shall have at least one ethics committee. All of them have to be notified to the Provincial State Office which keeps a register of ethics committees in their area. These can be joint committees or there can be several in one hospital district.[38]

The duties and the composition of the ethics committees are listed in the Act.[39] It is noteworthy that the ethics committees are under obligation to examine not only the ethical but also the legal acceptability of research projects by taking into consideration the Medical Research Act, the data protection legislation,[40] the international obligations covering the status of research subjects, and the rules and guidelines that govern medical research. The ethics committees shall also monitor and direct the handling of issues in research ethics for their region. International multicentre trials are processed by the Sub-Committee on Medical Research Ethics of the National Advisory Board on Health Care Ethics, which is situated within the realm of the Ministry of Social Affairs and Health. The Sub-Committee can, however, delegate international multicentre trials to the regional ethics committees and, in practice, at least half of the protocols are being delegated throughout the hospital districts in the country.

Although the duties of the ethics committee also include legal evaluation, there is no statutory requirement for a legal expert in the composition. According to the Act, the committees consist of a minimum of six members and a chairperson with an appropriate number of substitutes. At least two members shall be laypersons and the committees shall also contain representatives from areas other than medicine. The two primary principles that govern the functioning of the ethics committees are expertise and independence. If the ethics committee does not have the necessary expertise to evaluate a submitted research protocol , it can consult an external expert. Both the external experts and the permanent members must be free from bias.[41] In this respect, the provisions laid down in the Administrative Procedure Act[42] apply to research ethics committee members as well as to other civil servants, although the committee members are not considered to be employees of the hospital district or the Government *per se*.

The most efficient control mechanism outside legislation should, of course, be the private and professional ethical judgement of the researchers themselves. However, in Finland, medical or research ethics are not included in the curriculum of medical schools, and the courses made available to medical students are scarce. The information on ethical standards and the relevant legislation in the area is therefore disseminated to the researchers via supervisors, colleagues, conferences and professional literature. The ethics committees have a very important role to play not only with regard to evaluating the research protocols but also in guiding the researchers towards a better practice. Therefore, the interaction between research ethics committees and researchers is vital to the practice which calls for well-argued recommendations together with more general guidelines to be delivered by the ethics committees.

Conclusion

In some cases, the necessity of conducting research on minors is obvious. Research that is likely to be of direct benefit to the minor's health has rarely faced much opposition, but research without such benefit has raised discussion about acceptability. Defining the group of people for whose benefit the research is conducted and fulfilling the requirements of 'societal necessity' and 'minimal risk' form the basis for the compromise made in Finland. At the same time as allowing non-therapeutic research on minors, maximum measures for protection should be undertaken. The extent to which minors are subjected to non-therapeutic research procedures should be minimised. Also the Research Act actually imposes the requirements of societal necessity and minimal risk on research that is likely to be beneficial to the minor subject. This can be understood if it is thought that medical research always adds an extra risk compared with measures conducted in ordinary medical practice, although research adequately performed may lower the risks of health care in general. The Finnish solution tries to strike a balance between two good goals, protecting the individual and striving for scientific advances.

If medical research on minors is considered exceptional, medical research on minors without a valid proxy consent is much more so. The fact that the sole custodian is incapable of consenting to the procedure, or that both custodians are not present, should not tempt researchers to take an unduly liberal approach to the prerequisites for a free and valid consent. Consent is not valid if the person giving it has not the authority, capacity or enough information to do so. Lack of time must not be the only reason to apply the rule of urgency and to disregard the consent requirements; the focus must always be on the well-being of the child. In borderline cases, the custodians' power and position in evaluating the best for their child must be honoured, even though it would be contrary to the views of the researcher. However, the safety of the subject should not be compromised in any situation.

According to the present Act, research ethics committees cannot supervise medical research on any other basis than by relying on information given in research protocols, and therefore the main responsibility for the safety and well-being of the subjects is left to the researcher in charge. He or she is also responsible for the research personnel staying within the limits of legality and professional conduct. At the moment, there are two significant problems in enhancing safety and ethical awareness: research ethics is not part of the curriculum of medical schools and the research ethics committees are under-resourced for their task. Respect for human life and the safety of research subjects, as well as the credibility of medical science, are values which deserve to be adequately protected. In order to assist the ethics committees to serve their educating role, in addition to reviewing research protocols, the hospital districts or the Government should allot more funds for their activity. Although ethics committees are eligible to receive a moderate payment for their services, this fee is by no means sufficient to provide the resources that would enable the committees to dedicate themselves efficiently to the workload given.

Notes

1. Nr. 785 of Statutes, 17 August 1992. The translation is based on an unofficial translation by the Finnish Ministry of Social Affairs and Health.
2. See e.g. Raimo Lahti, 'Towards a Comprehensive Legislation Governing the Rights of Patients: The Finnish Experience' in Lotta Westerhäll and Charles Phillips (eds) *Patient's Rights - Informed Consent, Access and Equality*, Nerenius & Santérus Publishers (Stockholm 1994) p. 215 and Irma Pahlman, 'Potilaan itsemääräämisoikeus ja hoitotestamentti' (The patient's right to self-determination and advanced directives) in *Lakimies* 6 (1997) p. 820-825.
3. Nr. 488 of Statutes, 9 April 1999. Before the introduction of the Research Act, the law on medical research was mainly based on human rights conventions and international guidelines in the area, such as the Council of Europe Convention for the Protection of Human Rights and Fundamental Freedoms (1950), the UN Covenant on Civil and Political Rights (1966), the Council of Europe Recommendation (90) 3, European Community guidelines and guidelines provided by the World Medical Association. The Patient Act was applied if research was conducted on patients in the context of their treatment. Experimentation on pharmaceuticals and medical devices was and still is regulated by the National Agency for Medicinal Products (Regulation Nr. 6 (1993) and Circular Nr. 2 (1997)). The former National Board of Health also

issued circulars on ethics committees in 1980 and 1986, but they were abolished due to reorganisation of health administration in 1990 and 1993. Although the Research Act now covers most of the issues dealt with in the international codes mentioned above, they still have an authoritative status in the activity.

4. The translation is based on an unofficial translation by the Finnish Ministry of Social Affairs and Health.

5. Nr. 361 of Statutes, 8 April 1983. In Finland, custody and guardianship are separated by law. The concept of *custody* is used in connection to decision-making of the *person* of the incompetent and the concept of *guardianship* refers to *financial* decision-making on his or her behalf. However, in the case of minors, both are normally part of the parental powers unless otherwise is stated by law or by the court. (Guardianship Act (Nr. 442 of Statutes, 1 April 1999), section 4(1)).

6. Child Custody and Right of Access Act, section 3(1).

7. Child Custody and Right of Access Act, section 6(1).

8. Child Custody and Right of Access Act, section 5(1).

9. Markku Helin, 'Alaikäisen oikeudet potilaana' (The Rights of a Minor Patient) p. 96 in Jari Koivisto (ed) '*Potilaan oikeudet ja potilasasiamiestoiminta*' (Patient's Rights and the System of Patient Ombudsmen) Suomen Kuntaliitto (Helsinki 1994).

10. The translation is published by the Central Union for Child Welfare in Finland.

11. Markku Helin, '*Alaikäisen oikeudet potilaana*' (The Rights of a Minor Patient) p. 96.

12. Research Act, section 8(2), which makes a reference to withdrawal of consent of a competent person in section 6(2).

13. Section 6(1) reads: 'Medical research on persons may not be conducted without the research subject's informed consent in writing'. Further national regulation on consent is given on trials on pharmaceuticals and medical devices (Regulation Nr. 6 (1993) and Circular Nr. 2 (1997) by the National Agency on Medicines), but as they are secondary to legislation, no further reference is made to them here.

14. Section 7 of the reformed Constitution Act (Nr. 731 of Statutes, 11 June 1999) which comes into force 1 March 2000, states the right to personal integrity as a constitutional right which cannot be violated without a valid ground stated in law. Inviolability of a person has already been connected to the constitutional rights of patients and research subjects since 1972 in Finland by Professor Raimo Lahti, 'Potilaalta hoitotoimenpiteeseen hankittavan suostumuksen oikeudellista arviointia' (On the patient's consent to medical treatment from a legal point of view), in: *Rikosoikeudellisia kirjoitelmia* III 64 (Vammala 1972). The view expressed got authoritative support from the Parliamentary Ombudsman the following year in his annual report. (Report of the Parliamentary Ombudsman on his Activity in 1973, p. 19 (Helsinki 1974).

15. Research Act, section 6(3).

16. Medical Research Decree (Nr. 986 of Statutes, 29 October 1999), section 3.

17. For example, the Council of Europe Convention on Human Rights and Biomedicine (ETS 164), Article 5 which speaks of '*free* and informed consent'.

18. Research Act, section 21. The Ministry of Social Affairs and Health is in the process of setting up a schedule for payments for inconvenience incurred during research in order to prevent the misuse of this provision as an inappropriate incentive for potential research subjects. At the time of writing (March 2000), it has not yet been published.

19. Section 8(3) of the Research Act reads: 'Where the minor has reached the age of 15 and, in view of her age and maturity and the type of illness and research, is capable of understanding the importance of the research procedure and the research is likely to be

of direct benefit to her health, it shall be sufficient for her to give her informed consent in writing. In such cases the custodian shall be informed.'

20. Although the Research Act does not address the issue of the possible lack of capacity of the mother immediately after childbirth, there are provisions in Finnish law that regard the mother as being incapable or less capable of making decisions under these circumstances. For example, a mother cannot give a valid consent on giving up her child for adoption until 8 weeks from the delivery (Act on Adoption, Nr. 153 of Statutes, 8 February 1985, section 10(3)) and according to chapter 21, section 4 of the Criminal Code (reformed by a Statute Nr. 578 of Statutes, 21 April 1995), the maximum penalty for manslaughter is lowered by half if a mother has killed her child while being exhausted or anxious following childbirth. Naturally, the context in medical research is quite different from these examples.

21. The subjective standard is also used with information provided to patients in traditional health care. See e.g. Kaarlo Tuori '*Sosiaalioikeuden oppikirja*' (Textbook on Social Law), p. 338, Werner Söderström OY (Helsinki 1995) and Irma Pahlman, 'Potilaan itsemääräämisoikeus ja hoitotestamentti' (The patient's right to self-determination and advanced directives) in *Lakimies* 6 (1997) p. 825. See also, Paula Ilveskivi, 'Potilaan oikeusasema tiedonsaantioikeuden näkökulmasta' (The Legal Status of a Patient from the Viewpoint of Right to Information) Kansaneläkelaitos, *Sosiaali- ja terveysturvan tutkimuksia* 26 (Helsinki 1997).

22. As will be seen below, the Act takes into account urgent situations where exceptions to informed consent may be made. All exceptions should, however, be interpreted very narrowly, and not even ethics committee approval will protect the responsible physician from liability if illegal shortcomings are found in the research personnel's conduct. Section 27 of the Medical Research Act includes a sanctions clause for breach of consent provisions and sets a threat of a fine. Researchers may also face consequences for a breach of public duty or for disciplinary actions by the National Agency for Medico-legal Affairs.

23. Governmental Bill Nr. 229 (1998), p. 14.

24. Ibid.

25. Research Act, section 6(1).

26. Governmental Bill Nr. 229 (1998), p. 14.

27. Ibid.

28. Child Custody and Right of Access Act, sections 1, 2(1) and 4(1). See also the UN Convention on the Rights of the Child (1989), article 3.

29. Research Act, section 8(2).

30. Governmental Bill Nr. 229 (1998) p. 15.

31. Committee Report Nr. 39 (1998) of the Parliamentary Committee on Social Affairs and Health.

32. Research Act, section 8(1).

33. A more ethical approach to overcome the statistical problems would be, of course, to expand the design of the protocol and to include more research centres in order to enhance recruitment rather than enrolling minors in research.

34. A third aspect to the notion of 'societal necessity' may be added, although it does not apply only to vulnerable groups but addresses research ethics in general. It touches on the general aims and the quality of the project. For example, if the design of the project is flawed, if it is merely duplicating what has already been scientifically proven, or if the results are more directed to advance commercial rather than medical interests, the

reason for conducting the project is medically speaking futile and therefore cannot fulfill the 'societal necessity' criteria.

35. Council of Europe Convention on Human Rights and Biomedicine (ETS 164). At the time of writing (March 2000), the Convention has not yet been formally implemented into Finnish law, but is expected to be so within the course of the year 2000.

36. Explanatory Report to the Convention for the Protection of Human Rights and Dignity of the Human Being with regard to the Application of Biology and Medicine: Convention on Human Rights and Biomedicine CM (96) 175, paras 111-113. The list includes: 'replacing X-ray examinations or invasive diagnostic measures for children by ultrasonic scanning; analyses of incidental blood samples from newborn infants without respiratory problems in order to establish the necessary oxygen content for premature infants; discovering the causes and improving treatment of leukaemia in children (e.g. by taking a blood sample)'. The list is by no means complete.

37. Research Act, section 16.

38. For example, in the Hospital District of Helsinki and Uusimaa, there are at present nine ethics committees specialising in different areas of medicine or for special patient groups.

39. Research Act, sections 17 and 18.

40. E.g. Act on Personal Data (Nr. 523 of Statutes, 22 April 1999).

41. Research Act, section 19.

42. Nr. 598 of Statutes, 6 August.

10   The Regulation of Neonatal Research in Greece

PROFESSOR P. DALLA-VORGIA

In Greece, medical practice and research are governed to a great extent by the Hippocratic tradition. Greek legislation and jurisprudence are in favour of absolute respect for human life and protection of the human body from serious injuries, even if the person himself consents to them. The Constitution of Greece in Section 2, paragraph 1 states that 'the respect and protection of the value of the human being constitute the primary obligation of the State'. Moreover, the Code of Medical Ethics (Royal Decree 25 May/6 July 1955) states that the doctor is under an obligation to respect, in all cases, the honour and the person of his patient. He is not allowed to perform any therapeutic or surgical operation which under the specific circumstances is inappropriate, nor experiment when this may offend the personal freedom or the free will of mentally competent persons. He is under an obligation to protect and save human life.[1]

Research, however, is free in Greece and its value fully recognised even when its aim is the increase of scientific knowledge and not only the therapeutic benefit of the subject.

Research is not specifically regulated in Greece. Only clinical drugs trials on humans are regulated by a ministerial decree of 1984 which is based on the Helsinki Declaration with some innovations, such as regulation of research on pregnant women and provision for specific private insurance for death or injury during the research programme.

As far as minors are concerned the ministerial decree states that:

- The drug must be destined for the diagnosis or the prevention of diseases of minors.
- Research of comparable effectiveness cannot be carried out on adults
- Consent has been given by the legal representative of the minor.
- This consent is valid only when the legal representative has been fully informed by a doctor of the essence, the meaning and the possible risks of the clinical trial.

If the minor is in a position to understand the essence of the clinical trial, his written consent is also required.

The ministerial decision does not mention the requirement of the best interest of the minor, however this is a provision found in general legislation.

General legislation and the Code of Medical Ethics give the guidance for the conduct of research in Greece. However, two main problems are apparent:

1. Ethics Committees [1,2]

Although the increasing progress of medical research and the ethical problems in Greek hospitals make apparent the need for Ethics Committees, these committees do not function yet in Greece except in two or three hospitals or Scientific Societies.

The first attempt to establish an Ethics Committee took place in 1965 in the Institute of Child Health. The proceedings of this Committee were interrupted in 1981, due to a change in the government, and were started again in 1990. Other attempts for the establishment of Ethics Committees were made in 1973 with the Legislative Decree 97/73, section 2, paragraph 6, which concerned mainly the approval of clinical drug research by the Central Committee on the Control of Drugs. Later on in 1978 a Ministerial Circular (A2/oik.3061/5.6.78) imposed the establishment of Ethics Committees at a local level. However these attempts were not very successful.

In the past decade some positive steps were taken. Law 2071/1992 'On the modernisation and organisation of the National Health Service' provided for the establishment of the National Council of Medical Ethics and Deontology, as well as for local Ethics Committees. According to paragraph 4, local Ethics Committees will be established in public and private hospitals and clinics. Their task will be consultation on issues of Medical Ethics and Deontology for the Governing Board of the hospital or the clinic, as well as the monitoring of the Medical Ethics and Deontology regulations. However the necessary ministerial decisions for the establishment and functioning of local Ethics Committees have not been made as yet. However, it seems there has been some movement in the National Ethics Committees which are concerned with Medical Ethics in a general way.

The role of Ethics Committees is partly played by the *Scientific Committees* which function in Greek hospitals. These Committees deal not only with the scientific side of a problem but also with its ethical aspects. The Scientific Committees of the hospitals were set up by the law 1397/1983 on the 'National Health System' and have five members that come from the medical service of the hospital. The facts that these Committees are only composed of doctors and that their traditional role is mainly scientific, make them inappropriate for the ethical evaluation of research projects.

The need for the establishment of Ethics Committees in Greek hospitals is apparent.

2. Informed Consent [3]

As was mentioned above, Greece is a country where the Hippocratic tradition is still very much alive. Thus, doctors who care more for the well-being of their patients and less for the protection of their rights are very reluctant to inform them and seek their consent. Informing the patient means telling the truth and there are many cases where doctors do not disclose the truth about a serious illness and decisions are taken not with the patient himself but with his relatives. Also there are other cases where the patient himself waives his right to the doctor saying that 'the doctor knows best'. On the other hand, doctors do not feel the need to take all the necessary precautions by fully informing their patients and seeking their consent, since there are still few malpractice cases in Greece, although their number seems to be growing.

Greek doctors, however, have an obligation to seek the consent of their patients. This obligation comes from the Constitution according to which due respect should be paid to the person, and the autonomy of the individual should be respected. It also comes from the Code of Medical Ethics, mentioned above, and the new law 2071/1992 regarding the National Health System. According to this law 'the patient or his representative have the right to be fully informed in advance about the possible dangers deriving from any unusual or experimental diagnostic and medical intervention'.

Also the Greek Civil and Penal Laws have provisions which in a direct or indirect way establish the legal requirement for consent to diagnosis, therapy or research.

Very recently, in 1999, Greece ratified the Convention of the Council of Europe for the protection of the human being with regard to the application of biology and medicine.[4] This means that this Convention is now the internal law of the country.

According to this Convention, free and informed consent by the person concerned is necessary for an intervention in the health field. As far as persons who are not able to consent because of their age (minors) or their altered mental state are concerned, and for the sake of their protection, the Convention states that an intervention may only be carried out for their own direct benefit with the authorisation of their representative or an authority, a person or body provided for by law.

In an *emergency situation*, if the appropriate consent cannot be obtained, any medically necessary intervention may be carried out immediately for the benefit of the health of the individual concerned.

Scientific research in the field of biology and medicine shall be carried out freely, subject to the provisions of the Convention and the other legal provisions ensuring the protection of the human being. The necessary consent as provided for by the Convention must have been given expressly, specifically and be documented.

Research on a person without the capacity to consent is permitted only if it has the potential to produce direct benefit to this person if all the other conditions provided for by the Convention and the law are met (necessary authorisation etc). Exceptionally such research is permitted even if it does not have the potential to produce results of direct benefit to the health of the person concerned under very strict conditions.

According to the above-mentioned legal framework, informed consent is obligatory for any intervention in the health field; Greek doctors should comply with that, especially in research.

In the field of neonatal research, consent presents even more problems because the mother might not be in a position to give consent and the father might be absent. If consent is going to be strictly required and the evaluation of research projects by an Ethics Committee be a common practice, this research will be hindered even more. Doctors find that it is very difficult to talk with distressed parents and thus, if there are very strict conditions for consent, useful research, often for the benefit of the neonate, might not be feasible.

Research may be very important; however, equally important is the protection of the rights of the persons who take part in the research project. An equilibrium should be maintained, and the Research Ethics Committees, which should start functioning in Greek hospitals, could resolve the issue.

Notes

1. Dalla-Vorgia P., Garanis T. Hippocrates is dead, long live Hippocrates. *Bulletin of Medical Ethics* 66, 28-31, 1991.
2. Dalla-Vorgia P. Clinical Ethics committees: The Situation in Greece. In: *Ethical function in hospital ethics committees.* BIOMED II. Workshop 1. Brussels 3-5 June 1999.
3. Dalla-Vorgia P., Kalapothaki V., Kalandidi A. Bioethics in Greece. In: *The Quality of Life in the Mediterranean countries.* 1st Mediterranean Meeting on Bioethics. Acireale, 31 October-5 November 1992.
4. Council of Europe. Convention for the Protection of Human Rights and dignity of the Human Being with regard to the application of Biology and Medicine: Convention on Human Rights and biomedicine. *European Treaty Series*-No 164. Oviedo, Spain. 4 April 1997.

11 The Regulation of Neonatal Research in Ireland

DR C. CRAVEN

Legislation on Consent in General and Specifically for Neonatal Research and Proxy Consent

In Ireland, there is no specific legislation governing the issue of consent in general, except in relation to (a) the right to refuse to undergo any procedure on grounds of conscience/religious belief and (b) the age of consent (see: Health Act 1953 section 4 and Non Fatal Offences Against the Person Act 1997 section 23). Practitioners are bound by common law rules derived from case law.

The Supreme Court has determined that the duty of pre-intervention disclosure regarding the risks of a procedure or intervention, in the therapeutic setting, is an antecedent duty of care, similar to the duty of care in diagnosis and treatment. As to how the standard of care, however, is to be determined, the Supreme Court has divided, between the application of professional negligence and ordinary negligence principles (see: Walsh v. Family Planning Services & ors [1992] IR 496). Later decisions of the Superior Courts have not, thus far, decisively set out the proper standard to be applied (see, in particular: Bolton v. Blackrock Clinic & anor, Supreme Court, unreported judgement 23 January, 1997). Nevertheless, each approach recognises the existence of the therapeutic privilege. Thus, although some information may be withheld for this reason, the nature and the extent of what may be withheld is less certain in the therapeutic setting. Treatment without adequate disclosure amounts to negligence, claims of trespass being confined to cases where no consent is obtained to the particular procedure and where it is feasible to seek and obtain such consent.

The Supreme Court has further held that the requirement for consent to any intervention is rooted in the guarantee provided by unenumerated constitutional rights, whether articulated as a right to privacy or a right to bodily integrity, found in Article 40.3.1 of the Constitution of Ireland,

1937 (see: In the matter of a Ward of Court [1995] 2 ILRM 401, [1996] 2 IR 100).

The requirement for proxy consent in the case of minors, or others under a legal disability, is not expressly set out in Irish law but arises rather, by implication, from the terms of the Health Act 1953, section 4, the Non Fatal Offences Against the Person Act 1997, section 23 and the rights of the family, including those in regard to education, found in Articles 41 and 42 of the Constitution of Ireland, 1937. The 'test' of proxy decision-making seems to rely on the 'best interests' of the patient (see: In the matter of a Ward of Court [1995] 2 ILRM 401, [1996] 2 IR 100).

In Ireland, all pharmacological research is controlled by the Control of Clinical Trials Act, 1987, as amended by the Control of Clinical Trials and Drugs Act, 1990, and the Irish Medicines Board Act 1995. The Acts state the need for full disclosure and consent to participation in writing, prior to taking part in a clinical trial, followed by a six-day 'cooling off period' before the trial commences. The 'cooling off' period may be varied by the Irish Medicines Board. Consent may be withdrawn at any time, without the imposition of penalty or contractual liability. In the therapeutic setting, the exercise of constitutional rights might be validly restricted in certain circumstances. However, in the context of pharmacological research, the legislation has given full expression to the requirement for full and informed consent which seeks to vindicate the right of the participant/citizen to privacy and bodily integrity.

As far as proxy consent to pharmacological research is concerned, an ethics committee decides the competence of the proxy consent-giver, who must be independent of the person who applied for, or is undertaking, a clinical trial under the Acts. However, these provisions only apply where the subject of the clinical trial is suffering from 'an illness, the remedy for or alleviation of which constitutes an objective of the trial' and is 'incapable of comprehending the nature, significance and scope of the consent to be given ...'. It is further provided that the substance or preparation under trial 'is to be administered for the purpose of saving the life of such a person, restoring his health, alleviating his condition or relieving his suffering'.

The legislation is silent on the specific issue of neonatal research, which is simply subsumed into the general provisions and principles. Given the limitations on proxy consent, accordingly, non-therapeutic pharmacological research on neonates is prohibited. Constitutional protections (right to life, right to bodily integrity), of course, also accrue for the benefit of neonates.

Non-pharmacological research is not subject to statutory control in Ireland. However, regard must be had to common law principles, the constitutional rights of the individual and professional canons. In the setting of such research, including neonatal research, the therapeutic privilege would have no place and it likely that the Irish courts would adopt the full disclosure approach of the Saskatchewan Court of Appeal in Halushka v University of Saskatchewan 53 DLR (2d) 436 (1965). Furthermore, particularly in light of the statutory prohibition on non-therapeutic pharmacological research on neonates and having regard to the over-riding constitutional considerations, it must be considered that all non-therapeutic research on neonates is similarly prohibited.

In summary, consent is at all times required before a person can participate in a clinical trial, even if that trial is being carried out in a situation of clinical emergency - although 'necessity' may justify therapeutic interventions without consent, in such circumstances.

How the Law is Interpreted in Practice

The law on pharmacological clinical research, including such research on neonates, in Ireland, is strictly applied and practice conforms to the legal requirements. Only registered medical or dental practitioners are allowed to conduct clinical trials in Ireland, prior permission for which must be obtained from the Irish Medicines Board. For payments to participants to be lawful, the permission must so specifically provide. Adequate security for compensation for personal injuries to, or death of, a participant must be provided, and review by an ethics committee, approved by the Irish Medicines Board, for the trial must also be obtained. In granting its approval, the ethics committee must *inter alia* be satisfied that the risks incurred by participants are commensurate with the objectives of the trial.

Non-pharmacological research, including such research on neonates, regulated by common law principles and professional canons, is similarly carried out in accordance with legal and ethical requirements in practice.

The Reliance of the Law on Consent to Protect the Research Subject

Protection of the research subject in pharmacological research relies on the consent of competent decision-makers. A participant in a clinical trial must be capable of comprehending the 'nature, significance and scope of his consent' and give his consent in writing. The person conducting the trial must ensure that, prior to consent being obtained, the participant is aware of the objectives of the trial, the manner of administration of the trial substance, the risks and any discomfort involved in, and the possible side-effects of, the trial and whether or not some participants will receive a placebo. Although consent is central to the protection of the research subject, the prohibition on non-therapeutic research on those who are incapable of giving appropriate consent (including neonates), the nature of the constitutional guarantees upon which any citizen may rely, the creation of specific criminal offences for contravention (by act or omission) of the provisions of the Acts, the requirement for adequate security for injury to, or death of, a research participant and the potential civil liability for such death or injury also serve to protect those who take part in pharmacological research. Broadly similar considerations apply to non-pharmacological research also.

Extra-legal Controls on Research

All medical practitioners are bound by the provisions of *A Guide to Ethical Conduct and Behaviour and to Fitness to Practise of the Medical Council*, the State registration and disciplinary authority for all medical practitioners in Ireland (as with the General Medical Council in Britain). In accordance with the provisions of the Guide, whereby the Medical Council supports the formation of ethical committees in all institutions where human research is undertaken, practitioners are advised to seek approval from an appropriate supervisory organisation before undertaking any research project involving risks to human subjects. This provision is clearly in addition to the statutory requirements, which only relate to clinical trials, as defined, involving, in effect, the administration of pharmacologically active preparations. In this regard, the Medical Council supports the Declaration of Helsinki's recommendations guiding doctors in biomedical research involving human subjects.

How Doctors are Informed of Legal Controls on Research

Most undergraduate medical students in Ireland undergo formal taught courses in legal medicine and/or medical ethics, which deal with the legal and ethical requirements of clinical research. Given the highly publicised circumstances surrounding the introduction of the Act of 1987, there is a fairly high level of awareness of the existence of statutory control of clinical research (if not the actual details thereof) among the general public, in any event. Furthermore, as most clinical research in Ireland is sponsored or grant-aided by major pharmaceutical companies, or the State-funded Health Research Board, and carried out in major public hospitals (which represent the majority of Irish hospitals), institutional processes rapidly inform practitioners of the legal and ethical requirements of clinical research.

The Relation between Research Ethics Committees and the Law

The competence of ethics committees, for pharmacological trials, must be approved by the Irish Medicines Board and, as such, they are inextricably bound up with the legal requirements for the conduct of such trials. There are no statutory, or advisory, provisions as to their composition. In practice, however, most would include a lawyer in their membership. Insofar as non-pharmacological research is concerned, research ethics committees must be established, having regard to professional canons. There is no other formal direct relationship between such committees, and the law. Furthermore, there are no statutory, or advisory, provisions as to their composition, although most would include a lawyer in their membership.

The Legal Requirement for Consent for Research in the Situation of a Clinical Emergency

On any reasonable construction of the law, full disclosure and consent are, at all times, required before a person can participate in a pharmacological clinical trial (or non-pharmacological research) even in the situation of clinical emergency. Although 'necessity' determines the limits of therapeutic interventions in an emergency situation where the patient is incapable of consenting to treatment, such a criterion does not apply to clinical research.

The Most Significant Problems Raised by the Law on Neonatal Research in Ireland

Irish researchers have participated previously in several multicentre clinical trials in neonatology and, overall, it appears that proportionately more research is carried out on neonates than in paediatrics generally. No particular problems appear to arise in Ireland in relation to neonatal research and parental consent therefore, over and above those encountered in clinical research generally.

The statutory framework within which pharmacological research in Ireland must be carried out gives rise to practical problems common to all such research. Given the small population of the country, however, and thus the relatively small number of potential research subjects among neonates, the administrative and regulatory burden is proportionately greater than in analogous research in adults.

A major area of uncertainty related to the liability of ethics committees where a pharmacological trial was allowed to take place without provisions for adequate compensation for the subjects of the trial who suffered personal injury or death as a result of participating in it. Although the duty of assessing whether or not adequate security exists for the payment of such compensation fell to the ethics committees under the Act of 1987, the Act of 1990 imposed the duty on the Minister for Health and now, under the Act of 1995, it falls to the Irish Medicines Board (the State drug regulatory authority). In addition, there is now broad immunity (absent wilful neglect or default) for the Minister for Health and ethics committees in respect of proceedings for the recovery of damages for personal injury arising from the discharge of their statutory functions.

Issues in relation to the liability of research ethics committees sanctioning or overseeing non-pharmacological neonatal research, however, have not yet been the subject of judicial determination in Ireland.

12 The Regulation of Neonatal Research in Norway

DR JURIS M. HALVORSEN

Legislation on Consent, with Specific Regard to Research

1. Consent to Medical Treatment

Until the enactment of the Patient's Rights Act (PRA) of July 1999,[1] there were no specific provisions on consent to medical treatment in Norway. The field was mostly governed by general principles of law, the point of departure being individual autonomy. Consent or other valid legal authority is required for all infringements on someone's integrity, not only for medical interventions.

Consent is governed by PRA chapter 4, §§ 4-1 to 4-9. For a consent to be considered valid, it is required that the patient (or his/her representative) gives signs of sufficient understanding of the problem and the suggested measures, and is sufficiently informed as to possible alternatives, effects and side effects. The main rule is that persons over 16 years of age can give valid consent to treatment. The person responsible for giving health care must decide if the patient is capable of consenting. A refusal to accept the patient's consent must be given in writing, with the reasons for refusal stated. The next of kin must be informed of the decision.

If the patient is unable to give consent, because of age or mental incapacity, the PRA prescribes various remedies. Parents or legal guardians can consent on behalf of minors. For therapeutic medical purposes, the child will come of age at 16. Between 12 and 16 years of age, the child is entitled to take part in the decision. If the parents do not fulfil their obligation to provide medical care for their child - for example by refusing vital treatment - the Child Care Authorities (Barnevernet) can act in loco parentis and give consent. Parents can probably not overrule the child in therapeutic medical decisions when the child is 16 or older, albeit legal minority (for other than medical purposes) lasts until 18 years of age. Decisions concerning medical research may be different; many lawyers argue that parents may refuse to allow their children under 18 years of age to participate in non-therapeutic clinical research involving more than a negligible risk.

The PRA gives little guidance in case of disagreeing or divorced parents. If one parent has custody, he/she is competent to make all decisions on behalf of the child. In the (more and more frequent) case of joint custody, decisions concerning every-day matters are left to the parent with whom the child resides (Act on Children and Parents, § 34, sect. 3). Presumably, difficult medical decisions must be taken by both parents. There are no indications as to how possible disputes can be solved.

Treatment of an unborn child can only take place with the mother's consent. She can probably refuse any treatment at all. The father can probably refuse treatment that is experimental or very risky for the child.

As the Act is not yet in force, it is impossible to say anything about how it is interpreted in practice. As for the current legal situation, where the law on consent is based on general principles of autonomy, care, respect for individual integrity and the duty to give necessary medical treatment, practice seems to take the view that consent is important; however necessary medical interventions, performed *lege artis*, usually will be lawful even if the consent is faulty or missing, providing that the patient did not refuse treatment altogether, and the refusal must be respected. There are few court decisions on the issue.

2. Consent to Research

There is no specific regulation of consent to medical research. The Declaration of Helsinki offers guidelines that are used in practice. Norwegian courts will most likely presume Norwegian law to be in accordance with the Declaration of Helsinki, and thus apply its provisions.

It can be inferred from the Penal Code (Straffeloven) that an intentional act that results in what may be described as grievous bodily injury will not excuse the injuror from criminal prosecution, unless the injuror acted *lege artis* and with therapeutic intent. Medical research without therapeutic intent is illegal if grievous bodily harm is intended. Experimental treatment as understood in the Declaration of Helsinki, part II, 1 and 2, that is 'a new diagnostic or therapeutic measure, applied to patients because it is believed to be better than the existing measures', is legal.

Minors and mentally or legally incapacitated persons cannot give consent to research. Their legal guardian can consent on their behalf, but only insofar as the consent is in the best interest of the ward. This limitation must be inferred from the general provisions in the Act on

Children and Parents (§ 30, sect. 1), and from interpretation of the Act on Legal Guardianship.[2] This puts a restriction on consent to research without therapeutic intent unless there is insignificant risk involved. The question of how far the legal guardian's authority goes has not been tried in court. There is no consensus within the legal community on this issue, except perhaps that the younger the child, the less opportunity for parents to agree to include the child in a research project. Venepuncture is an example of a procedure that may be considered too risky. Some lawyers recommend that non-therapeutic research should never involve children as research subjects if any kind of physical intervention is part of the protocol. Others take a less rigid position, and argue that minor interventions with negligible risk may be allowed if the child at a later stage may profit from the knowledge gained, or if the research project can contribute important knowledge about the child's condition and thus be of benefit to other children. To use healthy children as controls is only acceptable if the procedure involves no risk to the child.

Research on neonates is not surrounded by any special legal framework, but the Research Ethics Committees (see below) use extra vigilance when reviewing such projects.

Research Ethics Committees

Since 1985, the five Regional Research Ethics Committees (Regionale forskningsetiske komitéer for medisin) (RECs) have given advice on ethical questions relating to biomedical research. The committees have eight members: two physicians, a psychologist, a nurse, a lawyer, an ethicist (theologian or philosopher), a lay member and a member representing a hospital owner (usually a politician; practically all hospitals in Norway are publicly owned). The members are appointed by the Ministry of Research, and the committees are administratively linked to the four University Medical Faculties. The Research Ethics Committees are not administrative agencies, and they have no superior body. Their decisions are only advisory, and have no legal bearing. There exists no means of enforcing the opinions of the Research Ethics Committees, except via 'peer pressure'.

The Research Ethics Committees have no statutory basis, and there is no legal duty for the researchers to present their projects to them. In practice, however, most biomedical projects are submitted. Partly, it seems that the research community has accepted the Research Ethics Committees, and partly, the major grant-giving bodies and authoritative journals demand that the projects are approved by an ethics committee.

The main source of reference for the practice of the Research Ethics Committees is the Declaration of Helsinki. The research subjects must give written consent, and the Research Ethics Committees will carefully evaluate the written patient information. It must contain a comprehensible description of the project, its justification, aim and methods, information on effects and side-effects, use of placebo, insurance, follow-up procedures etc. The consent form must state very clearly that participation is voluntary, that refusal to participate will have no bearing on the treatment, and that the patient can withdraw at any time, without giving any explanation.

If the patient is unable to give written consent, the Research Ethics Committees will evaluate the project according to the principles described above under 1 and 2. Non-therapeutic research will rarely be recommended. Therapeutic research where no effective treatment is known can be performed without written consent, but only if the risks and possible benefits are conscientiously weighed. Minors and mentally or legally incapacitated persons are always expected to receive such information as they are capable of understanding, and to give such consent as they are capable of giving.

Research projects including neonates are treated by the Research Ethics Committees on the same basis as other projects, with no special procedures to safeguard the interest of the infant. It is my impression that the Research Ethics Committees scrutinize projects involving neonates very carefully, and that they are quite restrictive, particularly when the project requires any kind of active intervention on the child. There are examples of Research Ethics Committees refusing to accept projects involving neonates, because the protocol required a blood sample (usually from the infant's heel) that would otherwise not have been taken. For the Research Ethics Committees to accept such research, the possible medical gain for the infant involved must be considerable.

Norway is a small country (4.3 million), so the research community is small and easily regulated. 'Everybody knows everybody.' It would be difficult to conduct research on any scale without the Research Ethics Committees knowing or being made aware. The compliance with the Research Ethics Committees' recommendations is probably good. However, there is not (yet) any system of reporting back the results of the research.

Legal Problems

In my opinion, the most significant problem raised by the law on neonatal research in Norway concerns how far parents should be allowed to consent to research being performed on their child. Parents have some authority to consent on behalf of the child. It is unclear what this authority really includes under the cover of 'therapeutic research'. Does parental authority encompass the right to inflict great pain and suffering in the hope of avoiding death? Is that in the best interest of the child?

Notes

1. Lov om pasientrettigheter, 2/7-99 no 63. Not yet (January, 2000) in force, but expected to be in force later this year or maybe in 2001.
2. Lov om vergemål for umyndige, 22/4 1927 no. 3.

13 The Regulation of Neonatal Research in Spain

PROFESSOR C.M. ROMEO-CASABONA

1. General Legal Framework

1.1 The Right of Patients to Information and to Informed Consent

The Spanish General Health Law of 25 April 1986 (*Ley General de Sanidad*) outlines patients' rights in a general perspective. Among them, it details the patient's rights to be informed and to give his or her informed consent to treatment (art.10.5 & 6):

> All persons enjoy the rights listed below in relation to the different public health administrations:
> 5. The right of patients and their next-of-kin or relations to be given full verbal and written comprehensible information on the process, including diagnosis, prognosis and alternative forms of treatment.
> 6. The right of a patient to choose freely between options given by the physician in charge of his case. The written consent of the user shall be necessary for all interventions, save for the following cases: (...) b) Where the patient is incompetent to take decisions, in which case the right shall pass on to his next-of-kin or those closest to him.

In the case where the patient is not qualified to take decisions, as in the case of a newborn, the consent will be given by his/her family or persons close to him/her (art. 10.6 b). But more exactly from a legal point of view, when it deals with minors, consent must be given exclusively by his/her legal representatives, that is to say, the parents, according to the rights derived from paternal authority, as the Spanish Civil Code establishes (art. 154).

1.2 Specific Rules for Research Involving Human Beings

The need for research is fully recognised in the Spanish legal system, but when it comes to experimentation on human subjects a series of provisions directly or indirectly seeks to prevent any injury or harm to the person, given that his or her most prized legal interests are at stake. Thus research in which human subjects are used must adhere to the strictest precautions in order that the interests of the individuals involved can be safeguarded. Regulations governing clinical trials of pharmaceutical products also address this issue in great detail, so much so in fact that they have even caused irritation among some researchers. Obviously these regulations also apply to experiments on human subjects with non-pharmaceutical products. There are also specific rules for some research fields: research and experimentation concerning human assisted reproduction or involving human gametes, in vitro human embryos, implanted embryos and foetuses, as well as clinical autopsies of human corpses.

1. Mention should also be made of the European Convention on Human Rights and Biomedicine provisions (see Chapter 8), which will be applied in Spain (it came into force on 1 January 2000).

2. The *General Health Law* provides the minimum precautions and guarantees necessary when it requires that the patient be informed and that he or she gives his or her consent prior to the experiment, that the doctor and the administration of the health care centre agree to the experiment and, above all, that 'under no circumstances should it involve additional dangers to health [that of the patient]'(art. 10, n° 4):

> All persons enjoy the rights listed below in relation to the different public health administrations: the right to be notified if the prognosis, diagnosis and therapeutic procedures applied to them is likely to be used as part of a teaching or research project. In no way shall the project entail any additional danger to their health and in all cases the patients' prior written consent must be sought and authorisation given by the physician and the management of the health institution concerned.

3. These requirements, together with the principles of preservation of dignity and privacy and the avoidance of discrimination, underpin more specific legislation, namely, the *Drugs and Medicines Law* (Law 25/1990 of 20 December, *Ley del Medicamento*) and Royal Decree 561/93 of 16 April, which set out the requirements governing the carrying out of clinical trials of medical treatments. In both regulations the specific requirements are set out for when the subject of the experiment is a minor and, consequently, they are applied to newborns too.

The Drugs and Medicines Law also established a number of basic principles regulating clinical trials (arts. 59 to 69), which have been developed further and completed by the aforementioned Royal Decree of 1993. It defined clinical trials as 'any experimental assessment of a substance or medication carried out through its application to human beings and directed to any of the specified purposes; such activity shall only take place within the limits of respect for ethical values' (art. 59).

Aside from the relevant administrative controls governing the trials themselves, their funding and the dissemination through publications that may result from the trials, the Law has created Clinical Research Ethics Committees (*Comités Éticos de Investigación Clínica*), with important functions in terms of laying down guidelines for the methodology to be employed, the ethical considerations and the risks and benefits that may be entailed in the trials; in fact, their most important task is to approve every trial to be carried out in hospitals and other health centres.

The Law also introduces measures to guarantee respect for ethical principles, with the specific requirement that trials 'must be undertaken in conditions which assure respect for the fundamental rights of the individual and the ethical considerations which apply to biomedical research involving human beings, in accordance with the Helsinki Declaration and subsequent declarations updating these ethical considerations' (art. 60.2).

Similar terms are used in article 10.2 of the RD 1993, which establishes also that norms for good clinical practice should prevail as well as normalised procedures of work (art. 44 f). Compliance with this standard provides public assurance that the rights, safety and well-being of trial subjects are protected, consistent with ethical guidelines and principles (i.e., with those of the Helsinki Declaration) and that the clinical trial data are credible.

4. The current Ethical Code of the Spanish Medical College Organisation, contains also some ethical rules concerning experimentation with human beings, assuming that this way of research is indispensable, but also that the health of the research's subjects should be a priority for researchers, and therefore the patient will not be deprived of valid treatment (art. 32).

2. Rules Concerning Research with Newborns: Purposes

There do not exist any specific rules concerning experimentation with newborns. In any case, the restrictive provisions established when minors are involved are equally valid for newborns and neonatal clinical research.

2.1 General Considerations

First of all, there are three conditions that we must address to justify the participation of minors or newborn children:

i.   Whether it is possible to equate the needs of research (acting in the best interest of the subject), with the societal need of obtaining new scientific knowledge, which can be used to treat other persons in the future;
ii. What the principle of proportionality is between the risks of the research and benefits for the subject; and,
iii. Whether it is possible to be certain of obtaining the consent of third parties on behalf of the subject concerned.

Each of these conditions may provide grounds for restricting the scope of, or even banning, experimentation. Note that the European Convention on Human Rights and Biomedicine of 1997 sets out the basic principle that the interests and welfare of the human being shall prevail over the sole interest of society and science (art. 2).

Generally speaking, the view taken is that experimentation in incompetent persons and minors should be permitted only where it entails, at the very least, a direct potential benefit for the health of the individual concerned (therapeutic experimentation).

Exceptionally, national bodies may authorise research involving an incapacitated person which does not have the potential to produce results of direct benefit to his or her health, when the research is to the benefit of persons in the same category and where the use of other individuals (i.e. adult persons) would not provide a valid model for comparison of experimental results.

In this way, the European Convention of 1997 exceptionally recognises that non-therapeutic research may be authorised, subject to some additional conditions: 'the research has the aim of contributing, through significant improvement in the scientific understanding of the individual's condition, disease or disorder, to the ultimate attainment of results capable of conferring benefit to the person concerned or to other persons in the same age category or afflicted with the same disease or disorder or having the same condition' (art. 17.2, i).

As a general principle, it is commonly accepted that a person can only endanger his own life or health voluntarily, in other words, if that person has previously accepted the risk that is involved. However, there are those who would argue that pure or non-therapeutic experimentation is also possible with these incompetent individuals, provided no risk or minimum risk is involved. In the words of the European Convention: 'the research entails only minimal risk and minimal burden for the individual concerned' (art. 17.2, ii).

As can be verified, in the particular case of persons not able to consent and when there is no direct benefit expected for them from the research, the principle of proportionality between individual risks and collective benefits is less of a consideration than a valuation of both the risks and other burdens by themselves.

2.2 Neonatal Clinical Trials with Therapeutic Purposes

In the first place, experimentation with minors and newborns can only take place when:

i.   it will have a particular benefit for the health of the minor, and
ii. it could not be carried out in cases not affected by these special conditions. Thus the illness investigated in the study should be one which is specific to and characteristic of children.

2.3 Non-therapeutic Neonatal Clinical Trials

Exceptionally, however, non-therapeutic clinical trials are allowed for children, as long as the following requirements are met, and the trial has been examined by a Clinical Research Ethics Committee (Royal Decree 1993, art. 11.3):

i.   All necessary measures will be taken to guarantee minimum risk.

It is important to note that the Royal Decree emphasises the need for risk prevention measures, as is only to be expected, but, unlike other legal instruments, does not stress that the trial itself should pose no risks or that these should be minimal. It is on the innocuous nature of the test itself that emphasis should be placed and not just on measures to counter any risks entailed, assuming that the latter are also necessary.

ii. The experiment to be undergone by the subject must be suited to his or her medical, psychological, social or educational situation.

This requirement is unclear and inadequately worded: it would appear to mean that the trial must aim to verify aspects of the person's medical, psychological, social or educational situation, in the case of an incapacitated person. This requirement brings out clearly just how inappropriate it is to place in the same category minors, mentally incompetent persons and those with diminished capacity as regards the legal treatment of experimentation, when clearly their situations are entirely different. Worse still, jurists are in no position to gauge whether an experiment is of interest and suited to the social and educational situation of the subject. The law refers exclusively to drugs and like substances, which merely serves to confirm the impression of uncertainty as to the objectives pursued by the Royal Decree.

iii.   Relevant knowledge shall be obtained from the trial with regard to the illness or condition under study, or information which will be of vital importance to understand it better, or to palliate or cure it.
iv.   The knowledge cannot be obtained by any other means.

From this it can be inferred that laboratory investigations or experimentation on animals will be used preferably, or adults with capacity for consent will be used if their characteristics are suited to the purpose of the research, without comparison of the results being necessary in an incapacitated person; similarly, it can be inferred that less onerous procedures will be used before others, if the former suffice to meet the objectives pursued. And,

v.   Guarantees must exist that informed consent has been obtained, in accordance with the provisions of the Royal Decree, which are the same as those established for therapeutic experimentation.

3. Obtaining Informed Consent

The research subject's informed consent (art. 12.1, RD 1993) constitutes the most important element in guaranteeing that the person may freely exercise his or her will and accept any risks involved. The subject may withdraw his or her consent at any time and is not obliged to give reasons for withdrawal, which under no circumstances will give rise to liability or loss of any kind (art. 12.7). Moreover, the exception provided for in emergency cases where it proves impossible to obtain consent from the subject or his or her legal representative is admissible only if the clinical test has particular therapeutic interest for the patient (art. 12.6).

The scope and efficacy of consent are conditioned by various factors, particularly relating to legal capacity to give consent, and the potential dangers to the subject's health.

There is no provision establishing a duty to provide information to the research subjects concerning the findings and final results of the trial, but in my view it should be compulsory for every research project that has been approved.

The method of obtaining consent when there is an attempt to do research in children or newborns, whether with therapeutic purpose or without (non-clinical biomedical research), is subject to the following requirements: the legal representative of the newborn must be previously informed about all the details of the research, according to the general conditions that are established for the information that must be given (Royal Decree, art.12.1); secondly, it must be verified that the legal representative has understood the information that has been given, and if the legal representative thinks that it is appropriate, he/she will give the consent, which must be in writing. Additionally, if the child has comprehension capacity (and always, if he/she is twelve years old), he/she must give his/her consent, although this is not the case for the newborn. Before starting the research, consent given by the legal representative will be communicated to the Public Attorney (Royal Decree, art. 12.5).

The consent given by the legal representative may be revoked at any time during the research process, without giving reasons for the decision and without affecting the treatment of the minor (Royal Decree, art. 12.7).

4. Pregnant or Breast-feeding Women

Given her relation with the newborn, we must point out that a pregnant or breast-feeding woman may only take part in a non-therapeutic clinical trial when the Clinical Research Ethics Committee determines that there is no predictable risk for the health of the woman, of the foetus or newborn, and that useful knowledge related to the pregnancy or lactation will result (Royal Decree, art. 11.4).

5. Clinical Emergency

In urgent cases, research in children and newborns can be done, under the following conditions:

i.   the researchers must inform the Clinical Research Ethics Committee and the sponsor of the research, explaining the reasons for the urgency;
ii.   this possibility must be anticipated in the research protocol approved by the Clinical Research Ethics Committee;
iii. the research must have a specific relevance for the health of the newborn patient, and
iv.   the legal representative of the child or newborn will be informed as soon as possible in order to give his/her consent, if he/she thinks it is appropriate (Royal Decree, art. 12.6).

Also, the so-called 'compassionate treatment' (where no standard treatment seems to be effective for a patient, but a drug [in a phase of research] could be more appropriate for him or her) is governed by Spanish law under strict regulations and is permitted for children and newborns (Law, art. 38.5).

6. The Legal Status and Functions of Clinical Research Ethics Committees

As we have seen above, Clinical Research Ethics Committees have to approve every research protocol prior to the start of the study, and their main function is to protect the subjects of experimentation. They must be set up in every public or private hospital or health centre intending to perform research involving human beings.

These Committees are responsible for evaluating the different features of a trial, not only from an ethical and legal focus, but also from a purely methodological and scientific perspective, as well as the balance of costs and benefits. In fact, all clinical protocols must conform to the previous evaluation report of the Committee concerned. Specifically, they have the following functions, among others:

i.   They will evaluate the suitability of the medical protocol in relation to the objectives of the research, its scientific efficacy (the possibility of reaching valid conclusions, with the minimum exposure to risk for the subjects) and the justification of the risks and anticipated burdens, balanced against the expected benefits for the subjects and society.

ii.   They will evaluate the suitability of the research team for the proposed trial. This will take into account its experience and research capacity to carry the study forward, paying attention to its duties of clinical care and current commitments in relation to other research medical protocols.

iii. They will evaluate the written information about the trial that will be given to the possible subjects of the research, or failing them, to their legal representatives, the way that such information will be given, and the type of consent that is going to be obtained.

iv.   They will check the provision of compensation and treatment that will be offered to the subjects taking part, in case of injury or death that could be attributed to the clinical trial, and of the insurance or indemnification to cover the responsibilities specified in article 13.2.

v.   They will be informed of and will assess the scope of the financial benefits that will be offered to the researchers and the subjects of the research for their participation.

vi.   They will monitor the clinical trial from its start until receiving the final report.

At least one lay person as well as a lawyer must be members of these Committees; the remaining membership is reserved for medical and nursing staff and experts. The Committees and their members are independent; they do not receive any kind of payment or material compensation for their work.

On the other hand, there is no formal link with Committees in other centres, so it might be that differing decisions are made when different committees are dealing with multi-centre clinical research. This is a very important and increasing problem, which should be resolved by the public health authorities passing new specific rules on the matter.

7. Controls by the Health Administration

There is also control on the part of the Health Administration (Directorate General for Pharmaceutical and Health Products), whose prior authorisation is required. Thus, there are two independent bodies which have to approve every research protocol: firstly, the Clinical Research Ethics Committee and, secondly, the Public Authority. Monitoring and inspections ensure that the entire clinical trial process is formalised, and that time periods and conditions are established for the carrying out of any such trials. That there is no connection between these two bodies is a matter for criticism.

In certain cases the Ministry of Health and Consumer Affairs may interrupt a clinical trial or insist that modifications be made to the protocol. This is possible in situations where the law has been broken, where the conditions under which authorisation was granted are altered, or where the above-mentioned ethical principles are not adhered to. The aim of such intervention is to protect trial subjects and to protect public health (art. 65. 5 of the Law and art. 31 of the Royal Decree).

An exception to the normal procedure for the therapeutic use of new drugs and medications, or those which are still included in a clinical trial, could be made when dealing with the so-called 'compassionate' use of medications (see above): this can be carried out under the practitioner's sole responsibility, the informed written consent of the patient or his or her legal representatives being needed, as well as the previous authorisation of the concerned centre and that of the Directorate General for Pharmaceutical and Health Products.

Needless to say, criminal liability may arise in serious cases involving both intentional or negligent homicide (arts. 138 and 142 of the Spanish Penal Code) or grievous bodily harm (arts. 147 and ff, and 152, Spanish Penal Code); also civil responsibility can be upheld in addition to any liability by the Public Administration. Notwithstanding, at the moment no prosecution at Spanish Courts has been recorded in relation to clinical trials.

8. Insurance and Payment to Trial Subjects

It is currently felt that all experimental subjects should have insurance cover for all the risks entailed. The Spanish Drugs and Medicines Law establishes this as a prior condition in all cases and makes the sponsor of the trial, the principal researcher or project leader and the medical director(s) of the hospital(s) where the trial is to be carried out, jointly liable for any injury sustained that is not covered by insurance, even where they are not at fault (strict liability for risk). The Law also establishes an assumption - although evidence to the contrary can be presented - that any injury to the health of the experimental subject occurring during the trial or up to a year later is the result of the trial, notwithstanding the support provided by the existence of administrative authorisation and favourable evaluation from a Clinical Research Ethics Committee (Law, art. 62 and Royal Decree, art. 13).

9. Final Considerations

Taking into account the strict controls on the undertaking of clinical trials, that have been set in place by Law and by Royal Decree, and the important function assigned for this purpose to the Ethics Committees for Clinical Research in every hospital where clinical trials take place, the existence of serious abuse does not seem likely. No serious problems have been detected in the practice of research involving children and newborns.

14 The Regulation of Neonatal Research in Sweden[1]

ASSOCIATE PROFESSOR E. RYNNING

1. Medical Informed Consent in General

1.1 General Provisions

In Sweden, the individual's general right to autonomy or self-determination is protected by the Constitution. The Swedish Instrument of Government thus recognises, among other fundamental rights and freedoms, the right of citizens to be protected against any physical violation or deprivation of liberty in their relations with the public administration.[2] These rights may only be restricted by a statute enacted by the Swedish Parliament, and only to the extent that this is necessary for purposes acceptable in a democratic society.[3]

The general health care legislation in Sweden does not contain any explicit demand for consent to medical care and treatment. As regards the patient's right to self-determination, chapter 2 section 1 of the Act on Professional Activities in the Health and Medical Services (1998:531) requests that medical care as far as possible shall be designed and conducted in consultation with the patient and that the patient shall be shown consideration and respect. A similar provision can be found in section 2a of the Health and Medical Services Act (1982:763). In the preparatory works, however, it is stated that the implications of these provisions are that nobody may be subjected to compulsory treatment or any other form of coercion in health care without a statutory provision and that, in principle, the patient's consent is required for all measures that are planned.[4] This does not preclude the possibility that in certain situations medical measures may be lawful without the consent of the patient.

With very few exceptions, Swedish law does not lay down any specific demands concerning the form for a legally valid consent.[5] Thus, oral consent will normally be sufficient, or even implicit consent. In certain statutes concerning particular medical measures, such as abortion, sterilisation and organ donation, a more explicit demand for the patient's consent is laid down. It may thus be required that the measure is demanded by the patient[6] or that a written consent to the measure is procured.[7]

In order for the patient's consent to be legally valid, he or she must be given the relevant information. Chapter 2, section 2 of the Professional Activities Act and section 2b of the Health and Medical Services Act, establish that the person responsible for the care of the patient shall ensure that the patient receives individually adjusted information concerning his or her state of health and concerning the existing methods for examination, care and treatment. It is quite obvious that it is the individual patient's need for information that shall be satisfied. Normally, this will entail information concerning the results of medical examinations and tests, diagnosis and prognosis, proposed methods for treatment or further investigations, alternative actions, expected results, risks and side-effects etc.[8] If this information cannot be supplied to the patient, it shall instead be given to a person closely connected to him or her.

Apart from situations where the patient is unable to receive or assimilate information, or does not wish to be informed, there are only two statutory exceptions from the duty to disclose information. These exceptions both refer to situations where the Secrecy Act (1980:100) stipulates confidentiality in relation to the patient himself or herself, and the health care personnel accordingly have a legal duty to withhold the information in question. This is the case when it is of particular importance, with regard to the purpose of the care or treatment, that certain information about the patient's state of health is withheld from him or her.[9] The patient may thus be protected from serious harm, e.g. attempted suicide or the outbreak of a psychosis, that might be brought about by disclosure of certain information. The other exception from the duty to disclose information concerns situations where a private person who has supplied information about the patient must be protected from serious acts of reprisal on the part of the patient.[10]

1.2 Incompetent Adults

There are no statutory provisions concerning vicarious health care decision-making for incompetent patients, even though it is understood that competence is a necessary prerequisite for a legally valid consent. As regards incompetent adults, it may first be established that Swedish law does not grant the patient's relatives any right to make decisions on behalf of the patient, even though certain provisions in our health care legislation prescribe that the relatives shall be informed and consulted.[11] Their task is primarily to supply the health care provider with information about what they believe the patient would have wanted. Neither do the Swedish courts or any other judicial body have any general authorisation to decide about medical treatment in an individual case.[12] The courts may, however, appoint different types of legal representatives or guardians - a Special Representative (*god man*) or an Administrator (*förvaltare*) - with the mandate to look after *inter alia* the personal needs of a person who is unable to do so by himself or herself due to, for example, illness, mental disturbance or a weakened state of health.[13] Such representatives are more often appointed primarily to manage the financial affairs of an incompetent person and the system has not been designed to solve the problem of health care decision making for incompetent patients. The power of these legal representatives, when it comes to consenting or refusing medical treatment on behalf of the patient, is thus rather unclear. Proxy consent to certain measures, such as organ and tissue donation or the participation in clinical drug trials, is regulated by special provisions.[14] Some measures, such as abortion or sterilisation, may only be carried out if the patient has the capacity to consent in person.[15]

1.3 Minors

When it comes to minors, i.e. children and adolescents below the age of 18, certain sections of the Parents and Children Code regulate the right and duty of the custodians - normally the parents - to decide in matters concerning the minor's personal affairs.[16] The custodians are responsible for the welfare of the minor, but the child must be treated with respect and must not be subjected to humiliating treatment. In keeping with the child's advancing age and development, increasing consideration must be shown for the child's own views and preferences with regard to his or her personal affairs. In some cases, the minor may have reached sufficient maturity to be considered competent to make a legally valid decision concerning a particular medical measure, but no particular age limit exists. In other cases, the consent of both the child and the custodian may be needed and in others again, the custodians may decide irrespective of the child's wishes.

If there are two custodians (e.g. the parents), decisions should in principle be made by both parents/custodians jointly.[17] In matters of lesser importance, the consent of one parent is normally sufficient, should the other parent not be at hand. The same applies when the decision cannot be delayed without inconvenience. If, however, the decision conveys far-reaching implications for the child's future, both custodians must take part in the decision-making, unless it is obvious that the best interests of the child demand that the decision be taken without delay. Should the parents disagree on a matter concerning the child, there is no general legal means of giving one parent's view precedence over the view of the other.

The power of the custodians may, however, be restricted if their decisions are found to be contrary to the child's best interests. If the custodians' refusal of consent to a certain medical treatment constitutes a palpable risk of the child's health or development being impaired, the right to decide may be transferred by court to the local social welfare committee, according to sections 2 and 6 of the Care of Young Persons (Special Provisions) Act (1990:52). This would also be the case if one out of two custodians does not agree to actions necessary for the welfare of the child.

As Sweden has ratified the UN Convention on the Rights of the Child (1989), the principle of the best interests of the child, as laid down in article 3.1, must be applied in all decisions concerning children. The legal implications of this, when it comes to different kinds of medical measures, would seem to be rather unclear. Even with adult patients, it certainly is not always easy to decide what is for the best, e.g. when it comes to prolonging a life of reduced quality, or carrying out a genetic test that will reveal information concerning the patient's disposition for a severe, untreatable disease. Deciding what really are the best interests of a particular child can be a difficult matter, where opinions are bound to vary. In the preamble of the Convention, the general importance of the family is underlined, as well as that of the traditions and cultural values of each people. This would seem to indicate that the best interests of the child should be consistent with the value system applied by its family, although the freedom implied by such a principle cannot be unlimited.[18]

The circumcision of baby boys for religious or ritual reasons, is a measure that may well illustrate some of the difficulties involved. These surgical interventions are considered lawful in Sweden and are sometimes performed in public hospitals, but are still currently being discussed. Parental consent as the legal basis for this measure could certainly be questioned, since this irreversible intervention causes pain and is not without risk.[19] In a recent decision by the Swedish Supreme Court, it was found that respect for religious or cultural traditions must yield if the pain inflicted on the child is 'too severe'.[20] Whether or not the circumcision of six boys aged 1½ - 7 years, without any analgesia, had involved such pain was not, however, made clear by the evidence presented in the case. The doctor, who had been found guilty of battery by the Court of Appeals, was thus acquitted. In the report from a Canadian study aimed at assessing the efficacy and safety of so-called Emla cream for pain during neonatal circumcision, it is stated that the intervention is often performed without analgesia and that the pain experienced 'may affect an infant's behaviour months after the event'.[21]

1.4 Medical Care and Treatment without Valid Consent

There are no statutory provisions dealing specifically with emergencies in health care, or other situations where for some reason it is not possible to obtain a valid consent to treatment.[22] The Swedish law related to actions performed from necessity can be derived from chapter 24, section 4 of the Penal Code. In this section, freedom from penal liability is granted for acts performed in emergency situations, unless the act is indefensible in view of the nature of the threatening danger, the damage that is caused and other circumstances. This general rule is not seldom invoked as the legal ground for medical treatment in cases where no valid consent can be obtained, even though it has not been especially designed for this purpose.[23] The necessity rule would also seem to constitute the legal ground for the assumption that a doctor may under certain exceptional circumstances be entitled to use experimental methods in order to save a patient's life, if the established methods available prove to be ineffective.

In cases where the parents of a child refuse to give their consent to vital health care measures, and there is not sufficient time to contact the social welfare authorities, the necessity rule can be invoked as the legal basis for life-saving or otherwise urgent treatment of the child, against the wishes of the parents. When it comes to competent adults, however, the necessity rule cannot be used to justify medical care or treatment against the wishes of the patient.[24]

In cases where the situation does not qualify as an emergency, urgent medical care and treatment without consent may sometimes still be performed in the best interests of the patient, under the assumption that this is consistent with due respect for the patient's right to self-determination. When no valid consent can be obtained, but there is a well-founded hypothesis that the patient would have consented if it had been possible to ask him or her, there is thus some limited scope for the performance of medical measures with reference to so-called hypothetical consent.[25]

2. Legislation on Biomedical Research

2.1 The Application of General Medico-Legal Rules in Research

According to chapter 2, section 1 in the Professional Activities Act, a person belonging to the health care personnel shall perform his or her work in accordance with science and proven experience. It is also required that patients shall be given expert and conscientious care satisfying these requirements. Clinical research and experimental treatment methods obviously cannot be considered to be in full accordance with both science and proven experience. The purpose of a research project will often be to establish whether or not a certain treatment is in fact sufficiently safe and effective. The Professional Activities Act does not, however, state any exception for clinical research, even though such activities are mentioned in other contexts and certainly are expected to take place. Nor is there any general Swedish legislation explicitly permitting or regulating biomedical research on humans, and no general statutory demand for review by a Research Ethics Committee (REC). At the same time, it is clear that the existence and activities of the RECs are officially counted on for the protection of research subjects.[26]

In medical research combined with professional care, the ordinary standards prescribed for medical care and treatment apply as far as possible. This means that the general requirements for information and consent described above must be fulfilled and that the custodians have the right to consent on the behalf of young children. The scope of this right would seem to be somewhat unclear, as regards the child's participation in research projects. For instance, is the consent of one custodian sufficient, or should the consent of both parents always be required for research measures?

The participation of minors in so-called non-therapeutic research gives rise to specific problems in this respect. Non-therapeutic research is usually conceived as research that has no potential direct health benefits for the research subject.[27] At least with very small children, e.g. new-borns, it cannot be said that the participation in such research is in the best interest of the child itself, since the psychological and social benefits of altruistic actions hardly apply to infants. It must be acknowledged that the participation of an infant in a research project that has no potential health benefits for the child itself, will as a rule imply that the best interests of that child have in fact been sacrificed, in the interest of other children, of science or society. This might, however, under certain circumstances be fully acceptable, e.g. if the risk and burden for the infant is minimal and the knowledge gained would be highly valuable. Article 3.1 in the UN convention on the rights of the child does not demand that the best interests of the child shall prevail in every situation, only that it shall be *a primary consideration*. A number of general prerequisites for medical research on incompetent persons are laid down in article 17 of the European Convention on Human Rights and Biomedicine (see Chapter 8). Research without potential health benefits for the person involved, is accepted only in exceptional cases, under additional demands concerning *inter alia* minimal risk and minimal burden. However, Sweden has not yet ratified the convention.

Another problem concerning consent to research on new-borns relates to the competence of the parents. Since neonatal research often involves premature babies or new-borns suffering from some illness or injury, the parents are likely to be under considerable stress. If the child has been delivered by a Caesarean section, the mother may not have recovered from the anaesthetic at the time when the research measures must take place. This brings us back to the question whether or not the consent of one parent - more often the father - is sufficient in cases where the other parent - normally the mother - is considered incompetent to decide? Could there even be situations where neonatal research may lawfully be carried out in the complete absence of any valid consent? If so, would this also apply to research without any potential health benefits for the new-born itself? According to article 17 of the European convention on human rights and biomedicine, the answer to the two latter questions is definitely 'no'. Swedish law does not give any clear answers, but it would seem unlikely that the unauthorised participation of infants in medical research - certainly research without any potential health benefits - could be justified under the general necessity rule.

2.2 Consent According to the Transplant Act

The Transplant Act (1995:831) regulates the taking of organs and other biological materials from a human being, for transplantation or other medical purposes. It applies also to very small samples of blood or tissue. The removal of biological material for the purpose of treating the patient himself or herself is excluded, and so is transplantation of gametes and organs producing gametes.[28] The taking of biological material from a living donor is only allowed if the donor gives his or her consent.[29] If the material taken is not regenerative, or if the intervention for other reasons may cause the donor considerable harm or inconvenience, a written consent must be procured.

When it comes to minors and persons with mental disturbances, specific demands on proxy consent - in addition to other particular prerequisites, such as permission granted by the National Board of Health and Welfare - are laid down in section 8 of the Transplant Act, with respect to the taking of material for *transplantation* purposes. As regards the taking of tissue from these donor categories for *other* medical purposes, such as research, section 9 of the Act only contains a provision forbidding the taking of non-regenerative material, as well as actions that may otherwise entail considerable harm or discomfort to the donor. This means that there are no specific statutory rules dealing with, for example, the taking of a blood sample or a small piece of tissue from a child, solely for research purposes, while the prerequisites for taking the very same material for transplantation purposes are regulated in detail! This issue is not discussed in the preparatory works and it would seem a reasonable conclusion that it has been overlooked in the legislative process.

Section 11 of the Transplant Act allows the use of tissue from aborted foetuses for medical purposes, with the authorisation of the National Board of Health and Welfare and the consent of the woman who has had the abortion (oral consent suffices, but it has to be an explicit consent to the intended use of the tissue). There is also specific legislation concerning embryo research *in vitro*,[30] but no provisions dealing with research on foetuses or unborn children. A few years ago, a lively discussion concerning the admissibility of research on foetuses that *are about to be* aborted, resulted in statements from several national ethics councils, that all foetuses should enjoy the same protection with respect to research.[31]

2.3 Consent According to the Medicinal Products Act

Section 13 of the Medicinal Products Act (1992:859) deals with clinical trials. Such trials may be conducted in connection with medical care and treatment, or without any such connection. Since 'connection with medical care and treatment' also may apply to control groups, the definition does not seem to be fully equivalent to therapeutic research, or research with potential health benefits for the research subject. Whether or not a clinical trial involving placebo could be considered potentially beneficial to all the research subjects involved may well be questioned. It could, however, be argued that the mere possibility of receiving a potentially effective treatment constitutes a certain potential benefit.

According to section 13, paragraph 2, the patients or experimental subjects intended to participate in a clinical trial shall receive such information that they are able to decide whether or not they wish to take part in it. When it comes to the matter of consent, paragraph 3 prescribes that consent shall always be obtained for participation in trials unconnected with the treatment of disease. Such trials may not be performed on a person who has a special representative or an administrator appointed by court, nor on a person receiving compulsory mental care or forensic mental care. As for trials connected with the treatment of disease, consent to participation shall be obtained unless there are special grounds for carrying out the trial regardless.

Regarding the participation of minors in clinical trials, no particular restrictions or safeguards are laid down in the Medicinal Products Act. In the preparatory works, however, the participation of children in clinical trials is discussed. It is declared that the custodians, as the legal representatives of the child, may consent on the child's behalf, but it is also pointed out that increasing consideration must be shown for the child's own wishes, in keeping with the child's advancing age and development. The particularly vulnerable position of children is stressed, and the RECs are called upon to keep this in mind when reviewing research projects involving children.[32] In certain provisions issued by the Medical Products Agency, it is stated that consent shall, where possible, be obtained both from the minor and in writing from the parents or guardians.[33]

The prerequisites for carrying out a clinical trial without informed consent are also discussed in the preparatory work.[34] Such actions should only be accepted in extraordinary situations. It is stressed, however, that the participation in a trial may involve potential benefits for the patient himself or herself. This would seem to lead us back to the discussion concerning the general necessity rule and so-called hypothetical consent as the legal basis for carrying out medical measures that are called for in situations where no valid consent can be obtained. In the guidelines of the Medical Products Agency it is stated that 'in the event that the patient is unable to give his informed consent, the patient may nevertheless be included in a trial which is linked to the treatment of illness, if the ethics committee has given its approval in principle and the investigator judges that it may be of benefit to the patient. This may apply for example to patients who are demented, psychotic or unconscious. Relatives should receive written information in such cases'.[35] Another situation referred to in the preparatory works is when there is no possibility of conducting the trial on persons who are able to give their consent, e.g. trials concerning medication aimed at reviving patients from unconsciousness. In situations of this kind, article 17 in the European convention on human rights and biomedicine would still demand written proxy consent.

2.4 Other Legal Safeguards for the Protection of Research Subjects

Swedish law does not rely solely on consent to protect research subjects. For some kinds of research, such as clinical trials concerning drugs, the permission of a specified national body - the Medical Products Agency - is requested by law.[36] Permission is granted only if the trial is considered ethically justifiable and will be conducted by an authorised physician or dental surgeon, with sufficient competence in the field to which the trial refers.[37]

As mentioned above, clinical research combined with professional care for patients must always be conducted in accordance with the legal demands on health care in general, as far as this is possible. The National Board of Health and Welfare monitors all health care providers and institutions, and may intervene if patient security is threatened. Health care personnel, who do not meet the professional standards demanded, may receive a warning or a reprimand from the Health and Medical Services Disciplinary Board, a national body presided over by a judge, which decides on disciplinary sanctions for health care personnel, in accordance with the Professional Activities Act. In cases of gross incompetence or if the health care employee has otherwise shown himself or herself manifestly unsuitable to practise the profession in question, his or her authorisation may be revoked.

Furthermore, according to Swedish penal law, consent does not as a rule grant freedom from liability when it comes to bodily harm of a certain degree.[38] It is uncertain where the courts would draw the line regarding the infliction of injuries in the course of medical research, since no such case has been tried.

3. Ethical Guidelines and the Research Ethics Committees

3.1 The Swedish System

The Swedish system of REC review is formally a voluntary advisory system, and their activities are not governed by any statute. Even so, the system is considered to cover practically all biomedical research on humans conducted in Sweden. No public health care provider will allow such research without the approval of an REC, and no financing will be granted from research councils etc. There are ten regional RECs, connected to the six different faculties of medicine. The committees have 11-16 regular members, out of whom two to three are lay persons (with the exception of one committee, where six out of 12 members are lay persons). The researchers elected by the faculties of medicine thus constitute a strong majority in most of the committees. Furthermore, the lay persons, who are usually appointed by the county council, are quite often nurses, health care politicians or persons otherwise connected to the medical profession, but they may also include clergymen and the occasional lawyer. In general, however, there are no legal experts on the RECs, although some of them do consult legal expertise when the committee itself recognises a legal problem.[39]

Even though the individual RECs are formally completely independent, a certain overview is provided for by the Medical Research Council's National Board for Research Ethics, which is a multi-disciplinary board with legal as well as other experts. The Board issues general recommendations and guidelines, although these are not binding and no appeal can be made to the Board in an individual case.

The RECs review research projects in advance, and have no resources for monitoring the actual performance of the research projects. There is no general statutory demand for review by a REC, but one of the prerequisites for clinical drugs trials, laid down in section 13 of the Medical Products Act (1992:859), is that the trial must be ethically justifiable. According to the preparatory works, this means that review by a regional REC will normally be necessary,[40] and the Medical Products Agency's regulation on clinical trials explicitly requires all trials to be approved by an REC.[41] There are also, however, different types of research, where no formal authorisation whatsoever need be obtained before a study is launched. This would be the case, for example, when new surgical methods are being tried out. Naturally, it would be expected that the project is submitted to the scrutiny of an REC - the county council governing the hospital in question might even demand it - but there is no explicit legal requirement. It is interesting to note, as a comparison, that legislation concerning ethical review for research on *animals* was introduced in Sweden decades ago.[42] Ethical review for such research is mandatory and the RECs for animal research are regulated by statute, as is the requirement for lawyers among the committee members!

Several parliamentary commissions during the past decade have suggested the introduction of statutory regulation concerning the REC system for research on humans,[43] but so far no bill has been put forward. In the latest report, presented in early Spring 1999 by the Commission on Research Ethics, the proposed legislation has been reduced to almost none.[44] A new provision in the University Ordinance (1993:100) should thus prescribe that research projects involving humans or human materials shall be reviewed by an REC, in accordance with the rules of procedure laid down by each university. The report can be expected to meet with some criticism on this subject, and it should be noted that there have been no legal experts on the Commission.

3.2 Ethical Guidelines

The ethical guidelines used by the RECs are mainly those laid down in the Declaration of Helsinki and other internationally accepted guidelines on research ethics, as well as the Swedish Code for Physicians and other professional codes of conduct. It may thus be assumed that the WMA Declaration of Ottawa, concerning research on children, will be observed in the future.

The Medical Research Council's National Board for Research Ethics has also published a booklet on research ethics policy and organisation in Sweden.[45] In these guidelines, it is said that the review carried out by the RECs can be divided into three main parts. Firstly, the scientific quality of the project is assessed (e.g. whether or not the methods used will produce reliable answers to the questions asked). Secondly, the ethical problems of the project are considered (risk - benefit calculations, financial compensation to participants etc.). Thirdly, the procedures for information and consent are examined.

The Swedish RECs do not seem to apply any specific ethical guidelines for neonatal research, but the guidelines regarding informed consent for medical research on minors are declared to be as follows:[46]

- Children of all ages have the right to be adequately informed/prepared, in relation to their age. The assent of the child should always be sought. When it comes to non-therapeutic research, the reactions of small children must be particularly keenly observed. Informed consent is given by the parents/custodians.
- Children aged approximately 7-14 years have the right to refuse non-therapeutic research even if the parents have given their consent. With

regard to therapeutic research (of potential benefit to the child's health) the consent of the parents overrules the wishes of the child.

- Children older than approximately 14 years of age have the right to give informed consent on their own behalf. The additional consent of the parents should also be sought.[47]

Even if the parents should give their consent, the guidelines demand that non-therapeutic research on children must not in any case be performed if the project involves more than a minimal risk. A vicarious consent must always be scrutinised more thoroughly than the consent given by a competent person on his or her own behalf. Parents may have their own motives for wanting their child to participate in the research project, motives that may not always coincide with the best interests of the child.[48] Certainly, most parents will primarily safeguard the welfare of their child, but there is always the possibility that some parents might have other reasons, for example, wanting to know more about the risk that the child will develop a certain disease, or that they might gain financial advantages from the child's participation. Having a new-born child, perhaps suffering from illness, also puts the parents under considerable strain and could make them vulnerable to the persuasive talents of physicians conducting medical research. Some parents might feel that they owe a debt of gratitude to the medical profession, members of which are saving the life of their child. In these situations, the voluntariness of the consent could of course be questioned.

4. The Law Applied in Practice

Clearly, there are uncertainties as to how Swedish law should be interpreted in practice, when it comes to research on minors. There are, however, no legal precedents in this area of law and not even the lower courts seem to have dealt with these matters. Previous legal research in the field is also practically non-existent. It is consequently difficult to determine how the law is in fact interpreted in practice.

As for research on incompetent adults, the medical profession would sometimes seem to grant relatives a stronger position - as proxies - than they are intended to by law. The custodians of a minor are, on the other hand, acknowledged by law as the legal representatives of the child. In this area the problems are presumably more related to the uncertainty concerning the implications of the general legal rules, when applied to medical research. To what extent can the custodians give a legally valid consent to the child's participation in research without any potential benefit for the child's own health? How do double-blind studies and the use of placebo rate in this context? When is it necessary to obtain the consent of both parents?

Even if the law is difficult to interpret, doctors need to be made aware of the legal rules and controls that do exist. In Sweden, this is done through various channels, such as professional organisations, employers, the research councils and other sponsors, information from the RECs, voluntary courses in research ethics and Good Clinical Trial Practice, etc. Decisions by the Health and Medical Services Disciplinary Board that are considered to be of general interest are regularly reported in the Swedish Physicians' Journal and other periodicals as well as the daily papers. The same applies to decisions by the Parliamentary Ombudsmen and the National Board of Health and Welfare.

Since 1985, there has also been a National Council for Medical Ethics in Sweden. This advisory body consists of representatives of the political parties as well as experts representing various disciplines, all appointed by the Government. The activities of the Council are aimed at elucidating matters of medical ethics from an overall society-oriented perspective, through reports and statements on different issues that may arise.[49] The Council is supposed to keep a look-out on the field of biomedical research and to function as a link between the scientists and the decision-makers in the Parliament, the Government, etcetera.

5. Concluding Remarks

The most significant problem raised by Swedish law on neonatal research – or research on humans in general and minors in particular – is the lack of clear legal rules and uniform legal control. This lack of clarity and control is of course particularly unsatisfactory in areas of research where the physical safety and personal integrity of incompetent and vulnerable persons may be endangered. It should be noted, however, that uncertainty regarding the ethical and legal prerequisites for research on children might also induce some researchers to abstain from carrying out such projects. Important knowledge regarding the health and medical treatment of children may thus unnecessarily be held back by the lack of satisfactory rules and guidelines.

As regards clinical drug trials, the legal situation is slightly different, since law requires the permission of the Medical Products Agency, and certain general prerequisites must be fulfilled. The more specific prerequisites for conducting clinical trials on small children are still, however, unclear. Furthermore, it is not very likely that the Medical Products Agency would raise legal objections concerning matters of consent, if a research project has passed the scrutiny of an REC, despite the fact that the committees have no legal expertise.

The RECs play an important role in securing the best interests of incompetent research subjects, but they lack interdisciplinary competence. Since the committees normally do not include any lawyers, the RECs do not have the necessary qualifications for even identifying the legal problems arising from research projects. When it comes to interpreting the law on a particular issue, their competence is of course even less adequate, although a legal consultant may be of help at that stage. Ethical review by an REC is furthermore not always mandatory by law, and the formal status of the REC's decisions are only advisory.

The need for clear rules and uniform control cannot be met in a satisfactory way by ethical guidelines alone. Such guidelines do not possess the same authority in society as statutory provisions, nor do they have the same democratic legitimacy. Medical research on human beings involve such important - and often conflicting - values and interests, that the basic principles and limits governing these activities should certainly be agreed on by society as a whole, and should not be decided by the medical profession alone. This does not mean that the content of the substantive rules would necessarily be very different. Good legislation must be founded on ethical considerations. Furthermore, within a legal framework, the ethical principles and guidelines are still indispensable. They are needed to supplement the legal rules in individual cases, but also provide a platform for the continued ethical and legal discussion. Such a public discussion is necessary for the awareness of both professionals and the public, as well as the further development of medical law and ethics.

In the present situation, Swedish law concerning medical research on minors, including newly-borns, does not seem to provide the minimum legal protection called for in articles 16-17 and 23 of the European Convention on Human Rights and Biomedicine. This is a regrettable state of affairs, but - it is hoped - one that can be changed. Despite the disappointing 1999 report by the Parliamentary Commission on Research Ethics, it must be assumed that biomedical research on humans will be governed by satisfactory legal rules within the foreseeable future.

Notes

1. This report has been produced within a research project supported by the Swedish Council for Social Research (project 95-0082).
2. Chapter 2, sections 6 and 8 of the Instrument of Government.
3. Chapter 2, section 12 of the Instrument of Government.
4. The government bill 1978/79: 220 p. 44.
5. Rynning, E, Consent to Medical Care and Treatment - Legal Relevance in Sweden. In: Patient's Rights - Informed Consent, Access and Equality (eds. Westerhäll, L & Phillips, C). Stockholm: Nerenius & Santérus Publishers 1994: 321-364. See also Rynning, E, *Samtycke till medicinsk vård och behandling.* Uppsala: Iustus 1994.
6. Section 1 of the Abortion Act (1974:595) and section 2 of the Sterilisation Act (1975:580).
7. Section 6 of the Transplant Act (1995:831), concerning living donors.
8. The goverment bill 1998/99: 4 p. 50, Rynning, op. cit.
9. Chapter 7, section 3 of the Secrecy Act.
10. Chapter 7, section 6 of the Secrecy Act.
11. E.g. sections 16-17 of the Compulsory Psychiatric Care Act (1991:1128), Rynning, op. cit.
12. There are, however, certain medical measures for which the permission of the National Board of Health and Welfare must be obtained, such as organ donation by incompetent persons and use of foetal tissue for medical purposes.
13. Chapter 11 sections 4 and 7 of the Parents and Children Code.
14. See sections 2.3 and 2.4 below.
15. Section 1 of the Abortion Act (1974:595) and section 2 of the Sterilisation Act (1975:580). This does not apply if such a measure is performed in order to save the patient's life or treat a serious disease.
16. Chapter 6, sections 1-2 and 11 of the Parents and Children Code.
17. Chapter 6, section 13 of the Parents and Children Code.
18. Under the Care of Young Persons (Special Provisions) Act, the children of Jehovah's witnesses may thus be given blood transfusions against the wishes and religion of their parents, should the life or health of the child be threatened. According to the Act (1982:316) on Prohibition of Genital Mutilation of Women, circumcision of females is explicitly forbidden, irrespective of consent and age. Obviously, Swedish law does not accept that the decisions parents may take, based on their religious or cultural background, will *always* be consistent with the best interests of the child.
19. In 1992, a two-year-old Swedish boy suffered permanent brain damage from the anaesthesia administered to alleviate post-operative pain after the circumcision, see *RiskRonden, Information om risker inom hälso- och sjukvården nr 1 1991-09-23: Hjärnskada vid rituell om skärelse.* Stockholm: The National Board of Health and Welfare 1991. At present, the case of a three-year-old who died after having been circumcised is being investigated.
20. NJA 1997 p. 636.
21. Taddio, A *et al.,* Efficacy and safety of lidocaine-prilocaine cream for pain during circumcision. The New England Journal of Medicine 1997 (vol. 336) pp. 1197-1201. Some of the conclusions drawn from the study, in which 30 of the 68 participating neonates were given placebo, were that even though the neonates that did receive the Emla cream still had pain - albeit at an attenuated level - and that other interventions that comfort the infant should also be used, the cream offers a safe and efficacious alternative to e.g. nerve block, which is more difficult to administer as well as being risky and painful in itself. Was it in their own best interest that these 68 neonates were not only circumcised, but also included in the double-blind, randomised trial - where half of them received no pain alleviation whatsoever - or did other interests prevail?
22. With the exception of statutes regulating compulsory mental care, forensic mental care etc.

23. Sahlin, J. *Om nödrätt i hälso- och sjukvården. Några anteckningar om juridiken på ett etiskt område. Svensk Juristtidning 1990* pp. 596-622, at 601.
24. Rynning, op. cit.
25. Rynning, op. cit.
26. E.g. the standing committee on social questions, 1991/92: SoU21 pp. 12 and 15.
27. See the preamble of the World Medical Association Declaration of Helsinki.
28. Section 2 of the Transplant Act.
29. Section 6 of the Transplant Act.
30. The Act (1991: 115) on Measures for Research and Treatment Purposes Concerning Fertilised Human Eggs.
31. E.g. *Forskning på foster som skall aborteras* (Research on foetuses to be aborted), Viewpoint of the National Council for Medical Ethics, December 1997.
32. The government bill 1991/92:107 p. 97 and the standing committee on social questions, 1991/92:SoU21 pp. 12 and 15.
33. Part 8, section 4 of the Medical Products Agency's Regulation and guidelines (LVFS 1996: 17) on clinical trials.
34. The government bill 1991/92:107 p. 97.
35. Guidelines to section 8, LVFS 1996: 17.
36. Section 14 of the Medicinal Products Act.
37. Section 13 of the Medicinal Products Act.
38. Jareborg, N, *Straffrättens ansvarslära.* Uppsala: Iustus 1994 pp. 177-179 and 91.
39. Rynning, E, *Etisk granskning av medicinsk humanforskning - lagstiftning behövs!* Stockholm: *Läkartidningen* 1997: 1771-1774. Until recently, some of the committees have been called 'local', but it has now been decided that they should all be considered regional, see Protocol of the Swedish Medical Research Council's National Board for Research Ethics, section 9, 12 January 1999.
40. The government bill 1991/92: 97 p. 94.
41. Part 3, section 1 of the regulation (LVFS 1996: 17).
42. Now in Section 21 of the Protection of Animals Act (1988: 534) and sections 41-49 of the Protection of Animals Ordinance (1988: 539).
43. The report of the Research Ethics Commission (SOU 1989: 74) and the final report of the Transplantation Commission (SOU 1992: 16).
44. *God sed i forskningen* (SOU 1999: 4).
45. *Riktlinjer för etisk värdering av medicinsk humanforskning, Forskningsetisk policy och organisation i Sverige (MFR-rapport 2 1996).* Stockholm: The Medical Research Council 1996.
46. Supra note 45 pp. 39-40 and Dahlqvist, G, De medicinskaforskningsetikkommittéernas organisation och verksamhet i Sverige. Kan forskningen bli mer etisk? Stockholm: The Department of Education 1996 pp. 13-20.
47. It should be observed that the age limits mentioned in the ethical guidelines do not have any equivalents in the *legal* rules, according to which the age and maturity of each child must be assessed and related to the complicity and seriousness of the health care decision in question.
48. Supra note 46.
49. See e.g. the Council's report dealing with research on foetuses that are to be aborted, *Forskning på foster som skall aborteras*, December 1997.

15 The Regulation of Neonatal Research in the UK

DR A. PLOMER

The regulation of clinical trials in the UK is the subject of numerous professional and administrative guidelines issued by the Royal Colleges, the Department of Health and public funding bodies such as the Medical Research Council.[1] Research trials on medicinal products are regulated by S.I. 1993/2538 implementing EC directive 91/507/EEC.[2] Otherwise, there is no general legislation specifically regulating the conduct of research on human beings. Neither are there judicial decisions specifically on clinical trials involving human subjects. So the legal limits on research are somewhat unclear and uncertain, and a matter of academic speculation based on inferences from well established common law principles in medical law.

General Common Law Principles Governing Medical Treatment

- A fundamental principle of English law is that each individual's body is inviolate. The courts have upheld the right of each individual to determine what happens to his or her body, to accept or refuse medical treatment.[3] This right has been said to be fundamental and absolute, it is protected by the criminal and civil law of battery and the tort of negligence which imposes on the medical profession duties to inform patients and disclose risks before treatment.
- In the case of an adult who is mentally competent, the courts have held that respect for the individual's right to self-determination requires a doctor to obtain consent for treatment. For consent to be legally valid, the doctor must explain to the patient, in broad terms and simple language, the nature of the treatment, its consequences, and any material risks.[4]
- Consent is not required in an emergency, or when the individual is an adult who is not mentally competent to give consent. Treatment which

185

is necessary either to improve health or prevent deterioration may lawfully be given. The doctor's duty is to act in the best interests of the patient.[5]

- The legal position of minors is somewhat complicated, and depends on their age and level of maturity which vary across England, Wales & Scotland.[6] In the case of a minor who is under 16, proxy consent must be obtained from someone who has authority to consent (e.g., a parent, guardian or the courts) but the courts retain the power to review any consent or refusal of treatment to safeguard the 'best interests' or welfare of the child. The child's welfare must be the paramount consideration in any decision affecting the child.[7]

Research

The implications of the above principles for clinical research depends on the nature of the research and its therapeutic or non-therapeutic value.

Research which is intended to have *therapeutic* value and to benefit the individual directly would come under the heading of 'medical treatment' to which the above principles apply. For the research to be lawful in the case of minors who lack the mental capacity to consent, the risk-benefits ratio must be such that the benefits to the patient should outweigh the risks so that participation in the trial could be deemed to be in the best interests of the individual concerned. A legal representative for the child must have given prior consent to participation in the trial. The consent must be specific and the representative should have been informed of any material risks. The consent must be free of any undue pressure or undue influence.[8]

Non-therapeutic research, where the intention is to obtain information through systematic enquiry so as to contribute to generalizable knowledge and where there is no intention to treat the person who is the subject of the research, is more problematic. The prevailing view used to be that non-therapeutic research involving human subjects who lack the capacity to consent was simply unlawful in English law, since such research is by definition not conducted for the benefit of the patient. But whilst the law is still uncertain, it is now thought that non-therapeutic research might be lawful if it does not expose the subject to more than minimal risks.[9] 'Minimal risk' is the American term defined in HHS Regulations on the Protection of Human Research Subjects 1990 (par. 46. 102 (g)), meaning that 'the risks of harm anticipated in the proposed research are not greater, considering probability and magnitude, than those ordinarily encountered in daily life or during the performance of routine physical or psychological examinations or tests'.

On the basis of the above, the legal limits on RCTs would depend on whether the trial falls into the category of therapeutic or non-therapeutic research. The welfare principle self-evidently prohibits denial of treatment which is of proven benefit to the child or substitution of treatment for a less beneficial alternative. The researcher must therefore ensure that the child assigned to the control group receives no less than the proven treatment which would benefit him or her most.

Dispensing with Consent

Would it be lawful in English law for a researcher to include a new-born baby in a trial without the parents consent, when the parents are unable to consent and the child's condition is dangerous and/or requires immediate or urgent medical attention?

Since the consent requirement is so fundamental, one would expect considerable judicial scrutiny of the circumstances under which it could be dispensed with. The *gravity* and *urgency* of the child's condition would no doubt be highly relevant factors. So would the circumstances which prevent the researcher from obtaining consent.

Dangerous and Urgent Conditions

If the child was suffering from a life-threatening condition, or some other highly dangerous condition which required urgent or immediate attention to save the child's life or prevent a serious deterioration of the child's health, then the researcher should be able to plead, in defence to an action for trespass to the person, that he had reasonable grounds to believe at the time that inclusion in the trial was medically *necessary* and in the best interests of a child.[10] Providing that at the time the child was entered into the trial there was clear evidence of the scientific soundness of the research project,[11] then the researcher would be protected even if the hypothesis tested in the trial subsequently turned out not to be proven. The defence is arguably restricted to therapeutic trials. It is difficult to imagine the circumstances under which it might be ethically and legally justifiable to expose a child suffering from a dangerous condition to even a minimal risk with no prospect of direct benefit and without the parent's consent. Researchers should beware of the concerns expressed by the Bristol Inquiry in the UK, over the profession's well-intended but cavalier disregard for obtaining consent.

Non-dangerous and /or Non-urgent

If the child's condition was dangerous but did not require immediate or urgent medical attention, then the researcher would no doubt be expected to take reasonable steps to obtain consent from an appropriate legal proxy for the child. Under the Children Act, such a proxy could be any person vested with parental authority by the Act or in default the Court.[12] *A fortiori*, there will be no lawful excuse under the principle of *necessity* for a researcher's failure to obtain proxy consent when intervention could reasonably be delayed because the child's condition does not require immediate or urgent medical attention to prevent deterioration of health.

Proxies

Finally, judicial scrutiny can also be expected of the circumstances which prevent the procurement of consent.

It is one thing for the researcher to proceed without consent because the parents (or other proxies) are unconscious, or cannot be contacted (for example in a car crash). But it is quite another to dispense with the parents' or proxies' consent because they are upset or emotionally disturbed. English courts have acknowledged that temporary factors such as confusion, shock, fatigue, pain or drugs may completely erode the capacity to consent.[13] But in view of the fundamental nature of the right of minors to have a legal representative, and the seriousness of curtailing such a right, clinical findings that the child's representative lacks mental competence have to be based on extremely tight safeguards and procedures. The parent's distress would have to be sufficient in law to impair the parent's legal capacity to give consent. The researcher's uncorroborated view is unlikely to constitute sufficient evidence without independent professional opinion.

Notes

1. See for instance *Research Involving Patients* (Royal College of Physicians, 1990), *Guidelines for the Ethical Conduct of Research Involving Children* (1992), *Department of Health Guidelines to LRECs* (DOH, 1991), *Guidance on Good Clinical Practice and Clinical Trials in the NHS* (Department of Health, 1999), *MRC Guidelines for Good Clinical Practice in Clinical Trials* (Medical Research Council, 1998), *The Ethical Conduct of Research on Children* (Medical Research Council, 1993).
2. Currently under revision. The proposed Clinical Trials Directive (*Official Journal of the European Community* - OJC 306, 08.10.97) in its final amended version adopted by the Commission in April 1999 (OJC 161, 08.06.99) is pending adoption by the Council.
3. *Re T* [1992] 9 BMLR 46.
4. *Chatterton v Gerson* [1981] 1 QB 432. *Sidaway v Board of Governors of the Bethlem Royal Hospital and the Maudsley Hospital Governors* (1985) 1 BMLR 132.
5. *In re F* [1989] 1 Med LR 58.
6. *Gillick v West Norfolk and Wisbech AHA* [1985] 3 All. E. R. 402.
7. Children Act 1989, s 1. For a detailed discussion of the legal position of children see Jane Fortin *Children's Rights and the Developing Law* (Butterworths, London, 1999).
8. *Re T* [1992] *supra*.
9. See R. H. Nicholson (ed.) *Medical research with Children* (OUP, Oxford, 1986), Kennedy & Grubb (ed.) *Principles of Medical Law* (OUP, Oxford, 1998). See also G. Dworkin 'Legality of Consent to Nontherapeutic Medical Research on Infants and Young Children' (1978) 53 *Archives of Disease in Childhood* 443 and B. Dickens, 'The Legal Challenge of Health Research Involving Children' *Health Law Journal* 6:131-148 (1998).
10. Under the principles enunciated by Lord Goff in *Re F* [1989] *supra*.
11. Prior approval of the research project by a LREC would constitute evidence of the scientific soundness of the trial.
12. See A. Plomer 'Parental Consent and Children's Medical Treatment' *Family Law* [1996] 739-742.
13. *Re MB (Medical Treatment)* [1997] 2 FLR.

16 Principles Underlying the Regulation of Research with Children in Europe: International Bioethics or Moral Bankruptcy?[1]

DR A. PLOMER

The regulation of clinical trials on neonates varies markedly across Europe.[1] Some countries have statutory regimes, whilst others do not. The procurement of consent prior to medical interventions is usually a legal requirement, but there is no uniform norm concerning the level of information that patients should be given to ensure that consent is adequate or informed. Neither is there a clear consensus on the circumstances in which consent can be dispensed with. Forms and procedures for obtaining consent vary. So do other control mechanisms, such as the legal status, role and composition of Research Ethics Committees. In the light of domestic variations in the regulation of clinical trials, the adoption by the Council of Europe of a Convention on Human Rights and Biomedicine (Oviedo, 1997) is an important step towards European and international harmonisation of norms in the field of biomedicine. But it has been suggested that harmonisation has the effect of driving down ethical standards to the lowest common denominator and diluting the rights of individuals in the fields of biology and medicine.[2] If true, this would fly in the face of the stated intention of the Council of Europe in the preamble of the Convention to maintain and further realise fundamental and universal human rights.

This paper seeks to explore the question of whether the rights contained in the Convention reflect universal ethical principles against which to judge domestic legal regimes on medical research with neonates in Europe. In the same year as the Convention on Biomedicine was adopted, the USA Advisory Committee on Human Radiation Experiments

(ACHRE, 1996) independently claimed to have identified fundamental ethical principles which are valid across all cultures and at all times and which can be used to judge the ethical soundness of experimentation with humans retroactively if required. A comparative analysis of the two frameworks throws up some revealing insights into the strengths and weaknesses of the Convention and the extent to which it has the capacity to address the most sensitive issues regarding the regulation of medical research on children/neonates in Europe today. The first part of the paper outlines and critically evaluates the ACHRE ethical framework. The second part compares the ACHRE principles with the rights protected by the Convention and argues that some of the weaknesses of the ACHRE report are duplicated in a different form in the Convention. The final part argues that consent is central to the moral and political legitimacy of medical research and discusses the circumstances in which the proposed weakening of consent requirements in emergency trials is morally permissible.

I. The ACHRE Report

The origin of modern international bioethics has been traced to the brutal abuse of human lives in the holocaust.[3] At the Nuremberg 'Doctors Trial' (1946-47) medical researchers were convicted of 'crimes against humanity' on the basis of principles which were said to be so *fundamental* that they were universally applicable to all eras and cultures.[4] Fifty years on, the philosophical soundness of 'moral fundamentalism'[5] was revisited on the occasion of President Clinton's appointment of the Advisory Committee on Human Radiation Experiments (ACHRE) to investigate allegations of unethical experiments conducted on human subjects by American researchers between the end of WWII and the early 1970s. The experiments that had been sponsored by government departments, including the Department of Defence involved up to 4000 human subjects. The experiments reviewed by the Radiation Committee included experiments with hospitalised patients suffering from chronic or terminal illnesses who were injected with plutonium and uranium to obtain metabolic data related to the safety of those working on the production of nuclear weapons (Ch. 5). There was no expectation that the patients would derive any medical benefit from the injections and the experiments put the subjects at risk of developing cancer in ten or twenty years' time. With only one exception, the records show that the subjects were not told of their involvement in the experiment. In the Cincinnati experiments in the mid 60s and early 70s, cancer patients underwent total body irradiation (TBI) with an expectation of low benefit. The experiments were sponsored by the Department of Defence which was interested in the study of the after-effects of radiation. These studies were not intended to benefit the patients. The patients were either not informed or not adequately informed (Ch. 8). Non-therapeutic experiments were carried out on institutionalised children, including some with mental impairment, at the Fernald School in the late 1940s and early 1950s. The experiments conducted by MIT involved feeding the children with food (Quaker oats) which had been irradiated with radioactive iron and calcium. Parental permission was sought, but the parents were told that the project was intended for the child's benefit, which was not true. Neither were the parents informed of the (minimal) risks to which the children were being exposed.

The ACHRE Ethical Framework: Six Fundamental Principles

Part of the brief of the Radiation Committee was to develop an ethical framework to evaluate, retroactively, the ethical soundness of the experiments under suspicion. In its report, the Radiation Committee, which contained two prominent moral philosophers Tom Beauchamp and Ruth Macklin, claimed to have identified six basic ethical principles which are morally binding on medical researchers, in all societies across time and space. The report grounded the validity of the principles on their acceptability to 'all morally serious individuals' and the fact that they are:

> ... widely accepted and generally regarded as so fundamental as to be applicable to the past as well as the present (Ch. 4, p. 1).

The principles are:

1. One ought not to treat people as mere means to the ends of others.
2. One ought not to deceive others.
3. One ought not to inflict harm or risk of harm.
4. One ought to promote welfare and prevent harm.
5. One ought to treat people fairly and with equal respect.
6. One ought to respect the self-determination of others.

The Committee regarded these principles as 'basic' because 'any minimally acceptable ethical standpoint must include them' (Ch. 4, p. 2). The principles are not lexically ordered and indeed 'all moral principles can justifiably be overridden by other basic principles in circumstances when they conflict' (Ch. 4, p. 2). The Committee claimed that the principles reflect a social consensus about the validity of certain moral *norms* as opposed to moral theories. Moral theories may differ in their metaphysical or epistemological basis and provide different justifications for a basic principle. But theoretical divergence need not, and *de-facto* does not, preclude convergence at the level of principles which in turn provide the grounding for more specific moral rules. For instance the requirement for informed consent may be based on the principle that one ought to promote welfare and prevent harm, which may in turn be grounded in the view that individuals are generally most interested in and knowledgeable about their own well-being. By contrast, an approach based on self-determination may assume that being able to make important decisions about one's own life and health is intrinsically valuable, independent of its contribution to promoting one's well being (Ch. 4, p. 4). Hence, it was claimed, cultural and ethical diversity need not preclude moral convergence on princ iples and particular moral rules such as the rule that competent individuals ought to be allowed to accept or refuse participation in experiments (Ch. 4, p. 5).

Application of the Ethical Framework

Applying the above ethical framework, the Committee drew a distinction between non-therapeutic experiments without the subject's consent and therapeutic experiments without the subject's consent.

Non-therapeutic research without consent This was held to be not only a violation of the basic principles listed above but also a violation of the Hippocratic principle that was the cornerstone of professional medical ethics at the time (Ch. 4, p. 8). The Committee found that in 11 out of the 21 experiments conducted on children which it reviewed, the risks (of cancer) were in a range that would today be considered as more than minimal and thus as unacceptable in non-therapeutic research (although the Committee emphasised that often these non-therapeutic experiments on unconsenting patients constituted only minor wrongs because often there was little or no risk to patient-subjects and no inconvenience).

Included in this category were experiments conducted on children who were sick or mentally handicapped, often confined to an institution such as a special needs school. The children were intentionally exposed to harmful radiation without adequate consent having been obtained from the parents or guardians. In these cases, the Committee argued, the children were being used as a mere means to the ends of the investigator conducting the experiment and the institutions sponsoring the experiment (breach of principle 1). The parents were not fully informed if informed at all (breach of principles 2 and 6). The infliction of harm was deliberate (breach of principle 3). Further, these children, the Committee argued, suffered the additional injustice of unfair and discriminatory treatment (breach of principle 5) as the evidence collected revealed that whilst there was a strong tradition of seeking consent with healthy subjects for research that generally offered no prospect of medical benefit to the participant, the same was not true in the case of subjects who were sick, paediatric patients, especially those who were institutionalised and/or subjects whose mental capacities were impaired.

Therapeutic research without consent The Committee argued that 'much the same can be said of experiments that were conducted on patient-subjects without their consent but that offered a prospect of medical benefit' (Ch. 4, p. 9). To the extent that the physician's intention was to benefit the patient, then 'the less blameworthy the physician was for failing to obtain consent. However, where the risks were great or where there were viable alternatives to participation in research, then the physician was more blameworthy for failing to obtain consent' (Ch. 4, p. 9).

The Charge of Moral Bankruptcy

In one of the most fascinating academic polemics to date Baker, a philosopher and historian of medicine, has argued that the search for universal moral principles is fundamentally misguided and charged the findings of the ACHRE report with moral bankruptcy. In the first of two articles published in the *Kennedy Institutes of Ethics Journal* in 1998, Baker presented a devastating attack on what he described as the 'moral bankruptcy of fundamentalism', the thesis that 'cross-cultural moral judgements and international bioethical codes are justified by certain "basic or fundamental" moral principles that are universally accepted in all cultures and eras'. The second article offers Baker's alternative model of a 'negotiated moral order'.[6]

The main gist of Baker's criticisms is this: Moral fundamentalism is essentially a rhetorical thesis with no social or historical basis. In the post-war era, the thesis has come under pressure from both multiculturalism and postmodernism. The former points to empirical evidence of the diversity of ethical norms in different cultures. The latter denies the possibility of normative convergence, as values or norms are seen as a reflection of the agents' perspective, gaze or narrative, and their hegemony is a function of power not of principle. In order to justify cross-cultural and cross-temporal judgements, moral fundamentalists presume that a culture or era *accepts* or *agrees* as 'basic' or 'fundamental' principles of which its members are ignorant or '… which are inconsistent with the principles that the culture forthrightly avows' (Baker, p. 218). But Baker contends that the thesis is historically untenable as the ACHRE report itself shows. American researchers involved in the radiation experiments with humans in the post-war era did not at the time recognise the ethical centrality of the requirement to obtain consent. They were prevented by a form of 'cultural blindness' from recognising the moral blameworthiness of their wrongdoing. Baker argues that the report's failure to attach moral blame to individual researchers, as opposed to government departments or regulatory agencies, shows the 'moral bankruptcy' of moral fundamentalism. On a postmodernist analysis, Baker claims, 'cultural blindness' could have equally excused the Nazi medical researchers indicted at the Nuremberg trial. If '… moral fundamentalism cannot justify the Nuremberg verdict, it has no *raison d'etre* and moral fundamentalism is philosophically bankrupt' (p. 216).

In a separate article,[7] Baker argues that moral fundamentalism must be abandoned and replaced by a contractarian theory derived from Rawls and Nozick in order to provide a theoretical framework for international bioethics which *can* bridge transcultural and transtemporal moral judgements in a way that withstands the multicultural and post-modern critique (p. 225). International bioethics can be reconstructed as a negotiated moral order which is consistent with traditional ideals about human rights, whilst respecting cultural difference but recognising defined areas of non-negotiability.

Baker's charges have been vigorously contested by Beauchamp and Macklin.[8] Both their responses contend that Baker has distorted the central postulates of moral fundamentalism and misrepresented the findings of the ACHRE report. Moral fundamentalism, they have argued, is not an empirical thesis. It does not postulate that universal principles find *de facto* acceptance across all cultures and times. It is a normative thesis. Further, Baker has seriously misrepresented the findings of the ACHRE report. The Committee did not find that American researchers who had conducted experiments found to be wrong could be excused on the grounds of cultural blindness. Quite the opposite. It was considerations of justice, partial evidence, absence of individual representation, etc, ... which prevented the Committee from ascribing individual blame. The principles identified by the report remain intact. What is more, Baker's alternative theory is but a contractarian version of moral fundamentalism. Who is right?

Beauchamp and Macklin's rebuttal carries some force. Moral fundamentalism does certainly purport to be concerned with moral ideals rather than historically held values as suggested by Baker. Further, Baker does appear to have misrepresented the finding of the ACHRE report. Individual researchers were not exonerated on the grounds of cultural blindness but ostensibly on procedural grounds. On the other hand, Baker's thesis that the legitimacy of international norms ultimately lies in *acceptance* by contracting parties of a negotiated moral order offers an attractive alternative reading of normative frameworks such as the Council of Europe's Convention on Biomedicine. Baker points out that the Convention is framed in terms of *rights* rather than principles.

But the theoretical differences between Baker and moral fundamentalists are arguably less significant than the points of convergence. Both sides of the debate agree on the possibility of transcultural and transtemporal moral judgements, but they do so on the basis of different theories. In practice then, it is the substantive principles or rights identified by the theories which will have to bear the burden of critical examination. In this respect, Beauchamp and Macklin's theories are more developed than Baker's, as the former have committed themselves to the six basic principles enunciated in the AHCRE report whilst Baker offers some interesting but limited views on emergency trials (see infra). How do these principles stand up to critical scrutiny? To what extent do they coincide with or reflect the principles underlying the Council of Europe's Convention on Biomedicine?

Coherence, Conflict and Moral Priorities

Most of the principles contained in the ACHRE report are unremarkable and not contentious. Principles 1 and 6 which justify the moral obligation imposed on medical researchers to obtain informed consent have not always been clearly distinguished in deontological theories such as Kant's. The advantage of distinguishing the two principles is that the requirement not to treat individuals as a mere means to an end is broad enough to extend protection to individuals who lack the capacity to make choices for themselves and who are therefore not caught by the requirement to respect self-determination. The ACHRE report specifically relies on the principle that one ought not to treat other humans as a mere means to an end to condemn the radiation experiments conducted on institutionalised children who were mentally handicapped (Ch. 7).

The principle that one ought not to deceive others presumably requires qualification but otherwise provides another uncontentious justification for the requirement to obtain informed consent. Whether the principle is truly basic is perhaps more questionable. It could conceivably be argued to derive its force from principles 1 and/or 6 which also happen to be the principles usually invoked in the ACHRE report to evaluate the radiation experiments.

The principle of non-maleficence is common to all ethical theories. The principle has a major limiting effect on the conduct of non-therapeutic research. ACHRE invoked it to condemn non-therapeutic research that carried risks more than minimal.

The principle of fairness and equal respect is a central pillar of liberal theories derived from Kant. Modern theories such as Rawls' have expressly situated themselves in opposition to welfare-based theories such as utilitarianism, which they claim cannot consistently meet the requirements of fairness and justice. The ACHRE report specifically applied the principle of fairness and justice to condemn trials without informed or adequate consent on research subjects which were particularly vulnerable or at risk of exploitation, such as children or institutionalised mentally incapacitated individuals, seriously ill and comatose patients.

Finally, the principle that one ought to promote welfare and prevent harm is also claimed to be a basic or fundamental principle for the conduct of research (the welfare principle). But as stated the principle admits of several interpretations, some of which are controversial. The crucial ambiguity here rests on the absence of a clear indication of *whose* welfare medical researchers are supposedly under a moral obligation to promote: the individual's welfare or the welfare of society? The two are not necessarily compatible, and whilst the former may be uncontentious, the latter is not.

The report's ambiguity or evasion in the formulation of the 'welfare principle' is particularly problematic in the light of the further interpretation principle proposed by ACHRE which denies any lexical priority between the six stated principles and endorses the possibility of *any* principle overriding another in the event of conflict (Ch. 4, p. 2). This opens the theoretical possibility of conferring moral legitimacy on medical experiments that are conducted primarily for the collective benefit of society rather than the benefit of the individual. In the hands of oppressive political regimes, individual rights could then be sacrificed to the interest of society and the State in biomedical research. But arguably it is precisely such forms of abuse of individual rights which truly universal and basic principles should be able to condemn. Examples of medical experiments prioritising collective over individual benefit can be found in the ACHRE report itself. In the great majority of cases the experiments reviewed were conducted to advance medical science or national interests in defence or space exploration (Finding 1). The Committee also found that the human radiation experiments 'contributed significantly to advances in medicine and thus to the health of the public'. And yet, the Committee found not only that some of the research subjects were exposed to unacceptable risks (Finding 2) but also that during the 1944-1974 period, especially through the early 1960s, physicians engaged in clinical research generally did not obtain consent for therapeutic research, and where the research was not therapeutic *it was common* for physicians to conduct research on patients without their consent (Finding 10). These practices on the part of the medical profession were condemned as morally wrong (Finding 11b)[9] and the Committee's recommendations also highlight the need to ensure that the individual's right to privacy and self-determination are protected in experiments conducted primarily for the purpose of promoting national security. But it is not clear how the findings or recommendations are logically consistent with the Committee's expressed view that *any* of the six principles can override the others in the event of a conflict.

Non-therapeutic experiments on individuals who lack the capacity to consent are another possible category for abuse. ACHRE actually reported that it was 'troubled' by the selection of subjects in many of the experiments reviewed as these subjects were often drawn from relatively powerless, easily exploited groups, and many of them were hospitalised patients (Finding 9). The finding that biomedical experiments had been conducted on institutionalised children, seriously ill and sometimes comatose patients was said by the Committee to be 'ethically troubling' (Finding 9). But whilst the principle of fairness and equal respect may indeed be relied upon to query the justice of these experiments (as the report itself argued), the ACHRE ethical framework cannot show why the pursuit of collective interests should not prevail over fairness as *any* principle can take priority over the others in the event of conflict.

The fundamental difficulty evaded by ACHRE is to provide an acceptable ethical justification for the conduct of medical experiments on human subjects who lack the capacity to consent, when the experiments are not intended to directly benefit the individual involved and the primary purpose instead is to advance knowledge for the collective benefit of society. Such a justification would require two things. On the one hand it is necessary to show why individuals are under a moral obligation to act for the benefit of others or the collective benefit. Theoretical justifications for welfarist programmes may certainly be found in utilitarian theories but these theories do not command widespread acceptance, neither are they clearly consistent with political regimes committed to the protection of individual rights. Secondly, even if an adequate justification for the welfare principle was forthcoming, it is also necessary to show why in the event of a conflict between individual and collective welfare it is acceptable for latter to prevail. The main weakness of the ethical framework advanced by ACHRE is that it does not adequately address either issue.[10]

II. International Bioethics: The Convention on Biomedicine

General Provisions

How do the rights protected by the Convention on Biomedicine compare to the ACHRE principles? Does the Convention avoid the weaknesses of the ACHRE ethical framework?

The stated purpose of the Convention on Biomedicine is to 'protect the dignity and identity of all human beings and guarantee everyone, without discrimination, respect for their integrity and other rights and fundamental freedoms with regard to the application of biology and medicine (Ch. I, Art. 1). Chapter 1 states three additional general provisions or principles:

- **The primacy of the human being** protected by Art. 2 requires that 'the interests and welfare of the human being shall prevail over the sole interests of society and science'.
- Contracting states shall take appropriate measures to provide **equitable access to health care** taking into account health needs and available resources (Art. 3) and
- Any intervention in the health field, including research, must be carried out in accordance with relevant **professional standards** (Art. 4).

Additional substantive detailed provisions on Consent and Scientific Research are detailed in Chapter II and Chapter IV respectively.

General rules on consent Medical interventions without the person's informed consent are prohibited by Article 5. An intervention in the health field may only be carried out after the person concerned has given:

1. free and informed consent, and
2. the person shall beforehand be given appropriate information as to the purpose and nature of the intervention as well as on its consequences and risks

When the individual is *a minor who lacks the capacity to consent*, then the general rule is that:

1. the intervention may only be carried out for the person's direct benefit (art. 6.2) and
2. with the authorisation of a legal representative (art. 6.2).

The meaning of the word 'intervention' is not restricted to 'medical treatment' and includes scientific research. The Explanatory Report stresses that 'one of the important fields of application of this principle concerns research' (para. 21). But the Convention contains additional specific rules on research.

General rules on research Article 16 imposes three general requirements on the conduct of research. There must be no alternative of comparable effectiveness to research on humans, the risks must not be disproportionate to the potential benefits and the project must have received prior approval by a multidisciplinary and independent research ethics committee.

Children Children who are unable to consent to biomedical research fall into the general category of 'persons unable to consent' whose rights in respect of research are further detailed in Article 17. Article 17 draws a distinction between:

1. Research which has the *potential to produce real and direct benefit* to the individual and

2. Research which has the *aim of contributing ... to the ultimate attainment of results capable of conferring benefit to the person concerned or to other persons in the same age category or afflicted*

with the same disease or disorder or having the same condition (Art. 17.2.i).

Although the terminology used is different, these two categories of research broadly map onto the traditional categories of therapeutic and non-therapeutic research. In addition to the general consent requirements imposed by art. 5 and 6, both types of research are subject to the further (evidentiary) requirement that the authorisation of the legal representative be given specifically in writing (art. 17.1.iv). Non-therapeutic research must only carry *minimal* risk and burden for the individual concerned (art. 17.2.ii).

Ethical Convergence?

To what extent do the rights detailed by the Convention on the conduct of medical research on children reflect so-called fundamental ethical values or principles contained in other normative frameworks such as the ACHRE report?

In some respects the values expressly espoused in the Convention are broader and vaguer than the ACHRE principles. Where ACHRE talks of respect for self-determination, and the prohibition on treating human beings as mere means to ends, the Convention endorses instead the need to safeguard human dignity without further elaboration on what the concept entails. Presumably justification for the rules on consent lies in respect for human dignity, but as the concept is left unanalysed the precise link is a matter of academic speculation. The Convention also contains what may be called a 'speciesist' slant which is lacking in the ACHRE principles, as it enjoins respect for the human being both as an individual and as a member of the human species. The closest equivalent to ACHRE's welfare principle is to be found in the preamble of the Convention which affirms that 'progress in biology and medicine should be used for the benefit of present and future generations' but the emphasis here is on the uses to which research should be put. This is quite different from the ACHRE principle which imposes on medical researchers a moral obligation to carry out research to promote welfare. However, the crucial difference between ACHRE and the Convention is that the latter unequivocally asserts the moral priority of the interests of the individual over those of society, whilst the former as we saw earlier does not. In the event of a conflict, as envisaged above, the Convention clearly asserts that the interests of the individual must prevail over those of society. In theory then, the general principles endorsed by the Convention should avert the problems of the

ACHRE principles. In practice, the specific rules on scientific research appear to resolve the conflict with which ACHRE had wrestled, in favour of societal over individual interests.

The Convention legitimises the use of human subjects for research which will not directly benefit the individual and which may even inflict harm, albeit *minimal*, on the subject concerned. It is far from clear how this rule can be consistent with the principle of the primacy of the individual unless the research is restricted to the investigation of a condition from which the individual concerned suffers. Whilst the wording of article 17 begins by introducing a restriction to that effect, the same section goes on to permit as an alternative research on 'other persons in the same *age* category'. In practice then, the Convention could condone some variants of the experiments on institutionalised children condemned by ACHRE.

Ultimately, neither the ACHRE ethical principles nor the Convention offer a coherent system of principles or values or an adequate ethical justification for prioritising the interests of society over those of mentally incapacitated individuals, be they adults or children, in non-therapeutic biomedical research. To that extent, moral fundamentalism has failed to deliver. Notwithstanding this, both ACHRE and the Convention have allowed academic and public debate to move on and identify some of the most sensitive issues concerning biomedical research on children. What is more, a protocol on research is to be added to the Convention and the ACHRE recommendations have a valuable contribution to make to the European debate.

III. Future Issues in Europe

The Centrality of Consent

Notwithstanding the absence of convergence in the normative theoretical basis of the ACHRE and Convention rules, there is clear and unequivocal convergence on the importance of the rule for informed consent. Under either framework, medical researchers are under an obligation to obtain *informed* consent from a research subject in advance of the trial. Arguably, the rules under both systems impliedly use informed consent as the main moral grounding for the conduct of therapeutic and non-therapeutic experiments on human subjects. Whilst ACHRE and the Convention are impliedly committed to the view that the collective interest of society can take moral priority over the interests of the individual, both sets of norms fall short of requiring that individuals be *compelled* to act for the collective benefit of others. Non-therapeutic experiments involving minimal risks are permitted but only subject to strengthened consent requirements. Mentally competent adults or children can simply decline to enter such experiments, and there is no question of their refusal being overridden. Similarly, non-therapeutic experiments on mentally incompetent children and adults may legitimately be conducted but only with the (proxy) permission of the subject's legal representative. In either case, moral legitimacy is conferred by the *acceptance* by the subject or the subject's proxy of the terms under which they will take part in the experiment. Further, the moral legitimacy lent to medical research by the subject's (or proxy's) consent also carries significant political implications. By giving primacy to individual (or proxy) consent, both sets of rules impliedly favour the political regimes of liberal societies which are committed (at least formally) to the primacy of individual liberty and rights.[11]

Neonates   In the case of children who cannot authorise medical research intervention for themselves, there is no dispute that consent has to be obtained from a legal proxy instead (usually the parents). Whilst it was not uncommon up to the 1970s for paediatric research to be conducted without the parents' permission 'Certainly today, any use of a child in research would not be ethically acceptable or legally permissible without the parent's permission' (Ch. 7). The ethical justification briefly canvassed by ACHRE is twofold. Parents are viewed as a mechanism for valuing and fostering the institution of the family and the freedom of adults to perpetuate family traditions and commitments. Alternatively or in addition, parents are thought not only to be in the best position but generally motivated to act in the best interests of the child (Ch. 7). This latter justification also points to the ethical limits of parental authority and rights: they are to be exercised for the benefit of the child.

Emergency Research: the Permissible and Impermissible

In the light of the moral and political centrality of consent, proposals to weaken or lift consent requirements in emergency trials require very careful scrutiny. The ACHRE report does not address the issue. The Convention does authorise medical interventions without consent in an emergency (Article 8) but interventions are limited to those which are *medically* necessary and have to be carried out immediately for the benefit of the health of the individual concerned. Circumstances under which consent cannot be obtained are illustrated in the Explanatory Report. The individual concerned may be unconscious and his/her representatives not available. The precise scope of Article 8 is unclear but the wording suggests that the proposed medical interventions may not extend to research.[12] If Article 8 does extend to emergency research, then it is clearly limited to *therapeutic* research which is capable of conferring an immediate and direct benefit on the individual concerned and subject to the further constraints already mentioned.

Moral arguments in favour of emergency research have been advanced by Baker.[13] Baker distinguishes between what he terms 'optimising revisions' to weaken consent requirements, and 'marginalizing rebellions'. An example of the latter is the US suspension of the CIOMS rule that cross-border research should abide by the same ethical standards as the sponsoring country at home. By contrast, Baker sees the revision of emergency standards as an 'optimising reform' because the reform is a direct response to a specific problem – the likelihood that surrogates will be unavailable to consent to therapeutic experiments on incapacitated patients admitted to hospital emergency departments. Further, the proposed lifting of consent requirements in emergencies in the USA has been further accompanied by heightened IRB scrutiny for monitoring therapeutic experiments in the emergency department.[14] In addition, the hospitals involved have adopted innovative procedures – such as notification to the community that experiments are being conducted in certain emergency hospitals – which indicate sensitivity to the problematic nature of the researcher-subject relationship.[15]

By contrast, the proposal to dispense with consent in an emergency when the proxy *is* available but consent may be difficult to obtain because the proxy is emotionally distressed, has the negative profile of a 'marginalising rebellion'. Presumably researchers will seek to rely on the beneficence principle coupled with the view that their expertise and experience puts them in a privileged position to unilaterally determine the child's best interests. But this is precisely the kind of paternalistic argument which has led to the widespread charge of professional arrogance and disregard for the patient's right to self-determination in Western liberal societies.[16] Emotional distress is a normal human reaction to tragedy whether the tragedy affects the individual herself or her children. Society is entitled to expect from the medical profession that they will have received appropriate training to deal sensitively with individual subjects and/their children who are suffering from emotional trauma in an emergency. No doubt in some cases shock and trauma can be such as to disable the individual or proxy altogether from weighing information and making a reasoned choice. But such judgements must be supported by strong clinical evidence and can only be reached on an individual case-by-case basis. There can no question of a whole class of individuals (emotionally upset parents/guardians) being divested as a group from their parental right to consent to treatment in an emergency.

Notes

1.   See Chapter 8.
2.   See for instance S. McLean and S. Elliston 'Bioethics, the Council of Europe and the Draft Convention' in *European Journal of Health Law* (1995) Vol. 2, 5-13.
3.   R. Macklin 'The Universality of the Nuremberg Code' in G. Annas and M. Grodin (eds) *The Nazi Doctors and the Nuremberg Code*, New York: OUP (1992).
4.   Nuremberg Tribunal (1948). *Trials of War Criminals before the Military Tribunals. The Medical Case*. Washington DC: US Government Printing.
5.   The expression 'moral fundamentalism' was adopted by R. Baker, in 'A Theory of International Bioethics: Multiculturalism, Postmodernism, and the Bankruptcy of Fundamentalism' *Kennedy Institute of Ethics Journal* (1998) Vol. 8, No. 3, 201-231.
6.   R. Baker, 'A Theory of International Bioethics: The Negotiable and the Non-Negotiable' *Kennedy Institute of Ethics Journal* (1998) Vol. 8, No. 3, 233-274.
7.   *Supra* note 6.
8.   T. Beauchamp, 'The Mettle of Moral Fundamentalism: A Reply to Robert Baker' *Kennedy Institute of Ethics Journal* (1998) Vol. 8, No. 3, 389-402. R. Macklin 'A Defense of Fundamental Principles and Human Rights: A Reply to Robert Baker' *Kennedy Institute of Ethics Journal* (1998) Vol. 8, No. 3, 403-422.
9.   Although the Committee attributed moral fault to government agencies rather than individual medical researchers (Finding 4 and 5, 9, 11).
10. For a useful discussion of the opposing ethical perspectives on children's participation in clinical trials see L. Friedman Ross, *Children, Families and Health Care Decision Making*, Oxford: Clarendon (1998).
11. A similar and much more detailed argument on the moral and political significance of consent to *medical treatment* may be found in H. Teff *Reasonable Care: Legal Perspectives on the Doctor-Patient Relationship* Oxford: Clarendon (1994).
12. This point is argued in more detail in A. Plomer 'Participation of Children in Clinical Trials: UK, European and International Legal Perspectives on Consent' in *Medical Law International* Vol. 4, (2000).
13. See *supra* note 5.
14. Wolpe, Paul and Merz, John (1997). Hospital Errs on the Front Line in the Informed-Consent Debate. *Forum for Applied Research and Public Policy*: 127-31.
15. Baker, Robert 'A Theory of International Bioethics: Multiculturalism, Postmodernism, and the Bankruptcy of Fundamentalism', 201-233 and 'A Theory of International Bioethics: The Negotiable and the Non-Negotiable', 233-275 *Kennedy Institute of Ethics Journal*, vol. 8, no. 3, (September 1998).
16. ACHRE report.

PART IV
INFORMED CONSENT IN
NEONATAL RESEARCH

17 Is Obtaining Informed Consent to Neonatal Randomised Controlled Trials an Elaborate Ritual? Interviews with Parents and Clinicians[1]

DR S.A. MASON, MR P.J. ALLMARK, DR C. MEGONE,
PROFESSOR D. BRATLID, PROFESSOR P. DALLA-VORGIA,
DR A.B. GILL, MRS P. MORROGH, PD DR S. REITER-THEIL,
DR V. FELLMAN, DR G. GREISEN, DR L. HELLSTROM-
WESTAS, DR G. LATINI, MRS N. LEROUX, DR N. MODI,
PROFESSOR M. MOYA, DR N. NELSON, DR S. PETMEZAKI,
MRS A. PHILLIPS, DR G. RUSSELL, DR C.A. RYAN, DR E.
SALIBA, DR A.M. WEINDLING, ON BEHALF OF THE
EURICON STUDY GROUP

INTRODUCTION

It is normal practice to obtain informed consent from parents for research on newborn infants. For consent to be valid parents must be deemed to be mentally competent, have received appropriate information, and be able to understand the information and give consent voluntarily.[2] However, the research may need to be carried out urgently, be potentially life saving, be complex (e.g. a randomised controlled trial), and/or there may be significant risks. As a result of these problems, it has been suggested that the process undertaken does not always lead to valid informed consent; indeed it has been described as a ritual[3] and a sham.[4] Nonetheless, it is legally necessary in Europe[5] and is seen as ethically vital by some commentators.[6]

The aim of the Euricon study was to examine the validity of obtaining informed consent for neonatal research across Europe (to our knowledge the first time this has been done), and suggest practical improvements if necessary. This paper reports on the experience of parents asked for consent and of clinicians seeking it.

METHODS

Subjects

Between January 1997 and September 1998, semi-structured interviews were performed with the parents of 200 infants and with 107 neonatologists in nine European countries (see Table 1). The sample of countries was designed to be geographically representative; accordingly, neonatologists of the European Neonatal Brain Club (an informal, pan-European organisation) were invited to take part in the study. The resulting participating countries were representative of Scandinavian, Western, Central and Mediterranean Europe. To avoid selection bias of interviewees, strict sampling criteria were set out in a study specific interview manual. (The interviewer was asked to select names randomly from lists of eligible patients and neonatologists, drawn up by the consultant on each unit. One list was of parents who gave consent for their baby to be entered into a trial and the other of parents who declined.) In four centres approach was by a single invitation letter, in the remainder it was face to face. Response to the letter was 90% in one centre, 55% in another and unknown for the two remaining. In total, four clinicians and 13 parents refused to be interviewed (of these, two were due to telephone problems).

Parents Parents whose infant was alive and who had been asked during the previous year for consent to allow their baby to take part in clinical trials on a neonatal intensive care unit (NICU) were eligible. Both those who had given their consent and those who had refused it were approached. One hundred and forty two interviews were held with one parent alone and 53 with two parents. (For five interviews the number of parents is unknown.)

The educational status of parents was categorised according to whether they had attended higher education or only compulsory education. (This was defined appropriately for each country, e.g. in Italy compulsory education is eight years in length and in the UK it is twelve.) Of the 200 fathers, 78 (39%) had received compulsory education and 103 (51.5%)

higher education (no information for 19 fathers). Of the 200 mothers, 84 (42%) had compulsory education and 110 (55%) were educated to a higher level (no information for six mothers).

Clinicians 107 neonatologists were interviewed who all had experience in obtaining consent from parents for neonatal research. Except for Greece, where only clinicians were interviewed (see table 1), the neonatologists worked in the same neonatal units as those to which the babies of the parents interviewed had been admitted. (Neonatologists among the Euricon partners were excluded.) Forty-nine (46%) were senior clinicians, 39 (36%) were middle grade and the clinician status for 19 (18%) was not recorded. Two-thirds of the clinicians were involved in obtaining consent to neonatal research at the time of interview.

Interviews

The interviews were conducted by bi-lingual English/native language speaking research assistants who were unknown to the parents. Each interviewer received instructions for the conduct of the interviews both from the study partner and by means of a comprehensive, study-specific interview manual. (This contained background to the ethics of informed consent in neonatal research, information on interviewee eligibility and sampling, and detailed instructions on the conduct of the interview; parent and neonatologist information sheets, consent forms and interview schedules, including prompts and the rationale for each question.) Questions were mostly open-ended, in keeping with the qualitative research strategy needed to explore this under-researched area.

Parental interviews took place either at home, following hospital discharge, or in private on the NICU when the baby's condition was stable. Taped, face-to-face interviews were encouraged, but telephone interviews were permitted in countries where such an approach was considered to be an accepted procedure for interviewees (e.g. Scandinavian countries). For the latter, the answers to questions were written onto the interview schedules during the interview whilst the taped, face-to-face interviews were transcribed later onto the schedules by the interviewer. Most interviews were face-to-face, 73 (68%) clinicians and 97 (49%) parents, with 23 (21%) clinicians and 101 (50%) parents being interviewed via the telephone. (There was no information on mode of interview for 11 (10%) clinicians and two (1%) parents.)

Approval was sought and obtained from all relevant Research Ethics Committees and consent was obtained from participating parents and clinicians.

Analysis

Translations of interview transcripts were performed in each country by either the interviewer, the study partner or an independent translator. Original transcripts of the interviews were reviewed to perform quality checks. To ensure reliability of the qualitative analysis, each interview was analysed independently by two people in the Management Team (mainly SAM, PJA, AP, CM) using a structured analysis document. This document was compiled by SAM and PJA analysing the first 40-50 transcripts and recording emerging themes using a well-accepted qualitative approach.[7] Firstly, the initial transcripts were reviewed to allow familiarisation. Secondly, key themes and issues were identified around which the data could be organised. These were both a priori researcher-identified themes and new themes identified by interviewees. The former specifically concerned the four criteria identified as necessary for a valid informed consent (competence, information, understanding and voluntariness as outlined in the section 'Definition of informed consent'). This structure, incorporating the themes, was produced as an analysis document. Thirdly, this document was used to analyse the transcripts in a systematic way, permitting pertinent answers to be extracted in a structured manner from sometimes long lengths of text. The two independent analyses were separately entered onto an Access database. Discrepancies were reviewed, again independently, by a third person and the decision on the analysis was then entered in a third review field. Care was taken not to force answers into categories and to represent answers in a faithful manner. Statistical inference was of an exploratory nature and thus used confidence intervals rather than p-values.

Parental numbers refer to parents of 200 infants. It is the parental unit which is referred to, irrespective of whether one or two parents were interviewed. Where consent for more than one trial was sought, the trial which had the highest risk and urgency was used in calculations.

Multiple answers to certain questions and some missing data meant that not all results added up to the total number of interviews and thus in some cases the numerical descriptions are not included, as they would be misleading or inappropriate. Multiple answers were treated as separate answers and described in the text. Disagreements between parents are treated as separate answers.

Definition of Informed Consent

The model of informed consent used in the study held that valid informed consent is obtained when all of the following criteria[2,8] are met:

1. Competence – the person giving consent is mentally competent to do so;
2. Information – sufficient information is received to make an informed choice;
3. Understanding – understanding is sufficient to make a reasoned choice;
4. Voluntariness – consent is given voluntarily.

All the interviews were analysed as being 'a problem', 'no problem' or 'equivocal' against each of these four criteria. We did not attempt to specify precisely the standards required for each criterion to be met. Thus we did not assess the consents and refusals given by parents, or the consents sought by neonatologists, in relation to some precise standards. Rather the interviews were analysed with a view to identifying factors that might put in question the quality of consent. For example, were a parent to say 'I was very emotional and couldn't think clearly', then we would record that there was a problem with competence, not that the parent was definitely incompetent. Similarly, a parent stating 'This was an emotional decision, but I thought clearly' would be recorded as not having a problem with competence.

However in some cases the interviews required a more difficult judgement, as where the parents claimed to have been fully informed about participation in a trial but then stated, for example, that they did not know they were able to withdraw. The presentation of the results requires interpretation in this light.

Characteristics of Research

Euricon clinician partners were asked to categorise the research protocols for which the parent interviewees' consent had been sought as being non-urgent or urgent and whether they contained no/minimal risk or discomfort

214 European Neonatal Research: Consent, Ethics Committees and Law

or risk or discomfort greater than no/minimal. These were defined as follows:

1. *Urgent* – If the protocol dictated that consent was needed from parents within 12 hours of approaching them. This was sub-divided into:
   a. Emergency – If treatment was also for a life-threatening condition in the neonate.
   b. Protocol Urgency – If the research protocol alone dictated the urgency.

2. *Risk or discomfort* – 'No/minimal risk or discomfort' was defined as such if the protocol did not entail risk or discomfort any greater than standard daily care on a neonatal intensive care unit (e.g. a feeding trial).

RESULTS

1. Background Data

The geographical distribution of both parental and clinician interviews are presented in Table 1. 164 (82%) parents were asked to consent to a single trial, 16 (8%) to two, three (1.5%) to three. For 17 (8.5%) the number is unknown.

Of the parents interviewed, 179 (89.5%) had agreed to their child taking part in a research study; 13 (6.5%) had declined. (This is broadly in keeping with the report by clinicians in their interviews that between 5% and 15% of parents generally decline to provide consent.) Two (1%) had agreed to one trial but declined another, five (2.5%) did not remember being asked and one (0.5%) was outside the time limit for eligibility to be randomised.

Parents of 149 (74.5%) infants made a joint decision as to whether or not to consent and 41 (20.5%) made a decision without reference to their partner. There was no information on this for parents of 10 (5%) infants.

Parents of 50 (25%) infants were asked for consent for urgent trials (of which 30 were emergency trials and 20 were for protocol urgency alone) and 135 (67.5%) for non-urgent trials (no information for 15 parents). 31 of the 200 parents (15.5%) were approached concerning trials which were of greater than no/minimal risk or discomfort and 154 (77%) for no/minimal risk or discomfort. (No information for 15 parents.)

The majority of parents were asked for their consent after their infant's birth, whilst on the neonatal unit. Three (1.5%) mothers were asked during their labour.

2. The Validity of the Process of Obtaining Informed Consent

59 (29.5%) parents were deemed to have 'no problem' with all four criteria of informed consent (competence, information, understanding and voluntariness). Thus over two-thirds had problems in one or more of the component areas. 29 (14.5%) had a problem with one criteria, 26 (13%) with two, 30 (15%) with three and 19 (9.5%) had problems with all four categories. (It should be noted that problem categories assessed as being 'equivocal' are not included in these figures).

In contrast, (but encompassing the many consent procedures with which clinicians were involved), only three (3%) clinicians were deemed to have 'no problem' with obtaining consent from parents whereas 97 (91%) clinicians considered consent to be problematic.

Table 2 provides a breakdown of the problem categories of the consent process.

The following results detail problems identified in terms of the four criteria:

Competence

Parents Sixty percent of parents were considered competent at the time of obtaining consent whilst 42 (21%) parents were deemed to have a problem with respect to competence.

The most common problems reported included that: they were overwhelmed by emotions and thus unable to think clearly; research at the time was a minor concern as they were preoccupied with the welfare of the baby; the mother was still under the effect of the anaesthetic or still unwell following delivery.

> Parent: *We were so shocked, we signed without knowing much.*

Clinicians Seventy-nine (74%) clinicians expressed a concern regarding parental competence.

Clinician concerns about competence included the fact that parents were in a vulnerable position and in their opinion did not have the ability to decide effectively, either through lack of knowledge/intellect or emotional state.

> Clinician: *If the baby is very sick they will tell you to do anything you like.*

Other clinicians thought that parents were able to decide for their baby despite adverse circumstances.

> Clinician: *I think that resources are found to make decisions in a tense situation*

a belief with which some parents concurred:

> Parent: *Yes, the situation makes you more concentrated, focused*

Information and understanding

Parents Forty-three (21.5%) parents reported a problem with information and 44 (22%) with understanding. Unsurprisingly, the main problems reported were essentially the same for both information and understanding and thus these criteria are reported together. These problems concerned lack of clarity/ understanding of information given: being unaware of some risks or that they could withdraw from the study; lack of time to decide or that the parents were not given an information sheet.

> Parent: *Perhaps if there are any downsides to the studies. I would have liked to know more about those. They concentrate on the positive results.*

The majority of parents thought that the clinician explained the research clearly to them in a considerate manner.

> Parent: *It is important that you are treated with dignity. It was very good that she did not just throw out a question 'Do you want to participate in a study?' but that she took it easy and discussed it with us.*

Complaints were of consent being requested at inappropriate times e.g. during labour, or in a rushed manner, such as whilst changing clothes prior to entering the NICU.

Almost half of parents (94, 47%) mainly relied upon the information provided orally by the doctor in order to reach their decision, with 18 (9%) mainly on the information sheet and 41 (20.5%) on a combination of the two. Eighteen (9%) parents said that they were not given a sheet. There was no information on this for the remaining parents (29, 14.5%). Many parents also stated that the value of the information sheet was that they could read it later to remind them about the trial.

Concerning parental understanding of ability to withdraw from the research, data is available from 145 parents. Of these, most parents (103, 71%) understood that they could withdraw their baby from the research once it had started.

Parent: *The exit door of being able to withdraw was very important.*

Thirty (21%) were unaware of the ability to withdraw. Seven (5%) could not remember and five (3.5%) implied other problems such as: treatment was given prior to consent, being unaware that their baby was in a trial or they did not feel that they could withdraw having signed the consent form.

Few parents were aware of Research Ethics Committees (RECs) and their role. Some parents reported that the burden they felt when faced with the decision would have been reduced if they had been made aware that the research project had been considered by such a body.

Clinicians Twenty-one (19.5) clinicians reported a problem with information and 52 (48.5%) with understanding.

Almost all clinicians (97, 91%) used an information sheet. 11 clinicians provided a variety of additional other responses (e.g. *depends on the parents; parents not allowed to take the sheet home; parents have to ask to keep it*). Seven clinicians did not use a sheet.

Positive clinician comments regarding the information sheets were that: they were a reassuring aid for parents in that they *legitimised* what the doctor had told parents; they helped the clinician to cover information in a structured way; they permitted parents to look at the information again at a later time when they were perhaps calmer. Negative comments by clinicians included that parents found them difficult to understand or that they forced disclosure of certain risks associated with the research to the parents.

Sixty-six (62%) clinicians thought that parents should be told all information about the research, while 47 (44%) believed that it was better for parents not to know certain information (in a question which had multiple answers). Some doctors reported limiting disclosure about risks either so as not to worry parents, or to obtain consent, and that information was often simplified (with the stated aim of providing the most appropriate information to parents).

Voluntariness

The majority of parents (73.5%) were deemed to have considered themselves to have given consent voluntarily. Only 21 (10.5%) parents reported a problem with voluntariness, yet 59 (55%) clinicians considered this to be a problem. Parents and clinicians reported a variety of problems, the main ones being as follows: lack of time to decide; 'moral obligation' to the NICU or society (this may not necessarily impinge on voluntariness and thus such cases were recorded as 'equivocal'); parents will try anything when desperate or vulnerable; feelings of guilt if they refused to consent; worried that baby's care might be adversely affected if consent refused; told treatment would proceed with or without consent; consent sought after randomisation; consent not sought at all from parents.

> Parent: *I was aware I could refuse, and it was repeated at the time of signature but I feel a moral obligation to help.*
> Parent: *They benefited a little from my weakness. They had just said to me that my child could die at any time. I immediately said 'Yes', then I did not seek other information.*

Informed consent problems compared to urgency and risk of research

See Tables 3a and 3b. Parents of children who were approached for urgent research and for research involving more than no/minimal risk had problems with competence, information, understanding and voluntariness in the informed consent procedure. Breakdown of urgent research into the subdivisions of emergency and protocol urgency, although numbers are small, indicates that emergency research was associated with more problems than protocol urgency alone. The point estimates for the proportion of parents with problems of informed consent suggest that two to three times more parents will have problems with urgent research and research involving more than no/minimal risk compared to non-urgent and no/minimal risk research. The confidence intervals are relatively wide, reflecting the small sample size for this type of analysis, however, even the lower limits still indicate meaningful differences between research which is urgent and non-urgent and that which has more than no/minimal risk or discomfort and no/minimal risk or discomfort. Voluntariness was the least problematic category overall, but differences between research types remain.

3. Views on Informed Consent for Research

The value which parents and clinicians attached to consent for neonatal research was as follows:

Parents Opinion was assessed via three questions (see Table 4). Responses showed resoundingly that parents valued the requirement for a consent process in research.[9] These results are backed up by many statements from parents such as:

> Parent: ... *the baby is mine.   It would be insulting to violate the parent's responsibility to decide. I should get very angry if I was bypassed.*
> Parent: *We thought that it was positive.   In the NICU you feel that you are in another world but we became participants when we were asked.*
> Parent: *The medical environment cannot do what it wants. It is necessary to ask the consent of parents, it is our child.*

It is interesting to note that these views were held despite the fact that 57 (28.5%) parents considered that it was a burden to be asked for their consent.

Clinicians Although frequently stating that informed consent for research was important, clinicians seemed less convinced of its value (see Table 5). The majority of the 107 clinicians stated that they always obtained written consent prior to research. Four obtained oral consent only, three stated that they did not obtain consent, and one stated that informed consent was obtained only if parents were available. Six clinicians stated that they sometimes obtained informed consent retrospectively, following entry of a baby into a trial in an emergency situation. Clinician comments were more varied than those of the parents:

> Clinician:*I don't think that one can experiment on babies without telling the parents what you are doing.*
> Clinician:*Parents are put in difficult situations, they are obliged to trust us and to sign a paper at the same time and that creates a doubt.*
> Clinician:*It is important that the doctor explains everything that occurs, but informed, signed consent is not essential.*
> Clinician:*In my opinion, it is not an informed consent but it is enlightened information which we ask them to sign.*

The clinician responses were perhaps influenced by the belief held by 50 (47%) that the requirement to obtain informed consent sometimes prevents 'some useful neonatal research'.

4. Parental Reasons for Consenting/Refusing to Provide Consent

One hundred and eighty-one parents gave 438 reasons for deciding to allow their baby to participate: 116 (64%) thought their own child would benefit (the decision being taken either rationally or out of desperation as a means of potentially providing help to their very sick baby); 88 (49%) held that it would benefit future infants (either as opposed to or in addition to their own baby), and 71 (39%) saw no risk/distress to their child.

> Parent: *What really convinced us was knowing that the little help from our part could help other babies.*

Reasons parents gave for refusing consent were the perceived risks/distress to their baby, their distrust of research/researchers, their dislike of the tone of approach by the doctor, their shock and inability to decide, the inconvenience of follow-up procedures. One parent refused because she knew the baby was in the control group prior to consent!

> Parent: *It was too much. I built up a fence because I couldn't take any more. I said no to everything that was not immediately good for X.*

5. Training of Doctors in Obtaining Informed Consent for Research

An overwhelming majority (102, 95%) had received no formal training. Most doctors learnt how to request informed consent by observation of more experienced colleagues. While some doctors felt this was adequate preparation, others did not.

DISCUSSION

Method

Inevitably limitations arose from the 'large-scale' design and size of the study, which had an exceptionally big sample for qualitative research. Thus, for example, there was no in-depth observation of the actual consent process and so neither the verbal information given to each parent nor the interactions involved were accessible; there was variability in the trials for which consent was sought, and babies varied in the severity of their illness. However, the reduced depth of data may be offset by the gain in breadth from this cross-cultural study and, therefore, in the validity of its findings.

The methodological limitations should be borne in mind when reviewing the results and their interpretation. First, due to the large, dispersed nature of the study it was not possible to employ planned theoretical sampling. The sample size and distribution varied due to different, practical interviewer resources and to the availability of eligible interviewees, however, this still allowed for saturation of categories in the analysis – that is, a stage was reached, in each country, where the last few interviews added little to the insights gained from earlier interviews. As is usual in a qualitative study, the sample aimed to be representative and not all-inclusive.

Second, there was no central check on the representativeness of the sample and thus there is the possibility that selection bias could have occurred (despite the strict guidelines outlined in the interviewer instruction manual), although we have no evidence to suggest this. Third, a number of interviewers with varying experience and competence were used. Therefore, there was variation in the quality of data gained, but this may also have reflected cultural differences in the length and content of answers. Usually the telephone interviews were shorter and contained less information than those that were face-to-face. However, results were not influenced by the mode of interview. Fourth, the design allowed for variations in the time that passed between the parental interview and the original consent or refusal to neonatal research, although it did stipulate a maximum gap of one year. This design was agreed to balance feasibility with the need to limit problems of memory recall. Although it could be assumed that those parents with the longest lag time had more difficulty remembering events, many of the longer, more detailed transcriptions were from such parents.

Quality of Consent and its Value to Parents and Clinicians

Our findings suggest that the quality of consent given by parents to neonatal research is often problematic; in over two-thirds of cases there was some impairment in at least one of the criteria for valid consent. Previous commentators have expressed the concern that informed consent to neonatal research was likely to be particularly impaired in situations where the infant was critically ill and/or where the time available for obtaining consent was short;[4,10,11] and there has been some research supporting this.[3,12,13] Our findings indicate that consent can be significantly

222 European Neonatal Research: Consent, Ethics Committees and Law

impaired where research is being conducted for emergency research and in research with more than no/minimal risk or discomfort. In these cases both clinicians and parents reported problems such as lack of time and the parents being overwhelmed by emotions (see Table 3). Interestingly, voluntariness did not seem to be as much of a problem for these parents. This may be because clinicians consider the voluntary nature of consent to be an important issue in these situations, to which parents should be alerted.

However, most of the parents we interviewed were approached regarding research projects, such as feeding trials, that were low-risk and where the need for consent was not urgent. The fact that consent to such research was often impaired was a notable finding.

Nonetheless, the process is perceived as worthwhile by most participants. The vigour with which parents protested against the notion of forgoing their consent was striking. This was so even where parents were aware of the limitations in the quality of their consent (e.g. because they hadn't been able to 'think clearly' at the time), or said that the request for consent was an additional burden. Clinicians also valued the process, although apparently less so. They were aware of some of the costs that attach to having a requirement for informed consent in research, such as that it may make some useful projects difficult or impossible to conduct.

One issue which our research left unresolved was the degree to which the four components of informed consent must be met in order for parents to retain their view of the value of the process. For example, it may be that what is of most value to parents is being involved in the decision-making. This requires further investigation.

Improving the Quality of Consent

What, then, follows if the consent being obtained for neonatal research is usually flawed? In a similar context, Edwards et al,[14] suggest that one could either disallow such research, do without consent, or try and obtain the best consent possible, albeit flawed. The latter is their favoured option. At least three areas of possible improvement to the consent process are indicated by our research.

First, in none of the countries examined do researchers receive training explicitly in the process of seeking informed consent. Many parents who had bad experiences were approached inappropriately (see results section 'information and understanding') or were recipients of poor practice (e.g. failure to provide an information sheet). Clearly those who seek consent for neonatal research should have a modicum of communication skills, as should those who seek consent for any medical procedures.[15] Some gaps in parental knowledge were surprising, e.g. 30% did not know that they were free to withdraw from the research at any time. It would seem desirable for key research personnel to receive guidance on legal and ethical constraints governing the process.

Second, when clinicians provide information about research to parents they should not be over-reliant on information sheets since we found that approximately half the parents did not use them prior to giving consent. Also, the level of understanding of the information parents received often fell below that assumed by RECs on the basis of the parent information sheet which had been submitted to them.[16] The best way to use such a sheet might be for the clinician to go through it systematically with parents so that the latter would be able to ask questions, and the clinician would be less likely to miss any points of importance.

Third, few parents were aware of RECs and their role. Some parents told us that the burden they felt when faced with the decision would have been reduced if they had been made aware that such a body had considered the research project. Indeed, a realisation that a research study had received peer review at a number of different levels (including REC review) might provide a comfort that the responsibility of safeguarding their child was to some extent shared, whilst others might regard this as an influence on the voluntariness of participation.

Non-altruistic Consent to Research

Some recent surveys have suggested that research participants consent for reasons of self-interest rather than altruism.[17,18,19] A study specifically focused on neonatal research found parental consent was strongly correlated with the perception of a probable benefit, negatively with a perceived probability of harm.[20] Our research did find that self-interest, in the form of perceived potential benefit over harm for the neonate, was the primary factor influencing parental consent. Altruism was second, with many parents evincing both reasons. For some commentators,[17,21] the fact that research subjects expect benefit is seen as problematic, as a fault of either information or understanding. The thought is that it is unreasonable for research subjects to expect benefit in a situation where there is clinical equipoise between a new treatment available within a trial and the standard treatment that they would receive outside a trial. However, we did not generally record the perception of self-interest as being a fault in information or understanding. It does not seem unreasonable to enter one's child into a trial with the hope that she or he may receive a treatment that turns out to be better than the standard treatment. After all, all trials of new treatments are undertaken by clinicians and scientists who entertain a similar hope.

Doing without Informed Consent

Informed consent in research has gained its place in research practice. It is seen as a vital defence of the welfare of the research subject against poor or unscrupulous research. Given that one of the functions of parental consent is to protect the welfare of the neonate, the fact that such consent is often attenuated is worrying. This supports the view that the key role of protecting the neonate's welfare in research should belong not to parents but to RECs, researchers, grant-giving and professional bodies, and senior staff within the hierarchical hospital structure.[14] Should we, then, do neonatal research without parental consent (sometimes, always, never)? Clearly our empirical research cannot answer this question, but some of our findings may be pertinent to the discussion.

Two main arguments are put forward to suggest that informed consent should not always be required in medical research. Both rely on the assumption that the research itself is scientifically sound and that the welfare of the participant can be protected by other measures. The first suggests that putting patients through the informed consent process is needlessly cruel and should, therefore, be by-passed.[21,22] The second suggests that valuable research is either slowed or prevented because of the informed consent requirement;[23] where such research is of sufficient importance the informed consent requirement should be weakened or forgone.[24]

The first argument is not supported by our findings or those of others.[13,25,26] Many parents did find the request for consent burdensome, but very few thought it unnecessary. It might be suggested that this is because parents were unaware of other protective measures in the research process, such as RECs. However, most of our parents seemed to trust the clinicians to act honourably. Their desire to be asked for consent often seemed to do with being involved in decisions about their child. In a similar way, parents may believe that professional educationalists might make the best decisions about, say, which school their child should attend. Nonetheless most would wish the decision to remain their own. This suggests that informed consent in the realm of neonatal research has an important function in addition to, perhaps even instead of, protecting the neonate's welfare. This may be called something like protecting the parental decision-making role. However our findings do emphasise that often what is being protected here is simply the parental authority to decide, not fully rational parental decision-making. Once again analogies with educational choice may suggest this is perfectly acceptable, but it will be useful for all parties, both clinicians and parents, to become clearer in the future as to what exactly it is that we are valuing here, and the limitations that may be unavoidable in this process.

Our findings are neutral *vis-à-vis* the second argument. Whilst it may be important to protect parental decision-making, it is a matter of discussion as to whether it is so important that research that is unable to do this should be ruled impermissible. Furthermore, we did not ask parents about specific types of situation where parental consent might be by-passed. Hence, it may be that parents would agree with the notion of doing without consent in emergencies, or in comparing two treatments that are already established. However, the fact that the parents we interviewed expressed a strong attachment to the principle of informed consent suggests that it is not something that should be by-passed without very good reason.

As one parent explained:

> *I'm sure there are times when you would want to say "You decide", but you can't. They're your children, your responsibility, right from the moment they're born. You should be involved in the decision, but you should have a lot of help making it. The more information you have, the easier it will be for you to make that decision.*

Notes

1. Chapter 17 has been reproduced in similar form in the *Lancet* 2000; 356: 2045-51.
2. Beauchamp T, Childress J. *Principles of Biomedical Ethics* 4th edn. New York OUP 1994: 142-146.
3. Levene M, Wright I, Griffiths G. Is informed consent in neonatal randomised controlled trials ritual? *Lancet* 1996; 347: 474.
4. Editorial. Your baby is in a trial. *Lancet* 1995; 345: 805-6.
5. Kennedy I, Grubb A. *Medical Law: text with materials* 2nd ed. London, Butterworths. 1994. 1052.
6. McLean S. Commentary: No consent means not treating the patient with respect. *BMJ* 1997; 314: 1076.
7. Moser C, Kalton G. Survey methods in social investigation. Heinemann, London. 1971.

8.   Neuberger J. Ethics and Health Care. The role of research ethics committees in the United Kingdom. King's Fund Institute, London 1992.

9.   The discrepancies between questions 4a and questions 4b and 4c are probably explained by the fact that for the first question parents took themselves to be speaking on their own behalf, whilst in the latter two respondents usually interpreted them as referring to parents in general and thus tended to qualify their answers; there were comments such as 'some parents might', 'people are different'.

10. Modi N. Letter – Neonatal Research. *Lancet* 1998; 351:530.

11. Morley C. Letter – Consent is not always practical in emergency treatments. *BMJ* 1997; 314: 1477.

12. Snowdon C, Garcia J, Elbourne D. Making sense of randomization; responses of parents of critically ill babies to random allocation of treatment in a clinical trial. *Social Science in Medicine* 1997; 45: 1337-1355.

13. Culbert A, Brown A, Davis D J.   Consent procedures for neonatal resuscitation research: A survey of parental preferences. *Pediatric Research* 1999: 45:34A.

14. Edwards S, Lilford R, Braunholtz D, Jackson J, Hewison J, Thornton J. Ethical issues in the design and conduct of randomised controlled trials. *Health Technology Assessment* 1998; 2(15) 1-132.

15. Wiltshire C. Letter – Communication with potential subjects needs to be effective. *BMJ* 1997; 314: 1477.

16. Williams C, Zwitter M. Informed consent in European multicentre randomised controlled trials - Are patients really informed? *European Journal of Cancer* 1994; 30A: 907-10.

17. Edwards S, Lilford R, Hewison J. The ethics of randomised controlled trials from the perspectives of patients, the public, and healthcare professionals. *BMJ* 1998; 317: 1209-12.

18. Singhal N, Oberle K, Huber J, Burgess E. Parents perceptions of research with newborns. *Pediatric Research* 1999; 45:35A.

19. Sugarman J, Kass N, Goodman S, Parentesis P, Fernandes P, Faden R. What patients say about medical research. *IRB: A Review of Human Subject Research* 1998; 20(4): 1-7.

20. Zupancic J, Gillie P, Streiner D, Watts J, Schmidt B. Determinants of parental authorization for involvement of newborn infants in clinical trials. *Pediatrics* 1997; 99(1): 117, e6 (www.pediatrics.org/cgi/content/full/99/1/e6).

21. Tobias J, Souhami R. Fully informed consent can be needlessly cruel. *BMJ* 1993; 307: 119-120.

22. Tobias J. *BMJ's* present policy (sometimes approving research in which patients have not given fully informed consent) is wholly correct. *BMJ* 1997; 314: 1111-4.

23. Truog R D, Robinson W, Randolph A. Is informed consent always necessary for randomized controlled trials? *The New England Journal of Medicine* 1999: 340: 804-807.

24. Collins R, Doll R, Peto R. Ethics of Clinical Trials. In: Williams C. [ed.] *Introducing New Treatments for Cancer: Practical, Ethical and Legal Problems*. Chichester, Wiley 1992: 49-65.

25. Singal N, Burgess E, Amin H. Parents make informed decisions for research in NICUs. *Pediatric Research* 1999; 45:35A.

26. Davis D J, Brown A, Culbert A.   Physician preferences for consent procedures in neonatal resuscitation research. *Pediatric Research* 1999; 45: 34A.

Table 17.1 Interviews by Country

Country	Parents	Clinicians	Geographical spread of participating Neonatal Intensive Care Units
Denmark	23	9	Aalborg, Arhus, Holbaek, Hvidovre, Kolding, Naestved, Rigshospitalet
Finland	34	11	Helsinki, Kuopio, Oulu, Tampere, Turku
France	30	19	Lille, Paris (Hopitals Beclere, Port-Royal & Institut Brune), Tours
Germany	6	6	Freiburg
Greece	-	10	Athens (Mitera Maternity, St Sofia's Children's Hospital, University of Ioannina)
Italy	38	15	Brindisi, Foggia, Padua
Spain	24	4	Alicante (Hospital Universitario de San Juan & Hospital Universitario de Alicante), Valencia
Sweden	20	16	Göteburg, Linköping, Lund, Stockholm, Uppsala
UK	25	17	Bristol, Leeds, Liverpool, London
Total	**200**	**107**	

Table 17.2a   Parental Interviews (n = 200) Breakdown of Problem Category

	Competence	Information	Understanding	Voluntariness
Problem	42 (21%)	43 (21.5%)	44 (22%)	21 (10.5%)
No problem	120 (60%)	95 (47.5%)	105 (52.5%)	147 (73.5%)
Equivocal	29 (14.5%)	35 (17.5%)	38 (19%)	25 (12.5%)
Insufficient data to categorise	9 (4.5%)	27 (13.5%)	13 (6.5%)	7 (3.5%)

Table 17.2b   Clinician Interviews (n = 107) Breakdown of Problem Category

	Competence	Information	Understanding	Voluntariness
Problem	79 (74%)	21 (19.5%)	52 (48.5%)	59 (55%)

Table 17.3a Part 1: Categories of informed consent for parents (n=200) approached for urgent (emergency and protocol urgency) and non-urgent research

	Urgent		Non-urgent (n = 135)	Unknown Category (n=15)
	Emergency (n = 30)	Protocol Urgency (n = 20)		
COMPETENCE				
Problem	15 (50%)	4 (20%)	19 (14%)	4 (27%)
No problem	9 (30%)	7 (35%)	95 (70%)	9 (60%)
Equivocal	5 (17%)	8 (40%)	14 (10%)	2 (13%)
Insufficient data to categorise	1 (3%)	1 (5%)	7 (5%)	0
INFORMATION				
Problem	17 (57%)	3 (15%)	21 (16%)	2 (13%)
No problem	11 (37%)	12 (60%)	67 (50%)	5 (33%)
Equivocal	2 (3%)	5 (25%)	23 (17%)	6 (40%)
Insufficient data to categorise	0 (0%)	0 (0%)	24 (18%)	2 (13%)
UNDERSTANDING				
Problem	16 (53%)	3 (15%)	22(16%)	3 (20%)
No problem	11 (37%)	11 (55%)	74 (55%)	9 (60%)
Equivocal	3 (10%)	6 (30%)	26 (19%)	3 (20%)
Insufficient data to categorise	0 (0%)	0 (0%)	13 (10%)	0
VOLUNTARINESS				
Problem	7 (23%)	3 (15%)	10 (8%)	1 (7%)
No problem	16 (53%)	11 (55%)	107 (79%)	13 (87%)
Equivocal	6 (20%)	5 (25%)	13 (10%)	1 (7%)
Insufficient data to categorise	1 (3%)	1 (5%)	5 (3%)	0

Table 17.3a   Part 2: A comparison of urgent versus non-urgent research on categories of informed consent using confidence intervals

% problem	Urgent	Non-urgent	Difference in %	95% CI for difference
Competency	9.6%(**19**)	14.8%(**19**)	24.7%	(9.6, 39.9%)
Information	40.0%(**20**)	18.9%(**21**)	21.1%	(5.7, 36.5%)
Understanding	38.0%(**19**)	18.0%(**22**)	20.0%	(4.9, 35.1%)
Voluntariness	20.8%(**10**)	7.7%(**10**)	13.1%	(0.8, 25.5%)

Note that for ease of interpretation of confidence intervals, the missing data have been excluded.

Table 17.3b   Part 1: Categories of informed consent for parents (n=200) approached for research with more than and no more than 'no/minimal risk or discomfort'

	Risk or discomfort (n=31)	No/minimal risk or discomfort (n=154)	Risk or discomfort unknown (n=15)
COMPETENCE			
Problem	13 (42%)	25 (16%)	4 (27%)
No problem	13 (42%)	98 (64%)	9 (60%)
Equivocal	4 (13%)	23 (15%)	2 (13%)
Insufficient data to categorise	1 (3%)	8 (5%)	0
INFORMATION			
Problem	14 (45%)	27 (18%)	2 (13%)
No problem	13 (42%)	77 (50%)	5 (33%)
Equivocal	4 (13%)	26 (17%)	6 (40%)
Insufficient data to categorise	0 (0%)	24 (15%)	2 (13%)
UNDERSTANDING			
Problem	16 (52%)	25 (16%)	3 (20%)
No problem	10 (32%)	86 (56%)	9 (60%)
Equivocal	5 (16%)	30 (19%)	3 (20%)
Insufficient data to categorise	0 (0%)	13 (8%)	0
VOLUNTARINESS			
Problem	5 (16%)	15 (10%)	1 (7%)
No problem	16 (52%)	118 (77%)	13 (87%)
Equivocal	8 (26%)	15 (10%)	2 (13%)
Insufficient data to categorise	1 (3%)	6 (4%)	0

Table 17.3b   Part 2: A comparison of research with more than and no more than 'no/minimal risk or discomfort' on categories of informed consent using confidence intervals

% problem	Risk or discomfort	No/minimal risk or discomfort	Difference in %	95% CI for difference
Competency	43.3%(13)	17.1%(25)	26.2%	(7.5, 45.0%)
Information	45.2%(14)	20.8%(27)	24.4%	(5.5, 43.2%)
Understanding	51.6%(16)	17.7%(25)	34%	(15.2, 52.6%)
Voluntariness	17.2%(5)	10.1%(15)	7.1%	(-7.5, 21.7%)

Note that for ease of interpretation of confidence intervals, the missing data have been excluded.

Parental Views on Informed Consent for Research

Table 17.4a

Question: Now that you have been asked for your consent for (name) to take part in a study, do you think it right in general for parents to be asked to give consent?

Yes	193	(96.5%)
No	4	(2%)
Don't know	0	
*Other	13	(6.5%)
Total replies	*210*	*(multiple answers)*

> * Must have consultation with parents
> Emergency is an exception
> Doctor is best person to decide
> Pointed out that general care is given by doctors without parental consent

Table 17.4b

Question: Do you perhaps think this is something parents might wish to be relieved of doing?

Yes	43	(21.5%)
No	120	(60%)
Don't know	9	(4.5%)
*Other	29	(14.5%)
No information	17	(13.5%)
Total replies	*218*	*(multiple answers)*

> * Answered in terms of parents in general, not necessarily themselves:
> Some might
> People are different
> In some circumstances
> If protocol is 'extremely complicated'

Table 17.4c

Question: Do you think that medical staff should be left to decide alone?

Yes	21	(10.5%)
No	151	(75.5%)
Don't know	0	
*Other	28	(14%)
No information	16	(8%)
Total replies	*216*	*(multiple answers)*

* Depends on study/situation
  For emergency treatment
  When parents unable to understand
  Could start trial then ask for consent
  Should be a joint decision between doctors and parents

Clinician Views on Informed Consent for Research

Table 17.5a

Question: Do you think that informed consent from parents should *always* be a requirement before RCTs involving neonates are undertaken?

Yes	75	(70%)
Desirable	5	(4.5%)
No	20	(18.5%)
Consent not always obtained	4	(4%)
Don't know	0	
*Other	20	(19%)
Total replies		*124 (multiple answers)*

* Is a legal requirement
  Equivocal
  Not for established/non-invasive/observational research,
  Post randomisation consent
  Retrospective consent for emergency/urgency trials
  Should have signature from both parents
  No need to have signature from both parents.

Table 17.5b

Question: Do you think that there are situations where you would prefer the decision to rest with the clinicians?

Yes	37 (35%)
No	56 (52%)
Yes and no	1 (1%)
Parents may want doctors to take responsibility	4 (4%)
Don't know	2 (2%)
*Other	7 (6.5%)
No information	9 (8%)
Total replies	*115 (multiple answers)*

* Consent is a legal requirement
  Would be easier
  Yes if supported by RECs

18 Is Parental 'Informed Consent' Always Necessary for Research Involving Newborn Infants?[1]

DR N. MODI

History of Informed Consent

> ... each potential subject must be adequately informed of the aims, methods, anticipated benefits and potential hazards of the study and the discomfort it may entail ... where the subject is a minor, permission from the responsible relative replaces that of the subject in accordance with national legislation. [Declaration of Helsinki, revised 1975, 1983, 1989 and 1996]

The requirement to obtain 'informed' consent from patients is a relatively recent development in the history of medical research. Article 1 of the Nuremberg Code, the first international ethical code for human medical research, drawn up in 1947, states 'the voluntary consent of the human subject is absolutely essential' but it was not until the 1960s that this requirement became widely acknowledged.

For much of history, dating back to the time of Hippocrates, the practice of medicine was largely authoritarian. The notion of beneficence, 'doing good', was believed to justify a paternalistic attitude. It was thought unnecessary to seek an individual's consent to treatment and to research. This view has changed. Although the shift in attitude is often attributed solely to recognition of the autonomy of the individual, it is also true that society is changing. The public is better educated; there is wider understanding of medicine and science. Perhaps one should say that we are now better prepared for the exercise of our autonomy.

238 European Neonatal Research: Consent, Ethics Committees and Law

What is the Purpose of Informed Consent?

For research involving competent adults, obtaining informed consent is a process that recognises and respects the autonomy of the individual. Its purpose is to enable adults to make informed choices about themselves and to safeguard their own best interests, in the full knowledge of risks versus potential benefits. Is the case the same when a parent makes choices on behalf of an infant? Rather than examining the issue of 'informed consent' from a legal, parental or purely 'ethical' perspective, as has been done all too often, I suggest that it should be approached with the question of how the infant might be protected from harm and how the best interests of the infant might be safeguarded.

Protecting the Infant from Harm

In general, parents are charged with responsibility for protecting their infant from harm. In reality they clearly receive help in this, in various forms, be it in the provision of safe water, consumer protection legislation, road safety measures and so on. The history of medical research makes it clear that patients do need to be protected from unscrupulous researchers. What is not widely appreciated by patients and parents is that safeguards do exist. Clinical research today is usually subject to peer scrutiny at multiple levels. In the UK, by the time a clinical research project begins, it will have been reviewed by a number of bodies, including for example, the investigator's departmental research ethics committee, an institutional research ethics committee, a grant awarding body and, in the case of multicentre trials, by a UK national multicentre research ethics committee.

McIntosh [1993] suggests that it is the research ethics committees that should shoulder a large part of the responsibility for ensuring that the infant's interests are being safeguarded. Parents should be told that these safeguards exist. This seems a sensible approach given that appropriately constituted research ethics committees are the bodies best suited to rationally consider the risks and benefits of proposed research, the validity of the hypothesis and the robustness of the methodology.

Randomised clinical trials should be preceded by systematic review of relevant published literature and by proof of professional equipoise. Observational research should only be acceptable if risks are negligible or minimal. In order for research ethics committees to take prime responsibility for protecting the infant from harm, they must be properly constituted to include the expertise necessary to make these and other evaluations, their function must be regulated and they must be consistent and not idiosyncratic in their approach. The Euricon study has shown that there is need for improvement in the constitution and functioning of research ethics committees.

Safeguarding the Best Interests of the Infant

A foremost concern is that an infant should receive the best possible treatment option. But what if, as is often the case, the best option is not known? If the best treatment is unknown and there is a choice of treatments, the only approach that apportions the risk of benefit and the risk of unexpected side effect equally, is the randomised controlled trial. In this situation doctors should be expected to regard the evaluation of treatments as a duty to patients not to continue to use treatments without doing everything possible to assess their true worth [Brewin 1985]. As this is the only approach that would protect patients from the continued use of ineffective or harmful treatments, treatment within a randomised controlled trial is in the patient's best interests. However instead of requiring doctors to make this point to patients, we have the present illogical position that not only allows a doctor to use a treatment that he or she merely *thinks* is best, but for which there is no clear evidence of benefit, but also positively forbids them from pointing out situations where entry into a randomised controlled trial is in the patient's best interests.

Parental Autonomy and the Rights of the Infant

The term autonomy means self rule. To accept a person's autonomy is to accept his right to make decisions about himself *even if those decisions are not in his best interests.* Translating the concept of autonomy to a newborn baby is difficult. Should a baby be regarded only as an extension of his or her parents? Do parents have a right to make decisions that are not in their infants' best interests? It can be argued that where entry into a randomised controlled trial is in an infant's best interests, to allow parents to refuse trial entry is to allow them to harm their infant. The problem is that society is ambivalent in its view of parental rights, or the exercise of parental autonomy to the detriment of the rights of the infant. There are parental behaviours that are harmful to children, such as smoking, that society is prepared to accept. There are others, such as refusing a diabetic child insulin, or, as in a current controversial issue in the UK, smacking children, that it is not.

The harm that can arise from failure to conduct research, for whatever reason, is worth emphasising. Collins et al [1992] contrasted what they considered 'humanely inappropriate' written informed consent procedures required in the United States in a trial of streptokinase and aspirin in acute myocardial infarction, with the United Kingdom where consent was obtained in the manner considered best for the individual patient. Recruitment was extremely poor in the United States and the resulting delay in completing the study probably led to thousands of deaths. There are many other such examples, spanning the history of modern neonatal care. An early, salutary example dates from the 1950s when favourable anecdotal reports led to the introduction of routine prophylactic administration of penicillin together with sulfisoxazole to newborn infants admitted to the Babies Hospital in New York to reduce the risk of infection. In 1954 a new prophylactic regimen, subcutaneous oxytetracycline, was suggested and a randomised trial of the two options commenced [Silverman et al, 1956]. Although the number of fatal infections was lower with the standard treatment (penicillin with sulfisoxazole), unexpectedly overall mortality was very much higher and was shown to be due to kernicterus, which occurred almost exclusively in this group. The mechanism for this unexpected association, namely the increased risk of bilirubin toxicity caused by sulphonamides, has since been unravelled. The lesson was quite clearly that had the then standard treatment been subjected to rigorous assessment prior to its routine introduction, many more infants would have survived or been spared brain damage. More recently a study addressing the use of acetazolamide and furosemide to treat post haemorrhagic ventriculomegaly in preterm infants has shown that though this combination of drugs has become part of the accepted approach in the treatment of the condition, it was not until it was tested in a randomised controlled trial that it became apparent that outcome was worse than with no drug therapy [International PHVD Trial Group, 1998].

Infants need to be protected not only from unscrupulous researchers, but also from the harm that may arise from being denied entry into a trial and being allowed to continue with an unevaluated treatment. Clinical trials are now regarded as an essential and routine part of good clinical practice [Baum, 1993], a view that has been endorsed by the Department of Health [1992]. This ought to be conveyed to patients and parents and the Research Ethics Committee that has approved the research should *take responsibility for the decision by advising parents with a positive recommendation.* Failure to advise that entry into a clinical trial is in the baby's best interests is wrong if it denies the infant justice, given that unevaluated new technologies are as likely to be worse as to be better than the existing treatment [Chalmers & Chalmers 1994]. It is also in direct conflict with two further principles integral to ethical medical practice, beneficence and non-maleficence.

The Requirements of Informed Consent

In order to give informed consent, a person must be given adequate information, must understand it and must be competent to use it. It is also held that there must be no coercion and that consent must be given freely or voluntarily. The Euricon study has shown that these requirements are met in full on only a minority of occasions.

Many adults [Cassileth et al 1980; Mason 1997] think that the main purpose of written consent is to protect those conducting the trial, that is, they do not appreciate their responsibilities towards their infant with regard to the conduct of research.

Parents may not really understand that they are being asked to consent to participation in research [Broyles, Tyson & Uauy, 1990; Elbourne, Snowdon & Garcia, 1997]. A problem found in the Euricon study was difficulty in understanding the difference between therapy and a therapeutic trial. Gallo et al [1995] compared classical informed consent and randomised consent procedures in surrogate patients. These were volunteers who had attended a scientific exhibition. They were educated, interested and uninfluenced by the pressures of illness or a clinical setting. Nevertheless, despite a poster display clarifying the basic principles of clinical research, failure to understand the issues was very common.

The Euricon project and other studies have shown not only that parents often do not understand the research but also that the extent to which the requirements for informed consent can be met varies between different types of trials. For example in a randomised controlled trial involving emergency treatment, the amount of information that can be conveyed and understood will be less than for a trial into which recruitment is not urgent. The importance of an information sheet that is given to parents after discussion of the research, so that it might be referred to later, was emphasised in the Euricon study.

Parents may experience anger and frustration from a feeling that they have little control over decisions, as well as from being put in the position of having to make a decision. Some parents reported being distressed by the consent process. They feared that participation in the decision would make them feel guilty if things went badly for their baby, a problem that has been reported by others [Broyles, Tyson, Uauy, 1990]. Others were under the impression that they had some sort of obligation to sign or that their baby's care would be adversely affected if they did not consent even though they had been told that it would not. When consent was required urgently, parents often spoke of events seeming out of control, of being overwhelmed with other emotions and of having to put their trust in the doctor. Unfortunately the Euricon study included only a few interviews from parents who refused consent (although the proportion of these was in keeping with the percentage of parents reported by clinicians as refusing consent (6%, 13/200)).

Caring for the Whole Family

The Euricon study found that many parents stated that one of the reasons that they agreed to participation was because they trusted the doctor to act in the best interest of their baby. However nearly all said that they did not wish doctors to make decisions without involving parents. Parents want to be involved but they also want good counsel. The need for patients, and parents, to receive counsel surfaces frequently. Good medicine requires that a doctor offer counsel, but in the context of research doctors are forbidden to advise honestly because some view this as coercion so that in this case the patient or parent would not be consenting freely. The perception that it is coercion to recommend participation in a research trial is not in accord with the philosophy that recognises the importance of the doctor/patient relationship, in which it is recognised that trust forms an essential element of good care. There is a double standard at work when it is legitimate to recommend and even prescribe an insufficiently researched drug, even though this puts the patient at risk, but not considered acceptable to recommend entry into a randomised controlled trial, when this is the only approach that allocates both the risk of harm and the chance of benefit equitably [Chalmers & Chalmers, 1994; Keatinge, 1993]. Given that the researcher believes that participation in the research is in the baby's best interests, there is an irreconcilable conflict if the doctor seeking consent from parents is also responsible for caring for their baby, and is unable to offer what to him is good counsel because this might be construed as coercive.

Every clinician is aware that it is not unusual for parents to want someone to advise them but there are very few studies addressing this objectively. Zupanic et al [1997], in a study of the determinants of parental consent, found that a third of parents agreed with the statement 'I would prefer to have the doctors advise me whether my baby should be in the study, rather than asking me to decide'. In an Australian trial of asthma therapy [Harth & Thong, 1995], 15% of parents had faith in their physician's advice and thought the consent procedure unnecessary. In the Australian study [Harth & Thong, 1990], consenting parents had a lower level of postsecondary education and professional occupation than those refusing, though the study by Zupancic et al [1997], which took place in a large Canadian centre, did not find any difference in sociodemographic characteristics.

The following passage [Ingelfinger, 1980] will testify to the fact that even doctors, when unwell, want to feel that the physician caring for them is able and prepared to make decisions on their behalf. It was written by the late Dr Franz Ingelfinger, editor of the New England Journal of Medicine for many years until shortly before his death from cancer. After he had learnt of his diagnosis he wrote:

> I received from physician friends throughout the country a barrage of well-intentioned but contradictory advice ... as a result not only I but my wife, my son, and daughter-in-law (all doctors), and other family members became increasingly confused and emotionally distraught. Finally when the pangs of indecision had become nearly intolerable, one wise physician friend said 'What you need is a doctor'. He was telling me to forget the information I had already had and the information I was receiving from many quarters, and to seek instead a person who would tell me what to do, who would in a paternalistic manner assume responsibility for my care. When this excellent advice was followed, my family and I sensed immediate and immense relief.

More information is needed about the extent to which parents would either prefer to be guided or to take sole responsibility for decisions. An exploration is also needed of the potentially adverse psychological effects on parents of being compelled to make decisions if they would rather be guided [Fallowfield, Hall, Maguire et al, 1994].

Parental Involvement

The Euricon study has shown that the process of seeking parental consent is important and is valued by parents. *The conclusion from the Euricon investigation was that what parents valued from the consent procedure was being involved.* Parents did not want to be asked for consent because it was

244 European Neonatal Research: Consent, Ethics Committees and Law

their right, or because it supported their autonomy, but because *they wanted to participate in decisions about the care of their baby.* The Euricon study has also suggested that parental consent does not play a key role in defending the best interests of the infant. This lends weight to the view that insistence on a rigid approach to parental consent may do harm by denying the infant's right to participate in research. Insistence that parents be 'fully informed' rather than 'sufficiently informed', as recommended by the Royal College of Paediatrics and Child Health [1999] may not only be impossible to achieve but may possibly harm parents themselves [Brewin 1997; Tobias & Souhami 1993]. A better approach would be to accept that different forms of consent are possible and valid. An emphasis should be placed on the need to discuss matters as fully as is possible and reasonable, whilst accepting the constraints of understanding, education, intelligence, clinical circumstance and time, all of which play a role in the world of real medicine.

A Flexible Approach

Clinical research takes several different forms and calls for different approaches. This is analogous to the situation in clinical practice and highlights the fact that good clinical research is an essential component of good clinical care.

For example, if the research in question is a trial comparing two treatments that are both used in routine clinical practice, neither of which require parental consent, there is a more appropriate requirement than that of consent. This is one that acknowledges the wish of most parents to be involved in their infant's care, by explaining to parents that all babies were being allocated to one or other option because it was uncertain which was best and that this approach would equitably apportion both potential benefit and risk of harmful or ineffective treatment.

A reasonable approach in non-interventional observational research that is without risk is to ask if parents wish to opt out of participation in research rather than opt in [Mutch & King, 1985]. This approach recognises that in many instances refusal of consent is in fact no more than avoidance of having to make a decision, an understandable human response, especially in times of stress.

Consent need not necessarily be an all or nothing matter but might be sought at different levels. For example a justifiable criticism of many randomised trials is that failure to include all eligible subjects limits generalisability. Parental refusal of consent to participate should not preclude requesting permission from them to collect information on outcome in order to determine to what extent participants differed from non-participants, which would allow some assessment of the extent to which the study was generalisable [Silverman & Altman, 1996].

Research involving emergency treatments is a clear example of a situation when obtaining consent may well not be possible. Levene et al [1996] suggest that in such studies, further information should be provided *after* randomisation at a 'rate commensurate with the parent's understanding'.

Methods incorporating an element of patient choice have been discussed by Silverman and Altman [1996]. Some such as the Zelen [1979] approach have been criticised on both methodological as well as ethical grounds. What does appear to be clear is that patients need to be both better educated and more involved in research design, that there is a distinction to be drawn between informed choice and subjective preference, and that there needs to be flexibility in research design.

The Way Forward

The Euricon study has shown that the 'informed consent' process as currently applied, is flawed. But given that the study has shown that it is the sharing of information and being involved that parents value, at this point we should pause and ask whether we are chasing the wrong goal. For rigorously scrutinised, randomised controlled trials that have received expert peer review, the informed consent process plays little part in protecting the infant from harm. It is also questionable whether 'informed consent' is necessary to support parental autonomy if this takes precedence over the right of the infant to participate in research.

Though I believe that it is unacceptable to involve infants in research without the knowledge of their parents, it appears no more than fact that a rigid approach to 'fully informed' consent is sometimes not achievable, sometimes not necessary, and sometimes harmful [Collins et al 1992]. A rational goal is 'reasonably informed consent' or for research in emergency situations, 'reasonably informed assent'. Evidence suggests that an informed public and involved parents are more, not less, likely to demand participation in clinical research [Baum1993; Elbourne1987; Forsythe 1994; Keatinge 1993; Thornton 1993]. At present, parents and the public are insufficiently aware of the reasons for and nature of research and about concepts like randomisation.

The question 'Is it ethical to conduct research in infants?' has no place today. It is an outdated view that incorporates the hidden assumption that research is more likely to cause harm than benefit. However, for research that is methodologically sound, expertly peer-reviewed, rigorously conducted, and closely scrutinized by both parents and professionals, this is untrue. Good medicine requires good evidence. Good evidence is best provided by good research. To paraphrase Sir Austin Bradford Hill [1990], a more appropriate statement for the twenty-first century is 'It is unethical to exclude the newborn from medical research'.

Note

1. This paper was presented by the author at a Euricon Colloquium held in Freiburg, Germany, on 8-10 October 1998, to promote discussion at the Colloquium.

References

Baum M. New approach for recruitment into randomised controlled trials. *Lancet* 1993; 341: 812-813.

Brewin TB. Truth, trust, paternalism. *Lancet* 1985; ii: 490-2.

Brewin TB. 'Blanket' consent to trials would be a good idea. *British Medical Journal* 1997; 314: 253.

Broyles RS, Tyson JE, Uauy R. Informed consent for clinical care and research: an unwarranted double standard? *Pediatric Research* 1990; 27: 200A.

Cassileth ER, Zupkis RV, Sutton-Smith K, March V. Informed consent - why are its goals imperfectly realised? *New England Journal of Medicine* 1980; 302: 896-900.

Chalmers I, Chalmers TC. Randomisation and patient choice. *Lancet* 1994; 344: 892-93.

Collins R, Doll R, Peto R. Ethics of clinical trials. In Williams CJ ed. *Introducing new treatments of cancer: practical ethical and legal problems*. Chichester: Wiley 1992; 49-65.

Department of Health, Advisory Group on Health Technology Assessment for the Director of Research and Development. Assessing the effects of health technologies: principles, practice, proposals. London, 1992.

Elbourne D. Subjects' views about participation in a randomised controlled trial. *Journal of Reproductive and Infant Psychology* 1987; 5: 3-8.

Elbourne D, Snowdon C, Garcia J. Informed consent. Subjects may not understand concept of clinical trials. *British Medical Journal* 1997 Jul 26; 315: 248-9.

Fallowfield LJ, Hall A, Maguire P et al. Psychological effects of being offered choice of surgery for breast cancer. *British Medical Journal* 1994; 309: 448.

Forsythe P. Research utilization and the consumers of care: The parent's perspective. *Journal of Obstetric, Gynaecologic and Neonatal Nursing* 1994; 23: 350-351.

Gallo C, Perrone F, De Placido S, Giusti C. Informed versus randomised consent to clinical trials. *Lancet* 1995; 346: 1060-64.

Harth SC, Thong YH. Sociodemographic and motivational characteristics of parents who volunteer their children for clinical research: a controlled study. *British Medical Journal* 1990; 300: 1372-5.

Harth SC, Thong YH. Parental perceptions and attitudes about informed consent in clinical research involving children. *Social Science and Medicine* 1995; 40: 1573-7.

Hill AB. Suspended judgement. Memories of the British streptomycin trial in tuberculosis. *Controlled Clinical Trials* 1990; 11: 77-79.

Ingelfnger FJ. Arrogance *New England Journal of Medicine* 1980; 303: 1507-11.

International Post Haemorrhagic Ventricular Dilatation Trial Group. International randomised controlled trial of acetazolamide and furosemide in posthaemorrhagic ventricular dilatation in infancy. *Lancet* 1998; 352: 433-40.

Keatinge R. Clinical judgement determines disclosure. *British Medical Journal* 1993; 307: 1496.

Levene M, Wright I, Griffiths G. Is informed consent in neonatal randomised trials ritual? *Lancet* 1996; 347: 475.

McIntosh N. Strengthen ethical committees' role. *Archives of Disease in Childhood* 1993; 307: 1496.

Mason S. Obtaining informed consent for neonatal randomised controlled trials - an elaborate ritual? *Archives of Disease in Childhood* 1997; 76: F143-F145.

Mutch L, King R Obtaining parental consent - opting in or opting out? *Archives of Disease in Childhood* 1985; 60: 979-80.

The Nuremburg Code. Reprinted in *Dictionary of Medical Ethics* (2nd edn) (eds Duncan AS, Dunstan GR, Welbourn RB) pp 130-2. Darton, Longman & Todd, London 1981.

Royal College of Paediatrics and Child Health. Safeguarding informed parental involvement in clinical research involving newborn babies and infants. RCPCH, London, 1999.

Silverman WA, Altman DG. Patient's preferences and randomised trials. *Lancet* 1996; 347: 171-74.

Silverman WA, Anderson DH, Blanc WA, Crozier DN. A difference in mortality rate and incidence of kernicterus among premature infants allotted two prophylactic antibacterial regimens. *Pediatrics* 1956; 18: 614-25.

Thornton H. Raise public awareness of the principles of clinical trials. *British Medical Journal* 1993; 307: 1496.

Tobias JS, Souhami RL. Fully informed consent can be needlessly cruel. *British Medical Journal* 1993; 307: 1199-1201.

World Medical Association. The Declaration of Helsinki. Ferney-Voltaire, France: The Association, 1964; revised in 1975, 1983, 1989 and 1996 (also *New England Journal of Medicine*, 1964; 271: 473-4).

Zelen M. A new design for randomised controlled trials. *New England Journal of Medicine* 1979; 300: 1242-5.

Zupancic JAF, Gillie P, Streiner DL, Watts JL, Schmidt B. Determinants of parental authorization for involvement of newborn infants in clinical trials. *Pediatrics* 1997; 99(1). URL http://www.pediatrics.org/cgi/content/full/99/1/e6.

19   Doing Without Informed Consent for Some Neonatal Studies?

PROFESSOR D. BRATLID

The practice of obtaining informed consent from patients involved in medical research was first clearly expressed in The Nuremberg Code,[1] which defined informed consent as an absolute condition for medical research. This principle was later modified by The Declaration of Helsinki,[2] first adopted by the World Medical Assembly in 1964 and last amended in 1996. This declaration made a distinction between therapeutic and non-therapeutic research, and also introduced the concept of informed consent *by proxy*. This approach has also made it possible to recruit patients who could not consent themselves, such as unconscious patients and children, to medical research. Informed consent *by proxy* is thus the term used to describe the form of informed consent related to research involving newborn infants. These views have been further expressed in the Council of Europe's 1996 Convention for the Protection of Human Rights and Dignity of the Human Being with Regard to the Application of Biology and Medicine.[3]

Informed Consent

The process of informed consent includes several separate elements that must be present if a consent, once obtained, is to be considered valid (see Chapter 1). Firstly, the person giving consent must be mentally competent to do so (competence); secondly, sufficient information must be given to the patient in order to make it possible for the patient to make an informed decision, based on possible benefits and possible risks involved in the project (information); thirdly, this information must also be understood by the patient so a reasoned choice can be made (understanding); and finally, giving consent must be a voluntary process (voluntariness), the patient or the parent must never feel an obligation to consent.

Informed Consent in Neonatal Research

Several studies have shown that the process of informed consent *by proxy* is highly appreciated by most parents when a newborn infant is eligible for a research project (see Chapter 17).[4,5] However, the validity of informed consent *by proxy* is also questionable because of obvious weaknesses; those related to the mental state of the parents shortly after the birth of a (unexpectedly) sick baby, as well as those related to the short time frame available for obtaining such consent, particularly in research protocols involving critically ill infants.[4,6] The Euricon project has shown that the quality of consent given by parents to neonatal research is often rather problematic (see Chapter 17); some impairment in at least one of the four criteria for valid consent was found in over two-thirds of the 200 cases evaluated.

Doing Without Informed Consent

Informed consent is seen as a vital defence of the welfare of the research subject against poor or unscrupulous research. However, the fact that the validity of such consent quite often can be questioned has to some extent resulted in a more flexible attitude towards the necessity of obtaining informed consent, particularly in research projects where informed consent would complicate, delay or even make research impossible. This development has been further influenced by distinguishing between therapeutic and non-therapeutic research, where the suggestion is that greater risk for the patient is acceptable in therapeutic research, as well as less need for obtaining a fully defined informed consent, since the patient would benefit from the study. This has further led to the introduction of alternative notions such as 'retrospective consent', 'delayed consent' or even 'presumed consent' (see Table 1).[7]

Table 1. Different forms of consent in medical research

Mode of research	*Modes of informed consent*
Therapeutic	informed consent informed consent by proxy delayed consent retrospective consent presumed consent hypothetical consent
non-therapeutic	informed consent informed consent by proxy

Source: Adapted from Ruyter 1997.

On this basis several arguments have been put forward to justify the claim that informed consent should not always be required in medical research. These arguments rely on the assumptions that the research is itself always scientifically sound and in the best interest of the child. Based on this it has also been argued that the informed consent process is needlessly cruel, particularly to parents suddenly faced with a critically ill newborn baby, and should, therefore, be by-passed. It has thus been argued that the priority must be to safeguard the infant, and this can be considered the responsibility and main objective of the research ethics committees in their evaluation of neonatal research protocols, and not the responsibility of the parents with limited knowledge of the problem. Thus, if the informed consent process can slow or even prevent valuable research, safeguarding the best interest of the infant must take precedence over the rights of the parents.[8]

However, a research ethics committee cannot take over the responsibility of the parents. The committee's main objective must be to ensure that the scientific-medical aspects and equipoise of a research project is such that it is ethical to perform a study, a question the parents usually will not have the skill to evaluate. The objective of the parents is then to decide what they, as responsible parents, feel will be in the best interest of their child. This decision is not only based on facts and figures about a research protocol, but will also depend on their impression of the standard and dedication of the health personnel who will be involved in the care of their child. This could (for some) be just as important for consent or dissent as the scientific quality of the research protocol. These are important factors a research ethics committee is not in a position to consider.

Informed Consent and Emergency Research in the Newborn

Important ethical and practical questions therefore arise with regard to emergency research on neonates, where a standard informed consent *by proxy* often is difficult to obtain. The Food and Drug Administration (FDA) Rules on Emergency Research (US) from 1995 have tried to define the basic criteria needed for including patients in research without informed consent.[9] The basic criteria for emergency research can be summarised as:[10]

- The potential subject enters into the clinical condition under study unexpectedly and suddenly.
- Once the clinical condition develops, the potential subject cannot give consent as a result of the condition.
- The legally authorised representative is not available to give proxy permission.
- To be effective, the intervention under study must be initiated before consent from legally authorised representative is feasible.
- The research could not practicably be carried out without forgoing consent.
- The state of knowledge has reached the point at which necessary answers can best be obtained through human trials.

These criteria are basically a general definition of the term 'emergency research' and should not cause much discussion. However, the FDA rules also give specific criteria that should be fulfilled by the actual research intervention to be studied. These criteria can be summarised as:

- The experimental intervention poses no more than appropriate incremental risk
- The research hypothesis is based on a foundation of valid scientific studies that support a realistic possibility of benefit over standard care.

Similar criteria are also expressed in the European Convention.[3] But how certain can one be that these two main criteria, 'no more than appropriate incremental risks' and 'a realistic possibility of benefit over standard care', will actually be fulfilled?

Therapeutic Research

Much of the confusion in distinguishing between the need for improved medical care and the patient's individual rights, between the safeguard of the individual infant versus the collective interest of all newborn infants, stems from the term *therapeutic research,* introduced by The Declaration of Helsinki.[2] The reason for performing a randomised controlled trial is that we actually do not know the performance of a new drug or intervention. If we definitely knew that the treatment or intervention to be studied had a benefit over standard care and that the incremental risk was no more than appropriate, it could be argued that it would be unethical to perform a randomised, controlled trial.

Therapeutic research is thus partly a misleading and unscientific word, it suggests that the desired aim of the study is already a reality. It could thus be argued that the term therapeutic research offers an alibi for researchers to expose patients to treatment and interventions that could possibly be less effective than standard care, or even have serious side effects.[11] Today's health personnel work less in contact with the patients and more in research laboratories than before, and a research career is often more prestigious than clinical work. The primary goal for many research protocols could become that of increasing knowledge of the pathophysiology of the human body rather than improving treatment, scientific curiosity being the driving force rather than patient care. By using the term therapeutic research we falsely imply that research (always) confers certain benefits on the patient; however, uncertainty constitutes the very nature of research.

Medical history provides several examples of how therapeutic modalities have been introduced into perinatal medicine and have gained widespread acceptance without having been evaluated critically. The present standard of not introducing any treatment before it has been thoroughly studied in randomised controlled trials is therefore to be welcomed. However, as long as the treatment has not been studied, we cannot be sure that the criteria put forward by the FDA Rules on emergency research are actually fulfilled. Thus, perinatal medicine has a record of therapeutic misadventures resulting in severe iatrogenic disorders of the newborn,[12] even if the basis for the interventions has always been the belief that the new treatment 'had a benefit over standard care' and 'the incremental risk was no more than appropriate'. Quite recently a multi-centre randomised trial with early dexamethasone, planned to include 1200 extrememly low birth weight infants, had to be stopped after 220 infants had been enrolled, because spontaneous gastrointestinal perforation quite unexpectedly occurred in 13% of infants in the treatment group as compared to 4% of control infants.[13] Against this background it would be unwise to accept that critical illness in the newborn, and the need for urgent intervention, constitutes an area of research where it is acceptable to conduct randomised controlled trials without informing the parents about the research protocol their infant might be enrolled in.

The Need for Medical Research in Children and Newborns

It is nevertheless in the interest of sick children and newborns that a similar scientific standard is adopted for their treatment as that for adults. Drugs and treatments that are used by adults undergo formal trials that assess the dose required, efficacy and toxicity. The situation in children and particularly in the newborn infant is very different. Recent studies of European children admitted to hospitals have shown that many receive unlicensed medicines and treatment regimens not evaluated by formal trials.[14,15] Restrictions on research in children will therefore not benefit children as a group if the restrictions on research, whether therapeutic or non-therapeutic, are too strict. The objective of the legal framework and guidelines concerning research in children[16,17] should not be to impede research which advances knowledge of childhood disease and its cure or which promotes child health, but to safeguard all participants.[18] Thus, too great a focus on the requirement for equipoise and the possible harmful effects of medical research might lead to a situation where parents are reluctant to have their infants enrolled in randomised controlled trials. Some hospitals have already noticed a reluctant attitude towards research amongst parents.[19] As a consequence of this there is an increasing gap between the scientific basis for medical treatment of adults and that for treatment of children.[15] This has led to the view that non-therapeutic research with some (minimal) risk should also be accepted, even if the research subject will not directly benefit from the research. But should this give any support to permitting some research in newborn infants to be performed without informed consent? Parents have a right to give informed consent to research involving their child. The question must therefore be how to redeem this right as much as possible.

The Possibility of Refusing

The term informed 'consent' describes the positive and active agreement of a person to be enrolled in a medical research project. The term 'assent' refers to acquiescence to the same procedure. In most medical research informed consent is probably a mixture of consent and assent. In both these responses to a research project the parents need to be informed before the infant can be enrolled in the trial.

If this is not possible, it is still not acceptable that other substitute forms of consent are sought, such as depicted in Table 1. From parents' evaluation of the informed consent process (see Chapter 17) it can probably be concluded that the most important element of the process is the right to be informed *before* their child is included in a research intervention, as well as *the opportunity to refuse such inclusion*. If a fully informed consent cannot be obtained, these two vital elements of the process must at least be taken care of. Furthermore, parents strongly agree that this decision should not rest with the medical profession alone.

Neonatal research is mostly performed in large hospitals such as university hospitals. In many institutions several projects are usually going on simultaneously, and several infants are usually eligible for such studies. It must therefore be possible to establish a system of general information for parents admitted to the hospital, whose unborn child might become a research object, about this possibility. The parents must also be informed that in some of the research, for instance research on resuscitation procedures for the newborn with asphyxia, the time element may make it impossible to obtain a standard informed consent after the infant is born but before treatment must start. Given such a system the parents will have been given some information about the research in which their child might be included. They will also have the opportunity to say 'no' to research on the conditions they have been informed about, and to ask for the standard treatment for their child instead. However, since this process must take place before the child is born, the information must not be given in a way that could scare parents unnecessarily. This could be taken care of by focusing on women and parents with pregnancies that have a higher probability of giving birth to a child eligible for the research.

A procedure like this might slow emergency research on critically ill neonates. The researchers will also have to put more work into enrolling infants in such studies. It can also be anticipated that even with such an approach not all parents will be informed beforehand. The number of infants eligible for studies might therefore be reduced, resulting in a longer study period before the results can be evaluated. However, with such an approach, the best interest of the infants as well as the parents and the researchers can be safeguarded. Researchers should not feel comfortable doing research on neonates behind the backs of parents, and informing them later on. It is to be hoped that researchers who accept this will continue to enjoy public support and co-operation for the benefit of sick infants and their families.

It is therefore concluded that medical research on newborn infants, without prior and open information to the parents, can only be accepted under rare and exceptional circumstances.

Notes

1. Nuremberg Code (1947) As cited in: Ruyter KW. Medical research ethics – Nuremberg 50 years on. *Tidsskr Nor Lægeforen* 1997; 117: 4383-91.
2. World Medical Assembly. The Declaration of Helsinki. Ferney-Voltaire, France, 1964; amended in 1975, 1983, 1989 and 1996.
3. Council of Europe. *Convention for the Protection of Human Rights and Dignity of the Human Being with Regard to the Application of Biology and Medicine.* 1996, Strasbourg: Directorate of Legal Affairs.
4. Culbert A, Brown A, Davis DJ. Consent procedures for neonatal resuscitation research: a survey of parental preferences. *Pediatric Research* 1999; 45: 34A.
5. Singal N, Burgess E, Amin H. Parents make informed decisions for research in NICU's. *Pediatric Research* 1999; 45: 35A.
6. Snowdon C, Garcia J, Elbourne D. Making sense of randomization; responses of parents of critically ill babies to random allocation of treatment in a clinical trial. *Social Science and Medicine* 1997; 45: 1337-55.
7. Ruyter KW. Informert samtykke forkledd *in absurdum. Etikkinformasjon* 1997; 6(4): 8-9. (in Norwegian). Norwegian Research Council http://home.sn.no/home/einfo
8. Modi N. Clinical trials and neonatal intensive care. *Archives of Disease in Childhood* 1994; 70: F231-2.
9. Biros MH, Lewis RJ, Olson CM, Runge JW, Cummins RO, Fost N. Informed consent in emergency research. Consensus statement from the coalition conference of acute resuscitation and critical care researchers. *JAMA* 1995; 273: 1283-7.
10. The term 'emergency' is used here where the Euricon project terms this 'urgent'.
11. Alderson P. Did children change, or the guidelines? *Bulletin of Medical Ethics* 1992; 80: 21-8.
12. Jain L, Vidyasagar D. Iatrogenic disorders in modern neonatology. *Clinics in Perinatology* 1989; 16: 255-73.

13. Stark A, Carlo W, Bauer C, Donovan E, Oh W, Papile L-A, Shankaran S, Tyson JE, Wright L, Saha S, Poole K. Serious Complications in a randomized trial of early stress dose dexamethasone (DEX) in extremely low birth weight (ELBW) infants. *Pediatric Research* 00; 47: 434A.
14. Conroy S, Choonara I, Impicciatore P, Mohn A, Arnell H, Rane A, Knoeppel C, Seyberth H, Pandolfini C, Raffaelli MP, Rocchi F, Bonati M, Jong G, van den Anker J. Survey of unlicensed and off label drug use in pediatric wards in European countries. *British Medical Journal* 2000; 320: 79-82.
15. Bonati M, Choonara I, Hoppu K, Pons G, Seyberth H. Closing the gap in drug therapy. *Lancet* 1999; 353: 1625.
16. British Paediatric Association. Guidelines for ethical conduct of medical research involving children. *Bulletin of Medical Ethics* 1992; 80: 13-20.
17. Royal College of Paediatrics and Child Health. Safeguarding informed parental involvement in clinical research involving newborn babies and infants. A position statement. Royal College of Paediatrics and Child Health, London, December 1999.
18. Editorial. Research involving children – ethics, the law, and the climate of opinion. *Archives of Disease in Childhood* 1978; 53: 441-2.
19. Pierro A, Spitz L. Informed consent in clinical research: the crisis in paediatrics. *Lancet* 1997; 349: 1703.

PART V
CONSENSUS STATEMENT

20 Consensus Statement of the Euricon Project

EURICON PARTNERSHIP

Status of Recommendations

Part of the purpose of the Euricon project was to suggest ways in which the process of obtaining informed consent can be improved. The aim of this chapter is to present those suggestions (or 'recommendations' as they are termed here). The recommendations are the result of reflection on, and discussion of, our empirical findings. The discussions took place mainly at three colloquia at which Euricon partners were present. The recommendations were presented at the third colloquium, the document was then circulated to all partners for comment, and final agreement was given to the document.

The background to these recommendations was given in the Introduction to this book. That should help clarify some of the rationale for the recommendations. The recommendations themselves are set out in full, interspersed with the summaries of the empirical results of Euricon's research that are relevant to each recommendation. Whilst there was a large area of agreement, there were also a number of points of importance where agreement amongst all partners was not reached. These points are presented in the final part of this document.

Many of the questions which Euricon sought to address were empirical; thus one aim was to find out facts about the process of obtaining informed consent to neonatal research. Answers to these questions are straightforward 'conclusions' of the project. For example, in response to the third question, 'How are health professionals trained in the process of obtaining informed consent?' it is possible to say that there is almost no formal training.

However, some of the questions were normative, in other words the aim was to suggest ways in which the process of obtaining informed consent to neonatal research could be improved. The answers to these questions are not straightforward 'conclusions' from our empirical work. Instead they are the result of reflection and discussion of the empirical work, much of it carried out at the three colloquia. We believe that these recommendations neither will nor should be implemented without further discussion but that they are suggestions for the practice of obtaining informed consent to neonatal research that are worthy of further consideration with a view to the implementation of some, or all, of them.

In the light of the above considerations, the Euricon team would now make the following consensus statement:

Consensus Statement of the Euricon Research Project

A. *The Requirement for Informed Consent*

Analysis of parental and clinician interviews has revealed that informed consent, as understood in the preamble above, was obtained unproblematically in approximately one third of parents asked for their consent. Furthermore, almost all parents valued their involvement in the process and the respect it paid to their decision-making role with regard to their children. In the light of this the following recommendation can be made:

> A1. It should be the standard practice for researchers to obtain informed consent from parents prior to neonatal research.

However, we have noted that the extent to which the different criteria for such consent are met will vary between trials and between parents. In relation to the variation between parents we have suggested that Research Ethics Committees (RECs) should consider the extent to which one could expect the informed consent criteria to be met by *most* potential candidates and insist that anyone who does not meet these requirements should be excluded from the trial. This is our next recommendation:

> A2. RECs should consider the extent to which one could expect the informed consent criteria to be met by most parents of eligible neonates. These should then be set as minimum standards for the particular trial. Anyone who does not meet these requirements should be excluded from the trial.

There seem to be particular types of trials that are likely to cause a significant reduction in the level at which the different criteria for informed consent can be met. Our research indicated that urgent trials (defined in this study as those in which consent has to be obtained within 12 hours) and emergency trials (in which consent has to be obtained within 12 hours and the research concerns a treatment for a disorder that is life-threatening) caused such a reduction. However, it should be restated that parents in these circumstances still valued being involved in the informed consent process.

> A3. RECs should consider the possibility that there is a significant reduction in the extent to which the criteria for informed consent can be met in urgent trials (where consent is required within a tight timeframe after birth, such as within 12 hours). RECs should set realistic minimum standards of consent for such trials. Further research is required to inform the setting of these standards.

Many clinicians dealing with urgent and emergency research used a 'step-like' process of informed consent. This involved giving parents a bare minimum of information prior to commencing the infant in a trial, then giving more information as time went on. Sometimes this process included obtaining oral informed consent at first, then obtaining written informed consent. The danger of such an approach is that parents will find out that something has *already* happened to their child that they find unacceptable. Thus, the best way to use the 'step-like' approach is to tell parents what the next stage of the research involves and to seek their consent, rather than tell them what it has already involved.

> A4. Where there is a significant reduction in the extent to which the criteria of informed consent can be met, researchers should consider gaining consent in stages. This should involve, as far as possible, getting parents to understand what the research involves in each impending stage. It may also involve beginning with oral consent that is followed by written consent at a later stage of the trial.

If the role of parental informed consent is to protect the neonatal research subject, then its presence to an attenuated degree would seem to imply that research subjects have reduced protection in such cases. This would not be acceptable. It is central to Euricon's recommendations that parental informed consent should not be seen as being the sole or main safeguard of the neonate's welfare in research. Parents should never be asked to consent for the neonate to be involved in bad research (nor are they, to our knowledge). It is up to researchers, RECs, and grant-giving bodies to make sure that this is the case.

> A5. It is not the role of parents to act as the sole or main safeguard to the welfare of their baby with regard to research. Researchers drawing up proposals, grant-giving bodies undertaking a scientific review process and RECs considering the proposals are also independently responsible for the welfare of the child.

Many parents expressed a desire to know the results of the research in which their child had been involved. This seems desirable, although there was some discussion of whether it was problematic for parents whose neonates had had a poor outcome. Parents who refused consent were thought unlikely to want to know, and to provide such information after refusal to consent would be a violation of the principle of informed consent, although an explicit request for information should be granted.

> A6. It should be commonplace for parents to receive feedback on the results of the research for which they provided consent. (See also D3.)

B. The Process of Obtaining Informed Consent

Euricon analyses revealed that in none of the participating countries do researchers receive training explicitly in the process of seeking informed consent. Furthermore, many clinicians seem unaware of the legal/REC guidelines governing the obtaining of consent in their country/geographical area. The analyses also revealed that many parents rely mainly on help from the person obtaining consent in reaching an understanding of the research in which they are being asked to allow their child to participate, and that many parents use the information sheet only as an *aide memoir* to remind themselves of points the researcher has made.

This led us to consider the question of formal training for researchers in the process of obtaining informed consent. It was thought that any such training would need to focus on two areas: (i) communication skills and (ii) guidance on the legal and ethical constraints governing the process. Regarding point (i) it was thought that, given that most researchers are clinicians, this training should be dealt with in earlier medical education. If someone is able to get informed consent to, say, surgery, then he/she should also have the communication skill to be able to get informed consent to neonatal research. Regarding point (ii) it was felt that this was information that should be available to the researcher, perhaps from the REC.

B1. Researchers involved in seeking parental consent need (i) communication skills and (ii) guidance on the legal and ethical constraints governing the process. The communication skills aspect should be covered in earlier medical training but formal training should be considered for those researchers who do not come from a medical background. The guidance on legal and ethical constraints governing the process should be available in the form of literature, perhaps from the REC. Where consent is required for an urgent trial (consent required within 12 hours of parents being approached), RECs should pay special attention to the competence of the researchers in this area.

B2. Those seeking consent should continue to give parents an information sheet but should not rely on this for dispensing information to parents. They should recognise that parents will want help in digesting the information on the sheet, and may not use it at all.

B3. Consideration should be given to the formal testing of the drawing up and use of information sheets. We suggest:

> i. The information on the sheets should be appropriate to the nature of the trial and circumstances of the consent. For example, where time available in which to consent is very short, the information sheet may contain less than where there is plenty of time. As a bare minimum parents must know that the treatment is being given as part of a trial, that their child may be receiving an experimental or unproven treatment, that they are free to say 'no' and to opt for the standard treatment. Parents should be informed that this is preliminary information only.
> ii. Where parents receive these 'minimal' information sheets these should be followed up with sheets telling them more at a time when they can deal with this information.
> iii. Information sheets should be drawn up with a *trial-specific* checklist of points which the researcher is to go through with the parents.
> iv. In cases where it is decided that there is a significant reduction in the extent to which the criteria for informed consent can be

met, a less demanding checklist would be appropriate. This should be followed by further information sheets to be given at a later point (see recommendations A3 and A4). RECs should develop guidelines to help researchers draw up information sheets in such cases.

B4. Researchers should go through a checklist of points with parents, drawn up in the light of the information sheet, to ensure that parents have understood the information presented.

B5. Information sheets should include the fact that the research proposal has been considered by an independent committee (an REC) which has approved the research. Parents should be aware that such approval is consistent with its being both reasonable to enrol the neonate, and reasonable not to enrol the neonate. Such a statement would need careful wording to prevent its coercing parents to enter children into trials.

C. The Structure of RECs

Analysis of RECs revealed considerable variations both within countries and across Europe in the composition, size and procedures of RECs. In the light of the role of RECs mentioned above this degree of variation needs to be addressed.

C1. Evidently RECs need sufficient expertise to assess the quality of RCT protocol designs and the likely risks and benefits attaching to individual trials. They also need the expertise to assess the trial from the subject's point of view, indeed from that of a sceptical subject.

C2. RECs should be composed of a core membership plus a peripheral membership. The latter should be composed of specialists in different fields of research and should be used solely to consider research in their specialised field. The core committees should aim to contain medical doctors, pharmacists, lay members, statisticians and ethicists, all with requisite expertise.

C3. There should be at least two lay-members on every committee. Part of their role should be to ensure that information sheets and checklists are comprehensible in lay terms (in practice, parents may need further clarification from the clinician obtaining informed consent).

D. The Role and Practice of RECs

Euricon analysis found considerable diversity in the attitudes of committees both within countries and across Europe. Few if any RECs in Europe conduct monitoring of Randomised Controlled Trials (RCTs) they approve. It found that, with regard to informed consent, committees focused mainly on the content and language in information sheets, even though our analysis also found these often not to be an integral part of the process of obtaining consent. It found that committees often lay great stress on the requirement for informed consent within neonatal research. However, when questioned about a RCT in which a significant reduction in the level at which the criteria of informed consent might be expected (because inclusion criteria required randomisation within four hours of birth), RECs tended not to acknowledge the problem. In the light of these, and other considerations, the following recommendations are made:

D1. RECs should continue to review information sheets and develop a checklist system to aid researchers in their use.

D2. RECs should seek to ensure that those who are charged with obtaining informed consent from parents are competent to do so.

D3. RECs should monitor research that they approve. Results of this monitoring should inform the development and dissemination of guidelines on good practice for those seeking informed consent from parents.

   i. Questionnaires could be sent to parents by principal investigators on behalf of RECs, seeking information on their experience of giving consent.
   ii. At the end of trial recruitment, research groups could review their RCT from an ethical point of view and send a short report and recommendations to the appropriate RECs.
   iii. RECs could randomly monitor the practice of obtaining informed consent in RCTs by direct observation of practice.

D4. In urgent and emergency trials the degree to which the different criteria of informed consent are met will be low, and in some trials they will not be met at all. RECs need to be especially stringent in assessing both the risk to benefit and the adverse event ratios of such trials.

D5. RECs should meet in national forums annually, in which best practice can be developed. In this forum a set of principles or general guidelines, providing a reasoned explanatory basis for decision-making, should be developed and published.

D6. National RECs should be guided by coherent national policies in the mode of appointment of members of RECs.

Points of Disagreement

The following issues were widely discussed at colloquia but no consensus was reached.

I. Where informed consent cannot be obtained two options should be considered: first, prenatal consent and, second, where that is not possible, proceeding without consent

In our discussions we asked whether there were any types of neonatal trials where no form of informed consent could be gained at all. There would, of course, be individual cases where informed consent could not be gained, such as those in which the mother is unconscious and the father unavailable. Given our recommendation A2 (above), in these individual cases the neonate should not be recruited into the trial. But Euricon asked the question whether there are cases in which most parents of eligible neonates would be unable to consent at all, or where their consent would be of such a reduced level in one or more of the criteria, that it could not be called an informed consent. It was suggested that the following pieces of information were central for parents to understand when asked for informed consent in an extreme emergency situation:

- The treatment we are proposing is being given as part of a trial.
- Your child might receive an unproven/experimental treatment.

- You are free to say 'no' to this course of action and receive standard treatment instead.

If most parents of eligible neonates could be expected *not* to be competent to understand these three things and/or if there would *not* be sufficient time for parents to receive and understand these three things, then it would be unrealistic to expect such trials to proceed with 'informed consent'. Are there any such trials? The answer seems to be that there are, although they are rare. They are trials where the need to give the trial treatment, is almost simultaneous with the recognition that it needs to be given. Usually this will be immediately following the birth of an ill neonate who needs a treatment (standard or experimental) straight away. In such cases there seem to be three options: first, get consent pre- or peri-natally; second, do not do the research; third, proceed without consent.

1a. *Pre-natal consent* is a good option where this is realistically possible. In our interviews, parents who had been approached pre-natally seemed to have a good understanding of what their consent involved. Thus whether or not this approach should be used depends upon whether it is 'realistically possible'. A problem arises where the experimental treatment is for a condition that is both rare and pre-natally unpredictable. In such cases, the application of this approach will involve giving large numbers of parents information that turns out to be irrelevant to them. This could be said to be inappropriate both because of the worry it may cause to many parents and because of the large amount of resources that it would require. Furthermore, the few parents for whom the information is relevant will receive it on the understanding that it is very unlikely to be relevant. Thus they may not give it the attention it needs. One last problem is that in some European countries (e.g. under Scottish law in the UK) parents cannot consent pre-natally because the foetus is not a legal person.

1b. *Peri-natal consent* is a more doubtful option. The stress of childbirth, particularly where it is complicated by a prospective neo-natal emergency, may make it impossible to achieve a reasonable level of understanding for informed consent. It may also make the consent process an unreasonable burden for the parents (as the interviews with parents indicated).

2. *Not to do the research* was thought unacceptable by the majority. There are well-known cases in the history of neonatology where both standard and experimental treatments have turned out to be harmful. It is imperative that such treatments are tested in all aspects of neonatology including those where informed consent is unobtainable. Without such testing, any progress in the treatment of certain neonatal conditions (those surrounding unpredictable emergencies at birth) would be haphazard at best.

3. *To do the research **without** informed consent* was also thought unacceptable by the majority, but some felt that neonatal research, in situations where both informed consent and pre- or perinatal consent was impossible, should proceed without informed consent. The REC would need to be convinced that this was indeed the case; that, for example, it was not possible to do the research in another way where informed consent could be obtained. They would need also to be convinced of the importance of the research and that the risk benefit ratio to the neonate (research subject) was satisfactory (although these conditions should apply in all neonatal research anyway). Nonetheless, it was felt that RECs would be required to provide extremely careful supplementary review of the protocol to provide an extra safeguard. One additional safeguard was that parents should be informed on admission that research occurs in the hospital and allowed to put in place a blanket refusal to all research straight away. It might also be worth considering an American model where, if non-consensual research is proposed, the proposal is put out to public debate first.

II. Financial reimbursement for REC members

Two alternative means of financial reimbursement were proposed:

1. Given the workload of RECs, payment of reasonable expenses (including time taken away from other work) should be given. It was recommended that this be paid by tax-payers, through central government to avoid potential biases from other sources, eg. the pharmaceutical industry.

2. REC membership should be seen as a civic duty, like jury service. This would mean that REC members should receive payment of reasonable expenses, and that employers should be required to give members the necessary time away from work to fulfil REC obligations.

III. It is in the best interest of an eligible neonate to be randomised into a trial.

There was a wide spectrum of views, from complete agreement to complete disagreement with this statement. The issue matters for at least three reasons:

1. In those rare cases where it is argued that neonates should be entered into trials without the consent of their parents, it is necessary that it be in the best interest of the neonate that this be done.

2. Much of legislation talks about therapeutic research as being in the best interest of the neonate. This needs to be clarified further.

3. If research is in the best interest of the neonate then this would be a telling point against one aspect of the Euricon recommendations. We have said that individual neonates should not be included in research if parental consent of the type normal for the particular trial cannot be obtained. If it is in the child's best interest to be randomised, and parental consent cannot be obtained, then it would seem that such children should be involved. Therefore we recommend further discussion and clarification on this point.

IV. The informed consent of parents need not be sought for trials that are comparing two standard treatments, either of which could be given without consent outside the context of a trial.

The majority seemed to be opposed to such a recommendation, but some felt there were points in its favour. First, a number of parents did talk of the informed consent process being an additional burden. Second, it might be said that nothing is at stake in such a trial. Either treatment could be given without parental consent outside a research protocol. However, the interview findings strongly emphasised the desire of parents to be asked for their consent.

V. Monitoring of approved research projects by RECs

Some partners felt that this would not be feasible for all projects whilst others felt that monitoring for all approved projects was needed.